I0441049

Stakes in Africa-United States Relations

Stakes in Africa-United States Relations

◆

Proposals for Equitable Partnership

Abdul Karim Bangura,

Ciyata Dinah Coleman,

Doyin Coker-Kolo,

Peter A. Dumbuya,

James T. Gire,

John Patrick Afam Ifedi,

George Klay Kieh, Jr.,

Oluseyi Kuforiji,

Guy Martin,

Mueni wa Muiu,

Ishmael I. Munene,

Godwin Ohiwerei

iUniverse, Inc.

New York Lincoln Shanghai

Stakes in Africa-United States Relations
Proposals for Equitable Partnership

Copyright © 2007 by The African Institution

All rights reserved. No part of this book may be used or reproduced by any means, graphic, electronic, or mechanical, including photocopying, recording, taping or by any information storage retrieval system without the written permission of the publisher except in the case of brief quotations embodied in critical articles and reviews.

iUniverse books may be ordered through booksellers or by contacting:

iUniverse
2021 Pine Lake Road, Suite 100
Lincoln, NE 68512
www.iuniverse.com
1-800-Authors (1-800-288-4677)

Because of the dynamic nature of the Internet, any Web addresses or links contained in this book may have changed since publication and may no longer be valid.

The views expressed in this work are solely those of the author and do not necessarily reflect the views of the publisher, and the publisher hereby disclaims any responsibility for them.

A publication of the African Studies and Research Forum, an affiliate of the Association of Third World Studies, under the auspices of The African Institution

ISBN: 978-0-595-45197-5 (pbk)
ISBN: 978-0-595-89506-9 (ebk)

Printed in the United States of America

† Nwafejoku Okolie Uwaclibie
A man who spent his life preparing future leaders in both Africa and the United States

Contents

Acknowledgments

We, and hopefully many readers, owe gratitude to:

Mwalimu Emanuel I. Udogu, Mwalimu Joseph Takougang and Mwalimu Olufemi Vaughan, for chairing the panels at which the essays in this book were presented and providing constructive feedback.

Mwalimu Harold Isaacs, for his unflinching support of the work of the African Studies and Research Forum.

Mwalima Shanelle Wells, for providing impeccable copyediting, research and keyboarding assistance.

The numerous families to which we belong, for offering their encouragement and prayers.

Preface

Stakes in Africa-United States Relations: Proposals for Equitable Partnership is our response to a 170-page report of the Africa Policy Advocacy Panel titled *Rising U.S. Stakes in Africa: Seven Proposals to Strengthen U.S.-Africa Policy.* The report was authorized by the United States Congress in early 2003 and was delivered to then Secretary of State Colin L. Powell in February of 2004 (Kansteiner III and Morrison, eds. May 2004). Two major shortcomings of the report motivated us to write this book. The first shortcoming is that none of the contributing authors of the report is an African. Consequently, an indigenous African perspective is missing from the chapters. The second shortcoming is that the report treats Africa only as an object of United States foreign policy. As such, the authors miss the fact that since the 1970s, Africa, as a new collective actor, has had an active role in international affairs. One need only recall the refusal by African states in the United Nations Security Council to vote in support of the United States' call for war against Iraq to underscore this truism.

The first decade of the new century is witnessing a continuation of the complex and profound changes in the international arena and the further advance of globalization. Development and peace remain the paramount issues of our times. On the one hand, promoting development, safeguarding peace and enhancing cooperation, which are common desires of all peoples, remain imperative. On the other hand, destabilizing factors and uncertainties in the global arena are increasing. Security issues of various kinds are interwoven. Development remains more pressing and peace more illusive.

Africa, which encompasses the largest number of developing countries, is an important force for global development and peace. Africa-United States relations face fresh opportunities under new circumstances. With *Stakes in Africa-United States Relations: Proposals for Equitable Partnership,* we wish to present the objectives for vibrant and lasting relations between Africa and the United States and measures to achieve them.

Africa, the home of humans, has a long history, abundant natural resources and huge potential for development. After many years of struggle, Africans freed themselves from slavery and colonial rule, wiped out apartheid, won independence and emancipation, thereby making a significant contribution to the progress of humanity. Africa still faces many challenges on its road towards development. With the persistent efforts of African states and the continuous support of the United States and the rest of the international community, Africa will surely overcome the difficulties and achieve rejuvenation in this new century.

Abdul Karim Bangura

1

Historical Overview of Africa-United States Relations

Peter A. Dumbuya

Introduction

Much, if not most, of the existing historiography depicts Africa as a marginal region of the world in the calculations of foreign policy and national security planners in Washington. For example, Henry Serrano Villard has written of the relationship in these terms: "With the exception of independent Liberia, for whom we acted as "next friend and attorney," we had no particular interest in what was to all intents and purposes an appendage of Europe and therefore a blind spot in our view of the international scene, where even the conventional duties of protecting American citizens and promoting American commerce were at a negligible low" (1965:65). Russell Warren Howe describes Africa as "A vast region where America had a special responsibility," but that "At the Washington level, Africa was still seen, principally, as being distant" (1975:40). According to Elliot P. Skinner, even though African Americans "tried to encourage often reluctant administrations to adopt policies toward Africa in keeping with their views of the nature of American national interests as well as what they thought would be helpful to Africa and its peoples" confronted by European imperialistic designs in the late 19th Century, the "United States government and most of its citizens sought to dissociate themselves from the plight of Africans" by adopting a "noninterventionist policy toward Africa" (1992:95,104).

This policy of nonintervention stood in sharp contrast with, for instance, United States policy toward Britain where "A shared language and a common historical inheritance of "Anglo-Saxon" polity created, for British and Americans alike, a set of immediately recognizable and axiomatically accepted habits of thought and behavior—especially in the conduct of public affairs" (Nicholas

1975:1). Trade, investment, and immigration (2.8 million British immigrants entered the United States between 1815 and 1860) were some of the ramparts of Anglo-American relations in the 19th Century. According to Nicholas, between 1821 and 1837, Britain invested more in the United States than in any other country in the world, and bought 80 percent of United States cotton, accounting for three-fifths of total exports by the 1850s. Furthermore, Immanuel Wallerstein (in Arkhurst 1975:14) has argued that the economic histories of Africa and the United States in the period from 1789 to 1960 did not overlap. United States "indifference" towards Africa was said to be linked to industrial Europe's perception of the African continent as a "peripheral area of the world economy," even though prior to the abolition of the trans-Atlantic slave trade African slave labor had provided the much-needed backbone of the cotton, coffee, and sugar plantations of the Americas and Caribbean islands.

The overall picture of marginalization, neglect, and nonintervention presented in these and other studies will benefit from a more rigorous examination of the historical context within which the United States and Africa interacted with each other for over two centuries. In this chapter, I argue that from 1787 when the United States signed a commercial treaty with the Kingdom of Morocco to the end of the Cold War in the 1980s, there have been noticeable shifts in relations between the two Atlantic regions over a wide range of issues (diplomatic, commercial, economic, philanthropic, cultural, and military). Instead of viewing African-United States relations as a continuum of marginalization, disinterest, and nonintervention, these thematic and chronological phases offer a rare insight into the challenges and opportunities both regions faced in a world that was constantly changing in so far as it concerns issues facing world leaders. These noticeable shifts will be grouped into five chronological and thematic phases and analyzed so as to present a more balanced and coherent account of African-United States relations than previous studies have succeeded in doing.

From Barbary Piracy to Liberian Colonization, 1787-1847

Industrialization and the abolition of the slave trade and slavery brought "legitimate trade" and European and American naval, cultural, philanthropic, and diplomatic influences to the shores of Africa. As Paul A. Varg (in DeConde 1978) has observed, cultural contacts, underscored by the presence of American missionaries, could not be separated from United States' foreign policy objectives in Africa. The intersection of religion and foreign policy informed Samuel Hopkins' plan (in 1772) for the training of free Blacks as colonizers and missionaries especially in Africa. This prompted the United States Congress, in 1821, to empower the President to make "proper negotiations" with the coastal peoples of Africa for the repatriation of Negroes. In the following year, President James Monroe chose Dr. Eli Ayers to head the mission that later founded the settlement of Monrovia. Between 1822 and 1827, the American Colonization Society (ACS) shipped more than 6,000 free Blacks to the West African settlement; and in 1847, the Republic of Liberia came into being. The founding of Liberia encouraged President John Quincy Adams to support the extension of education and "the true religion" [Christianity] as "the best and only means by which the prosperity and happiness of nations can be advanced and continued" (Varg 1978:569).

This religious, cultural, and philanthropic imperative in West Africa stood in sharp contrast with United States' policy toward North Africa which was shaped in large part by commercial interests. For their own economic survival, many European states, including Spain, France, and Britain, had concluded bilateral treaties with the Barbary States of Morocco, Algeria, Tunisia, and Libya. In 1787, the United States dispatched Thomas Barclay, its Consul General in Paris, to Morocco where he signed a treaty with Sultan Sidi Muhammad XVI (1757-1790) who agreed to curb piracy on the Mediterranean Sea. In 1825, the United States established a Consulate-General in Tangier to oversee its interests in the North African Kingdom. The United States made similar efforts in Zanzibar and the Congo (Hall 1971).

Thus, in the first phase, which ended with the proclamation of the Liberian Republic, United States' relations with Africa were shaped by philanthropic, cultural, economic, and strategic interests in key areas of the continent. In the second phase, which is discussed in the following section, the United States often responded to crisis situations involving rival European claims to African territories as exemplified by the Berlin Conference, or when Nazism and Fascism aligned themselves with the colonial lobby in Germany and Italy, respectively, to challenge key provisions of the Post-World War I peace settlement.

European Colonialism and United States Foreign Policy, 1865-1919

The period from the end of the Civil War in 1865 to the signing of the Versailles Peace Treaty in 1919 marked the second phase in African-United States interactions. This period was characterized by tacit American recognition of Europe's colonial interests in Africa and, therefore, constrained Washington's ability to interact freely with individual African states. This may also help explain why the United States did not pursue relations with Africa with a great deal of enthusiasm as the historiography has suggested. Such constraints aside, the United States interacted with Africa in other ways, such as by participating in almost every major international conference devoted to African affairs. In every instance, the United States used treaty rights obtained at these international conferences to share with Europe access to Africa's resources and markets.

The Berlin Conference, which gave birth to modern African nationalism, is a case in point. Hosting the conference was the German Chancellor Otto von Bismarck. Even though prior to 1884 Bismarck had expressed no interest in African colonial ventures, he, nonetheless, spearheaded the creation of German protectorates over Togo and the Cameroon (July 1884), in addition to the colonization of Southwest Africa (now Namibia, August 1884) and German East Africa (now Tanzania, February 1885). The "Iron Chancellor" was motivated to colonize these African territories for domestic (electoral gain) and foreign policy concerns (peace at home and prestige abroad) stemming from Germany's triumph over France in the War of 1870.

The Berlin Conference met from November 15, 1884 to February 26, 1885 without any African representative in attendance. It dealt with such issues as free trade in the basin and mouth of the Congo River, freedom of navigation on the Congo and Niger Rivers, and the formalities to be observed when taking possession of new coastal territories. The agenda of the Conference reflected a desire on the part of Germany and King Leopold's Belgium to forestall implementation of the Anglo-Portuguese Treaty of February 1884. The treaty, by which Britain was to recognize Portuguese sovereignty over the mouth of the Congo River, threatened the treaty interests Henry M. Stanley had negotiated on behalf of King Leopold, albeit fraudulently, with over 2,000 Congolese chiefs between 1879 and 1884.

The United States, which had recognized King Leopold II's claim to the territory in April of 1884 (Hochschild 1998), urged John Adam Kasson, its Minister in Berlin, not only "to fight for free trade and to have the Congo basin defined as widely as was possible-against the competing Portuguese and the commercial 'dead hand' of the French," but also for "humanitarian policies" that included access for missionaries to the Congo (renamed Congo Free State in May of 1885), a ban on the sale of illicit liquor, and the peaceful settlement of conflicts in the region (Howe 1975:34-39). The Final Act of Berlin (February 26, 1885) created two free trade areas known as the "conventional Congo basin," offered protection to Christian missions, banned the slave trade, and authorized the regulation of the liquor trade by local authorities. Furthermore, the Final Act sanctioned the "effective occupation" of new coastal territories and notification of such action to the other signatories. With this requirement, the Berlin Conference sought to minimize conflicts between and among rival European claimants to African territories. By 1914 when African primary resistance in the form of armed revolt against the imposition of colonial rule had been suppressed by imperial military and police forces, only Ethiopia and Liberia remained independent.

Prior to World War I, therefore, the United States gave tacit recognition to Europe's colonial empires on the continent. This was reflected in the fact that the United States had no clearly designated office in the Department of State (DOS) to handle its African affairs. All of this began to change during World War II when the DOS assigned North Africa, the strategic and commercial gateway to the East, to the Division of Near Eastern Affairs and sub-Saharan Africa to the Division of European Affairs, another sign that the United States continued to defer to its partners in Europe when interacting with Africa.

From Versailles to the End of World War II, 1919-1945

The exigencies of World War I and the emerging threats posed by such ideologies as Communism, Fascism, and Nazism competed with national self-determination in the third major phase/shift in relations between Africa and the United States in the interwar period. It began when the Allied Powers (Britain, France, Italy, and Japan) pushed back attempts by President Woodrow Wilson to demand self-determination for all colonial peoples and ended with the onset of the Cold War and decolonization. If Wilson had succeeded in his endeavor to make national self-determination for all colonial peoples one of the cornerstones of the post-war peace settlement, it would have ruptured not only the agreement reached at Berlin in 1885, but also called into question America's tacit recognition of Europe's colonial empires in Africa. Ironically, the United States' deferential policy toward its European allies undermined its commitment to African self-determination at the end of the war.

Nowhere was this more evident than during the Versailles Peace Conference of 1919. President Wilson believed that World War I had been ignited by, *inter alia*, European colonial rivalries in places like Africa. Therefore, on January 8, 1918, in the fifth of his Fourteen Points which he presented to a joint session of the United States Congress, he called for an "impartial adjustment of all colonial claims" and also suggested that "the interests of the populations concerned must have equal weight with the equitable claims of the government whose title is to be determined" (Wilson 1918). In speeches in May and July of 1918, Wilson continued to refer to national self-determination and the rule of law as "this great enterprise of liberty," while Secretary of State Robert Lansing warned, rather prophetically, that the president's statement on self-determination was "loaded with dynamite" that would create impossible demands on the peace conference, and raise false expectations among colonial peoples.

Wilson's domestic policies toward African Americans, in particular his executive order segregating Black and White employees in the federal bureaucracy, curtailed any success he might have had on the issue of self-determination for colonial peoples in Africa (Skinner 1992). The president's refusal to meet with and discuss colonial issues such as self-determination with people like W.E.B. Du Bois of the National Association for the Advancement of Colored People (NAACP) and Blaise Diagne, the Senegalese Deputy in the French National Assembly, both organizers of the Pan-African Congress that was held in Paris between February 19-21, 1919 to drum up support for African national self-determination, made it even more difficult for him to press the Allied leaders to grant self-determination to all colonial peoples consistent with his Fourteen Points speech. Moreover, Wilson's advisers such as George L. Beer, the expert on colonial issues, believed that Africans lacked the wherewithal to govern themselves, and pointed to Liberia as a case in point (Skinner 1992). The inevitable conclusion was that the African colonies were better off under some sort of international supervision than on their own as sovereign independent states in the turbulent post-war world.

Despite the fact that over one million Africans had fought against the Central Powers (Germany, Austria-Hungary, the Ottoman Empire and Bulgaria), while others handed in petitions demanding the right to self-determination and full citizenship (in the case of Muslim Algerians), the Allied Powers crafted a colonial settlement based not on the principle of self-determination for all colonial peoples but on security and geopolitical considerations. These were spelled out in two war-time secret treaties wherein they undertook to divide the German and Turkish colonies among themselves should they win the war: the Anglo-French treaty of August 30, 1914, relating to the division of the Cameroon and Togoland, and the Treaty of London of April 26, 1915, whereby the Allies (including Russia) promised Italy substantial lands in Africa as an inducement to join their war effort. In his memoirs, David Lloyd George (1939:1:8-9, 14-15), the then British Prime Minister, characterized the Treaty of London as a "very distinct violation of the principles of nationalities."

After protracted negotiations, Wilson (representing the only Associated Power) conceded the right of the Allies not only to maintain their respective colonial empires intact, but also to administer the German colonies they had occupied in Africa during the war subject to international supervision by the League of Nations (Dumbuya 1995). Article 119 of the Treaty of Versailles demanded that Germany hand over its colonies to the Allied and Associated Powers. South Africa's Jan Christian Smuts offered the blueprint for the League's mandate system: *The League of Nations: A Practical Suggestion* (1918). Memorialized in Article 22 of the Covenant of the League of Nations, the mandate system created three categories of mandates on the assumption that they were "inhabited by peoples not yet able to stand by themselves under the strenuous conditions of the modern world," and "that the well-being and development of such peoples form a sacred trust of civilisation and that securities for the performance of this trust should be embodied in this Covenant." The "A" mandates, colonies of the former Ottoman Turkish Empire in the Middle East, received recognition, albeit provisionally, as independent states subject to administrative supervision by Britain and France. The victors considered the "B" mandates (the German colonies of Togoland, Cameroon, and Tanganyika; and Ruanda-Urundi, awarded to Belgium for its war efforts) to be politically less advanced than those in the Middle East. The "C" mandates (German Southwest Africa and scattered German island colonies in the Pacific Ocean), viewed as politically the least advanced of all the former German colonies, were administered as "integral portions" of the respective mandatory powers.

In addition to the exigencies of the Great War, the emerging threat of Nazism in Germany's former African colonies (Tanganyika, German Southwest Africa, Togo, and the Cameroon) ceded to Britain, France, and Belgium as mandates under the League of Nations, brought the United States closer to formulating an African policy whose contours would become evident during the Cold War. Due to its size and location on the Indian Ocean, Tanganyika, in the eyes of German imperialists, lay at the core of a future German Central African Empire or *Mittelafrika* (Dumbuya 1995). Throughout the inter-war period, therefore, various German colonial associations and individuals denounced the Treaty of Versailles in general and the mandate system in particular as dictated settlements. The Italian Fascist leader Benito Mussolini threw in his support for the return of the former German colonies, forcing the government of British Prime Minister Ramsay MacDonald to issue a statement stressing the "permanence" of the mandates. As the United States' ambassador to Norway (from 1935 to 1937), A. J. Drexel Biddle, Jr., noted at the time, "Britain is adamant, and at present is determined not to yield the colonies—under any circumstances" (Biddle in FDR's Office Files 1933-1945, Part 2).

Following Germany's withdrawal from the League of Nations in October 1933, Adolf Hitler, who in May 1933 had announced that "our fate is not bound up with coasts or dominations, but with the east of our own frontiers," told the

Reichstag in 1934 that Germany wanted its former colonies as a source of raw materials, an outlet for German immigrants, and a market for German goods (Dumbuya 1995:197,199). The *Reichsführer's* instructions to Joachim von Ribbentrop, then ambassador at large, "to take up the colonial matter generally—but not to press the issue" induced Britain to counter with an offer to sell raw materials to Germany through the League of Nations and as "Part of the price of a general European settlement" that "will involve no territorial changes" to the Versailles peace agreement (Biddle in FDR's Office Files 1933-1945, Part 2).

Critical steps in the articulation of United States policy toward the "dependent" areas had more to do with perceived and real threats some European states posed to American interests than to the demands of African nationalists at Versailles or thereafter. The administration of President Franklin D. Roosevelt took the first step not only in articulating a policy, but also in institutionally de-linking Africa from the Department of State's European desk when Italy invaded Ethiopia in 1935. Ignoring overtures from the United States and Britain "to settle the dispute if that could be arranged" (FDR's Office Files 1933-1945, Part 2), Mussolini ordered the invasion of Ethiopia to safeguard or develop what he considered to be Italy's "legitimate interests" which included an Italian mandate over Ethiopia, fostering "amity" and "collaboration" with Ethiopia under the Treaty of 1928, minimizing French influence, and avenging the Italian defeat at Adowa in 1896. As Villard has written "When the thunderheads of Nazi imperialism began to rise over Africa—Hitler's grand design was to take over the continent's resources for the New Order in Europe—the way was paved for recognition of another area. The European Division, which had jurisdiction over the European colonies on the African land mass, transferred them—for want of a better place—to the Division of Near Eastern Affairs" (1965:18).

In 1938, the administration began this process by transferring responsibility for African affairs (with the exception of Algeria, South Africa, and Madagascar) within the DOS from the Division of European Affairs to the Division of Near Eastern Affairs, created in 1937 with responsibility for Ethiopia and North Africa, among others. In July of 1940, Villard became Assistant Chief of the African Section, and in January of 1944 Chief of the newly created Office of African Affairs in an expanded Division of Near Eastern, South Asia, and African Affairs. Villard assumed the position of Acting Deputy Director of that office in April of 1946. As Loy W. Henderson, Deputy Under Secretary of State for Administration, told the *Boston Herald* in December of 1956, the Roosevelt administration effected these institutional changes "In recognition of the increasing importance of Africa to the United States and the dynamic developments which were beginning to take place in the continent."

World War II not only highlighted Africa's role in the defeat of the Axis Powers (Germany, Italy and Japan) but also facilitated the eventual de-linking of African affairs from the European Division. On November 7, 1942, President Roosevelt articulated United States' military objectives which were "to prevent an occupation by the Axis armies of any part of northern or western Africa and to deny to the aggressor nations a starting point from which to launch an attack against the Atlantic coast of the Americas" (FDR's Office Files 1933-1945, Part 2: February 6, 1943). Nevertheless, his administration considered and rejected the establishment of a military base in Dakar (Senegal). Even though "Climate, health conditions, communications, base facilities and ease of defense, all favor Dakar" over Freetown (Sierra Leone), the operation would have required at least 100,000 army troops and 500 planes, and the earliest the troops could have deployed was November 1941. The War and Navy Departments concluded that "This operation would not contribute materially toward winning the present war and it is not vital to hemisphere defense," but also indicated that "For our participation in [the] present war, a base in West Africa would be useful only in the protection of friendly shipping in the South Atlantic" (FDR's Office Files 1933-1945, Part 2: May 7, 1941).

In December of 1941, the War Department had acknowledged West Africa's strategic significance in the "North Atlantic as our principal theatre of operations should America become involved in the war." The West African theater featured prominently in the scheme of things because it could be used to protect air and sea communications and supplies to Egypt, the Persian Gulf, and the Far East generally (including Australia, Singapore and China). It could also have been used "as a means of preventing Germany from reaching Dakar from which she would both block the trade route around Cape Horn and also threaten the South American continent" (FDR's Office Files 1933-1945, Part 1: December 20, 1941).

According to Villard, the United States settled for a policy that ensured that the French North and West Africa colonies remained friendly toward and supportive of the Allied cause. This was achieved in part by the Murphy-Weygand Agreement of 1941 under which France purchased consumer (tea, sugar, cotton cloth, petroleum, etc.) and durable goods (agricultural machinery) with funds frozen in United States banks. To make sure that these commodities did not fall into the hands of General Erwin Rommel, the commander of German troops in North Africa, General Maxime Weygand, Supreme French Commander in

North Africa, allowed the United States to station intelligence officers posing as vice consuls in Morocco, Algeria, and Tunisia. The Murphy-Weygand agreement, initially condemned because it seemed as though the United States was collaborating with Vichy France, cleared the way for "Operation Torch," the Allied landing in North Africa on November 8, 1942. This was followed by the Casablanca Conference of January 1943 where Roosevelt announced the "unconditional surrender" of all enemy forces as an Allied war aim.

Cold War, African Nationalism, and the Truman-Eisenhower Doctrines, 1945-1996

The fourth noticeable shift in relations began with the Cold War and ended with Secretary of State Warren Christopher's enunciation of the Clinton Administration's African Crisis Response Initiative (ACRI) in 1996. In the early phase of the Cold War, more precisely between the Roosevelt and Dwight D. Eisenhower Administrations, the United States responded more to national security crises situations than to the aspirations of Africans, often stepping in to bolster or replace the departing European colonial powers much as it did in southern Europe and the Middle East. As Under Secretary of State Chester Bowles informed the American Foreign Service Association in April of 1961, "for the first time in 200 years the British were really thoroughly incapable, simply by lack of power and capacity to balance out the power of Europe." The collapse of the European balance of power system was evident in Greece and Turkey where the United States began to be "exposed to all the force and ferocity of a new and revolutionary world."

Whereas in the Monroe Doctrine of 1823 the United States had asserted its hegemony in Latin America as Europe's colonial empires crumbled, the Truman (1947) and Eisenhower (1958) Doctrines provided the rationale for United States' entry into those countries and regions being vacated by Britain and France and which Washington considered prime targets of Communist subversion (Schraeder 1994). The Truman Doctrine was crafted to aid Greece, in the throes of a civil war, and Turkey, being pressured by the Soviet Union for territorial concessions and the right to erect naval bases on the Bosporus. By 1950, both countries had been stabilized by American economic and military assistance. Similarly, the Eisenhower Doctrine was predicated on the extension of American economic and military assistance to ward off the threat of Communist aggression in the Middle East following the withdrawal of Britain and France.

Of all the Communist parties in Africa (in Morocco, Algeria, Tunisia, the Sudan, Senegal, and Nigeria) in the first decade of the Cold War, the most effective was said to be the South African Communist Party (SACP). Although banned, the SACP was committed, along with other political groups like the African National Congress (ANC), to the dismantling of South Africa's apartheid structures and laws. Communist countries offered an alliance of mutual interest and an alternative source of badly needed development assistance. Nonetheless, as shown later, the assistance the Communist states offered was far smaller than that provided by the United States and its Western allies. West African leaders such as Ahmed Sékou Touré of Guinea and Kwame Nkrumah of Ghana embraced Communist/Socialism ideology not only as an economic system but also as a means of ridding the continent of colonialism and fostering pan-African unity (Nkrumah 1970).

Faced with an upsurge in African Nationalism on the one hand and the need to contain Communism on the other, the United States and its Western allies began to find ways to increase development aid while preventing what they considered to be a hasty and unwise transfer of power to African nationalists. It was feared that Africa's domestic problems could be exploited by Communist agitators at the beck and call of Moscow and Beijing. Almost overnight, Africa became "not only a fascinating part of the world, but what happens there is of very great importance to all of us" (Penfield 1959:841). Africa became an "emergent colossus" with great economic potential (Davidson 1951). As George Fielding Elliot pointed out, Africa's storehouse of strategically important resources (including industrial diamonds, cobalt, gold and palm oil) had enhanced America's fighting capabilities during World War II. The Congo's uranium was much sought after by the United States in the 1940s as it developed the atomic bomb (Elliot 1955).

Concern for the spread of Communism was not reflected in the amount of economic and technical assistance provided to African states. Compared to other parts of the world, American aid to Africa was very modest in part because most of the continent was still under European colonial rule. In the 1950s, pursuant to the Eisenhower-Acheson foreign policy commitment to roll back Communism, the United States accorded preferential treatment to those nations that renounced neutralism, which John Foster Dulles adjudged "immoral," and joined the crusade against Communism. For Dulles, development was not an end in itself but a tool for shielding the newly independent nations of Africa from Communist subversion. Beyond that, aid was meant to promote sound economic development both as an end in itself and as an important factor contributing to democratic political evolution (N.S.C. 5818, 1958). This East-West perspective dominated the thinking of the foreign policy and national security establishment since the enunciation of the Truman Doctrine in 1947.

The rhetoric of anti-Communism, however, far outstripped the amount of aid provided to African countries supposedly the targets of Communist machinations. For instance, between July 1, 1945 and December 31, 1955, the United States disbursed, without requiring the recipients to pay back, $46,142,423,000; African states received $71,595,000 or 0.15 percent of that amount. Of the $16,140,524,000 in United States loans, Africa netted $342,713,000 or 2.12 percent. South Africa alone received $151,714,000, and Northern and Southern Rhodesia (now Zambia and Zimbabwe, respectively) received $60,686,000. In 1956, less than $25 million of approximately $1,546,700,000 that was set aside for foreign aid for fiscal year 1957 went to Africa (Goldschmidt 1958).

Between 1945 and 1961, the United States provided $24 million in technical cooperation and $23 million in economic assistance to various African countries. Liberia, described by President Roosevelt as "the historic, unwritten protectorate," received $5.5 million in technical assistance during the same period. By the end of the fiscal year in 1961, special assistance had been furnished to advance military and political interests in Morocco ($302.2 million), Tunisia ($254.7 million), Libya ($179 million), and Ethiopia ($180.4 million) (McKay 1963). For the rest of Africa, the United States awarded $50 million in Mutual Security Funds. Military aid to Africa from the Communist bloc countries was far less than that provided by the United States and Western Europe. It totaled $101 million from 1959 to 1963. This figure did not include aid for para-military training and military assistance to nationalist groups. Most of the aid went to Algeria, Ghana, Mali, Morocco, Guinea and Somalia. For the same period, 1,340 African military personnel were trained in the Communist bloc countries.

As in the provision of development aid and technical assistance, overall United States' investments in Africa represented but a small percentage of the world total. Between 1943 and 1950, American investments rose from $104 million to $298 million. In 1954, investments stood at $568 million; and in 1959, they rose to $834 million. The lion's share went to South Africa which, it was estimated, had a more developed, stable and profitable market than the rest of Africa.

Prior to 1960, United States' trade with sub-Saharan Africa amounted to $1 billion annually. In 1955, the United States imported $618,702,000 worth of goods from Africa, representing 5.4 percent of its total imports from all countries. It exported $587,577,000 worth of goods or 3.8 percent of all exports. The shortfall in trade and investments was offset by the activities of missionary and philanthropic organizations, universities, and organized labor. The African-American Institute, the American Society of African Culture, and the American Committee on Africa helped to create and sustain an awareness in the United States of African issues. In 1958, philanthropic grants totaled $7 million. The economic indicators demonstrated that propaganda was more important than trade.

On the Soviet side of the equation, trade with Africa was quite minimal. In 1956, for instance, the Soviet Union's exports to Africa were valued at $24 million, while it imported $29 million worth of goods. Between 1954 and 1963, total Communist economic aid to Africa was $857.7 million in credits and $160.3 million in special drawings. Much of the aid went to Algeria, Ethiopia, Ghana and Guinea. These were all independent states by 1959, the exception being Algeria which gained its independence from France in July of 1962 after a bloody war of independence.

On May 8, 1950, Assistant Secretary of State George C. McGhee drew attention to the fact that there was "no comprehensive program of African area studies in any American university" (in McKay 1963: 289). Therefore, as part of the United States' interest to stimulate greater involvement in the continent, McGhee appealed to private financial interests, educational institutions and foundations for help in promoting an awareness of Africa. The result was the availability of African Studies programs in over 2,000 universities and other institutions of higher learning. By 1961, there were over 2,800 (out of 47,000) foreign students from Africa enrolled in American educational institutions. In 1963, that figure jumped to 6,000. In 1957, a $50,000 AFL-CIO scholarship program for trade union leaders was inaugurated. The aim of these various programs was to maintain a high profile that would discourage African reliance on the Soviet Union, China and their allies.

Even in the field of education, Communist bloc countries did not have an edge over the United States and its Western allies. They hosted 6,135 students, most of whom (3,385) were in the Soviet Union. Students from West Africa constituted 52.8 percent of the total. In fact, there were more African students in Britain (18,000) and France (12-15,000) combined than in the Communist bloc states.

Politics of Self-Determination

As the "wind of change" swept across Africa in the post-World War II era, the United States continued to advocate a policy of containment of Communism. This policy stimulated greater American involvement in those parts of the continent where it perceived a Communist threat. More often than not, the United States exaggerated the threat Communism posed to Western, as opposed to African, interests. Inevitably, it resulted in the crafting of a reactive policy to real and putative Communist threats that supported the continuation of European colonial rule in places like Mozambique, Guinea-Bissau and Angola.

When decolonization occurred in most of the continent in the 1950s and early 1960s, the United States was poised, as it did in Vietnam when the French withdrew, to step in and take the place of the departing colonial powers. This angered many African nationalist leaders who felt that the United States had turned its back on the issue of independence endorsed in the Atlantic Charter of 1941. Demands for independence became even more persistent with the Soviet Union lashing out at European imperialism. American support for the national aspirations of individual African states was tempered by much larger Cold War concerns and the unity of the Western world in the North Atlantic Treaty Organization (NATO) (Gleijeses 2002). What the United States wanted to see was a continent emerging from colonial rule in an orderly fashion and in cooperation with Britain, France and other European colonial powers. American thinking was based on what was perceived to be a symbiotic relationship between Europe and Africa dating back to the dawn of imperial rule in the 19th Century, centering on investments, trade, and the procurement of raw materials for Europe's industrial development.

Another United States foreign policy determinant was containment. The goal of containment in Africa was to deny the Sino-Soviet bloc any access to markets and sources of raw materials. In an address at Northwestern University (in Evanston, Illinois) on June 27, 1951, McGhee spelled out United States' policy toward African decolonization in the post-World War II era. It was premised on the achievement of individual and national aspirations in concert with what he called the free world. In caustic and paternalistic words, McGhee warned that independence for "primitive, uneducated peoples," unprepared to stand up to aggression, would have a negative effect on Western interests. He reckoned that the immediate concern of African colonies was not political independence but improvements in health, sanitation, education, and living and working conditions, and training for successful participation in government (Mcghee 1951).

From the outset, the United States and its NATO allies overestimated Communist interests in order to strengthen their influence throughout Africa. No American politician expressed the American viewpoint better than John Foster Dulles, President Dwight D. Eisenhower's Secretary of State. In a speech on June 1, 1953, following a tour of the Near East and South Asia, he made this candid assessment about decolonization:

Most of the peoples of the near east and Southern Asia are deeply concerned about political independence for themselves and others. They are suspicious of the colonial powers. The United States too is suspect because, it is reasoned, our NATO alliances with France and Britain require us to preserve or restore the old colonial interests of our allies.

I am convinced that the United States policy has been unnecessarily ambiguous in this matter. The leaders of the countries I visited fully recognize that it would be a disaster if there were any break between the United States and Great Britain and France. However, without breaking from the framework of Western Unity, we can pursue our traditional dedication to political liberty. In reality the Western powers can gain, rather than lose from an orderly development of self-government. I emphasize, however, the word 'orderly.' Let none forget that the Kremlin uses extreme nationalism to bait the trap by which it seeks to capture the dependent peoples (in Wallerstein 1975:16).

Dulles's statement revealed the primacy of United States' relations with its European allies over the question of self-determination for Africans under colonial rule. For instance, the White House Office of National Security expressed concern that American abstention on the Algerian vote in the United Nations General Assembly would strain the NATO alliance. France, the colonial power, would view it as a betrayal of a friend. Also, the United States would not come down too heavily against South Africa's apartheid laws and its illegal occupation of Southwest Africa (Namibia) because of defense, trade, and investment considerations. The need to maintain that cohesion with allies influenced America's equivocal attitude toward decolonization, even when all signs pointed to its inevitability.

When the inevitable happened, the United States established and maintained diplomatic and cultural ties with Africa's independent states. The number of embassies, legations, and consulates jumped from 16 before 1959 to 41 in 1960, and 61 by the end of 1962. As Undersecretary of State Douglas Dillon put it, "no matter how admirable our intentions, no matter how well-conceived our policies and programs, our success in the final analysis depends upon people" who would adequately represent the United States in Africa.

Self-determination and decolonization continued to fuel the East-West rivalry and influence-peddling. The political transformation of the continent from the outbreak of World War II to the 1960s was extraordinary and unsurpassed in the history of the modern world. In 1945, Egypt, Ethiopia, Liberia and South Africa were the only independent states in Africa. By the end of 1958, six more colonies (Ghana, Guinea, Libya, Morocco, the Sudan and Tunisia) had regained their independence from Britain, France and Italy. In 1960, 14 more colonies became independent, constituting the largest number of sovereign states to join the ranks of free nations.

By the end of the 1950s, the United States could no longer ignore the shrinking European colonial empires in Africa, and the strident anti-colonial stance of the Communist bloc states. These developments led to the establishment of a separate Division of African Affairs on July 1, 1958. Joseph C. Satterthwaite became the first Assistant Secretary of State for African Affairs. The wind of change swept through Africa in the 1950s, bolstered by the rise of independent states like Egypt, the Sudan, Libya, Morocco, Ghana and Guinea. These factors were responsible for the decision by the Eisenhower Administration to upgrade the African Section of the Department of State.

Post-Cold War Military Retrenchment, 1996 to Present

The end of the Cold War marks the fifth noticeable shift in relations between Africa and the United States. It is characterized by military retrenchment, as the end of the Cold War diminished the need for covert as well as overt military operations in support of friendly anti-Communist states and regimes, and calls for improved trade relations and the promotion of democracy. The Somali humanitarian debacle in 1992-93 kept the United States and other major powers from undertaking humanitarian interventions in even greater tragedies, namely the Rwandan genocide of 1994 and the Darfur genocide in the Sudan. Backed by Security Council Resolution 794 of December 3, 1994, Operation Restore Hope, the United States' humanitarian mission to ensure the safe delivery of food and other essential items to war-ravaged Somalis in Mogadishu, bogged down into gruesome street battles that left Somalis and many of the 28,000 American troops dead or wounded.

President George H. W. Bush's successor, Bill Clinton, withdrew American troops from Somalia at the beginning of 1994 and promptly instituted a tough new policy that emphasized a multilateral approach to peacekeeping operations. While Presidential Decision Directive (PDD) 25 stated that "Peace operations are not and cannot be the centerpiece of United States foreign policy," it also acknowledged that "peacekeeping can be one useful tool to help prevent and resolve such [regional] conflicts before they pose direct threats to our national security. Peacekeeping can also serve UNITED STATES interests by promoting democracy, regional security, and economic growth." A corollary to PDD 25 was Secretary of State Warren Christopher's African Crisis Response Initiative (ACRI). Inaugurated in October of 1996, the ACRI aimed at working "with international partners and African nations to enhance peacekeeping and humanitarian relief capacity" by training and equipping "African nations who seek to enhance their peacekeeping capabilities and are committed to democratic progress, principles, and civilian rule."

When Clinton signed PDD 25 on May 3, 1994, Rwanda was already engulfed in a genocide that claimed over 800,000 lives. As the Report of the Independent Inquiry into the Actions of the United Nations During the 1994 Genocide in Rwanda (December 1999) noted, the international community not only failed to prevent the genocide but also did not act to stop the killings once they began in April of 1994. In fact, the United Nations only acknowledged the killings in Rwanda as a "genocide" on May 31, 1994, when Secretary-General Boutros Boutros-Ghali issued a report on the situation in the central African state. The same situation prevails today in Darfur where former Secretary of State Colin Powell called the killings of unarmed civilians a "genocide" and yet nothing by way of a humanitarian intervention has been done. Under the 1948 Geneva Convention on Genocide, signatory states are not only obligated to punish the crime of genocide through appropriate legislation, but they are also required to bring such crimes to the attention of the United Nations Security Council.

In addition to defining the parameters for American involvement in multilateral peacekeeping operations in Africa, the Clinton administration also showcased the African Growth and Opportunity Act of 2000 (H.R. 434) as a way to increase American exports to Africa which then accounted for only six percent and expand Africa's access to United States markets. In addition to the entry into the United States of designated sub-Saharan African textile and apparel articles duty free, H.R. 434 also provided for the establishment of a United States-Sub-Saharan Africa Trade and Economic Cooperation Forum that would "discuss expanding trade and investment relations between the United States and sub-Saharan Africa," and deal with issues relating to free trade agreements, debt relief, poverty alleviation, trade liberalization, and fiscal and financial reforms.

Conclusion

This chapter has shown the historical context in which the United States has pursued its relations with Africa, paying particular attention to the noticeable shifts in those relations. United States' relations with Africa were predicated upon a recognition of Europe's colonial empires. As the Berlin Conference amply demonstrated, the United States acquiesced in the existence of those empires and sought to further its own economic interests by cooperating with the colonial powers themselves. Woodrow Wilson realized the shortcomings of the old diplomacy characterized by the balance of power, colonial rivalries and secret alliances, but he found himself isolated on the issue of self-determination at Versailles in 1919.

Before the 1930s, the United States had no clearly designated office in the DOS with responsibility for its African policy. Instead, the DOS's Division of European Affairs handled matters relating to Africa. The Italian invasion of Ethiopia in 1935, among other things, convinced the Roosevelt administration to rethink its African policy. In 1938, it began to institutionalize its relations with Africa by transferring responsibility for African affairs within the DOS from the European to the Division of Near Eastern Affairs.

The chapter has also explored the nexus between ideology and the institutionalization of America's foreign relations with Africa in the critical interwar and Cold War decades. The aim has been to provide as detailed an analysis as possible of the origins and the central themes of that relationship, the particular circumstances in which foreign relations were crafted, and the impact of those policies on relations between the Africa an the United States. The end of the Cold War and the Somali humanitarian debacle led to a reassessment of America's involvement in peacekeeping operations. Instead of unilateral humanitarian interventions, the United States opted for multilateral operations that are in the national interest. Africa and America also realized that democracy and free trade can go a long way toward minimizing or avoiding conflicts.

2

Energy Policy

John Patrick Afam Ifedi

Introduction

This chapter is a response to David Goldwyn and Robert Ebel's chapter in the edited report by Kansteiner III and Morrison (2004) that spurred this book. Goldwyn and Ebel offer two salient priorities for United States' policy in the area of United States energy security relative to African sources of energy and four recommendations aimed at realizing the objectives set forth in the policy proposals. The proposals allude to the paramount importance of Africa, especially sustainable stability of the oil producing countries, to the United States in the area of energy security. The two salient priorities it identifies are: (1) Risks and Challenges to African Energy Development—under this objective, certain key factors are identified: poor governance, civil unrest, terrorism, oil price volatility, HIV/AIDS. (2) The Sources of Leverage for Meeting the Objective of Energy Security; these include reputation, debt relief, electricity, investment, and trade financing. Furthermore, it outlines specific policy recommendations that are important to attaining energy security. They include (a) the organizational structure of the State Department relative to the management of multi-sector policy; (b) social, political and economic rewards for meeting specified benchmarks for regional behavior in Africa; (c) pursuit of bilateral policies with the countries of Nigeria, Angola, Equatorial Guinea, Chad, Sao Tome and Principe, Cameroon; and (d) public diplomacy to educate Americans on United States' energy stakes in Africa, and use of the United States—European Union Transatlantic Dialogue, Asia-Pacific Economic Cooperation (APEC) and the G-8 (Group of Eight) in seeking to reach agreement with other nations on a common approach to energy development and transparency in Africa.

This author submits that the proposal presented by Goldwyn and Ebel provides an excellent span and depth of coverage of perspectives on how United

States' energy security policy should be crafted and pursued, but significant analytical shortcomings and omissions remain, which prompts the responses and perspective presented in this chapter, and they center around the following: (a) African perspective is absent in the report, as no indigenous African contributed ideas or perspective or had their views sought in the course of authoring the proposal; hence, an authentic African view is missing from the report; (b) the study treats Africa only as an arena of United States' foreign policy rather than as an integral player and partner in African and global affairs, as Africa is increasingly becoming in the area of energy production; and (c) the proposal is silent on some crucial issues and factors that the United States should take into consideration in working for its energy security in Africa.

This chapter, from the African perspective, systematically identifies and addresses the shortcomings and omissions found in the priorities and policy recommendations set forth in the proposal by Goldwyn and Ebel. Additionally, it contributes to the analysis of the respective points raised in each key priority, as well as the recommendations, and also introduces and analyzes some salient factors that are not mentioned by Goldwyn and Ebel, but considered germane to United State's energy security. Implicit in this analytical response is the refutation of some of the analytical insights presented, and offering of practical alternatives meant to present a more balanced analysis and solutions to United States' energy security interests. Since the central focus of this response is energy policy, it is useful to analytically buttress the imperative of energy security to the United States; hence, this writer begins with a brief sketchy review of United States' attempt to establish a coherent energy policy.

United States Initiatives on Energy Policy

Clamor in the United States for energy policy grew or actually developed after the 1970s oil shocks. Hitherto, supply of oil was plentiful and price was nominal. This scenario ended in 1972 and a new reality materialized. The need to secure a reliable source of energy became imperative in the wake of the OPEC oil embargo of 1973/74 and the ensuing volatility of the Middle East region. In regard to the focus of this response, the central energy concern of the United States in Africa is crude oil and perhaps natural gas. The combination of regional instability in the Middle East and competition from China and India for global oil resource have compelled the United States to elevate the need for energy policy to a level of vital priority. Although the United States is endowed with large deposits of all sorts of energy sources, including oil, its extraordinary appetite for oil has gradually led to dependence on imported oil. Importation of petroleum increased rapidly in the early 1970s and has continued to increase steadily since 1985, accounting for some 60% of the United States domestic needs; it is expected to reach 75% by 2020 (Energy Information Administration 2000:88).

Prior to the initial oil shock in 1973-74, federal energy policy consisted essentially of uncoordinated industry specific support policies: tax subsidies for oil, leasing of federal lands for oil exploration, prospecting and quotas on imported oil to protect domestic industry from cheap imports. Moreover, in the past three decades, several bursts of political activities have occurred relative to responses to "energy crisis." They focused chiefly on import reduction by developing national policies aimed at increasing domestic production of oil, as well efficiency of energy use.

Following the first oil shock in 1973-74, President Nixon enunciated project independence, directed at attaining energy self-sufficiency by 1980. This initiative entailed the reorganization of federal agencies involved in energy research and development, new energy price regulations, data gathering and policy initiatives. It proved to be unsuccessful in realizing the stated objective of energy self-sufficiency, as demand for imported oil continued to grow. In 1975, President Gerald Ford signed the Energy Policy and Conservation Act, extending price controls on oil, establishing automobile fuel efficiency standards, and authorized the creation of the Strategic Petroleum Reserve.

Coming on the heels of President Ford's effort was Jimmy Carter who, upon assuming the presidency, signed many Acts and implemented a plan meant to reduce consumption of oil and reduce dependence on foreign energy sources, especially oil: Emergency National Gas Act of 1977, in response to increasing shortages in gas; National Gas Act of 1977, in response to increasing shortages in gas; and a National Energy Plan, calling for the creation of a new Department of Energy, which is to consolidate dispersed federal agencies involved in energy policy, research and development programs. This plan led to the passage of the National Energy Act, which entails the National Energy Policy and Conservation Act, the Power Plant and Industrial Fuel Use Act, the Public Utilities Regulatory Policy Act, the Energy Tax Act, and the Natural Gas Policy Act. Essentially, the policy was meant to regulate energy prices, reduce dependence on foreign sources of oil, and increase energy efficiency. A few months after President Carter signed the laws making up the National Energy Act, Iran stopped exporting oil following the Shah's overthrow, leading to a worldwide shortage of oil and a dramatic increase in oil prices. Consequently, President Carter, in 1979, responded to growing oil shortages by introducing gradual decontrol of oil prices. He also followed this by signing the Energy Security Act, consisting of many pieces of legislation essentially directed at encouraging energy security and efficiency.

Furthermore, there were few significant new federal energy policy initiatives during the Reagan Administration and the first few years of the George H. W. Bush Administration. Presidents Reagan and Bush completed essentially the process of deregulating oil prices, as oil prices peaked in 1981 and fell gradually until 1985 and dramatically in 1986. The 1990s dawned with the invasion of Kuwait by Iraq, precipitating the curtailment of oil export from the area, with attendant rapid and significant increase in oil prices in the mid-1990s. Since then, the United States has experienced episodically a collective hand wringing about rising oil prices, dependence on Middle East oil, and absence and or need for sustained coherent energy policy. Moreover, the Bush Administration, in 1991, developed a national energy policy aimed at increasing oil supply, exploration in the United States—centered on the Arctic National Wildlife Refuge (ANWR). The proposal was controversial and vehemently opposed by environmentalists. Although debated for a considerable length of time by Congress, it was finally rejected.

The United States continued to grapple with the issue of energy policy as 1992 dawned, although public angst over oil prices, potential shortages and dependence on imported oil lifted quickly with the end of the Gulf War. In the 1990s, the only major piece of energy related legislation passed was the 1992 Energy Policy Act; it grew out of the National Energy Efficiency Act of 1991. Its focus was to create tax and direct subsidies for energy efficiency and renewable energy technologies and on encouraging the general implementation of integrated resource planning programs for utilities in all states. Although, the 1992 Energy policy Act considered all energy—nuclear, coal, solar, electric, hydro—sources, the major focus was on crude oil. In that regard, the focus of the policy was on conservation, efficiency, and environmental protection. No new energy policy legislation was passed for the balance of the decade of the 1990s. Hence, the energy policy for the rest of the decade hinged on the framework of policies embodied in the energy Act of 1992. Nonetheless, net import of energy, oil, increased significantly by about 50 percent during the decade.

In the interim, the United States faces energy challenges that are likely to linger for many years and require critical policy changes to come to grips with the challenges. The success of any acceptable public policy crafted to manage the energy security issue must entail at least a decided repositioning of the United States' approach to Africa and possibly a paradigm readjustment, given the increasingly significant level of oil import from the region. The preceding sketchy analysis of United States' initiatives sets forth a framework for understanding the run up to the sort of energy policy imperative articulated by Goldwyn and Ebel.

Critical Analysis of the Salient Shortcomings and Omissions of the Proposal

Turning to the issues and factors raised in the proposal, Goldwyn and Ebel are on firm ground relative to their articulation of the energy challenges facing the United States; but in analyzing the solutions proffered by the proposal purely from African perspective, it is evident that there are some shortcomings and omissions. Hence, this review would systematically identify and address these areas of shortcomings and omissions. They include the conduct of United States transnational energy companies, the need to address environmental issues attendant to energy sourcing, and necessary readjustments in the diplomatic approach taken by the United States in Africa.

At the outset, Goldwyn and Ebel assert that the United States' energy stakes in Africa are on the rise. Specifically, they write that "the United States has burgeoning energy interests in Africa.... Today, Central and West Africa, with proven reserves of more than 60 billion barrels, double the estimate of a decade ago, provides one in four barrels of oil coming into world markets from outside the Persian Gulf. The region's energy-endowed countries supply 13 to 14 percent of U.S. oil imports, positioning the region as the fourth-largest source of imports" (Goldwyn and Ebel 2004). The insights set forth by the proposal about the growing commercial and investment value of Africa is well founded, especially in the energy sector, which accounts for about 90 percent of the about one percent of Africa's commercial relations and trade with the rest of the world. The report is also generally correct in indicating that "Africa could enjoy enormous wealth this decade (Joskow n.d.). But, this analysis is clearly inadequate because it is overly generalized, as it fails to pinpoint that this new African wealth accrues only to the small number of oil producing countries such as Nigeria, Gabon, Angola, Equatorial Guinea, Chad, Sao Tome, and Principe, Cameroon and, to some extent, the Congo (Brazzaville). Furthermore, the prospects of these increased earnings from oil notwithstanding, many, if not all of these countries, remain poor in terms relative to their populations, socio-economic and infrastructural needs, as well as due to unbridled graft and corruption often engendered by the "curse" of oil. Corruption undermines economic and political institutions necessary for economic prosperity and social stability.

Policy makers and leaders in the United States find that the sustained development of Africa's energy sector is crucial to America's energy and security goals;

hence, it is central to its policy to encourage its development. The United States, therefore, considers it imperative to understand and develop strategies to manage and/or ameliorate factors that pose risks and challenges to the extraction and delivery of African oil. The proposal argues that improvement of these factors—poor governance, civil unrest, terrorism, oil price volatility, HIV/AIDS—are necessary to ensure United States' energy security. While the factors identified are salient, the United States' approach to assuring that they do not continue to pose problems to its energy interests has been inadequate. This view is pervasive in Africa, and it tends to govern the attitude of Africans towards all American efforts and pursuits in Africa.

Take poor governance, coups, misrule, and fraudulent elections, for instance, this has been the bane of governance in Africa for a considerable length of time, actually since the end of colonialism. Hardly does any African country escape culpability in this regard. Yet, the United States did little or nothing about the problem, and even in many cases overtly and covertly encouraged and condoned it, so long as its interests are advanced by such governments—Nigeria and the Democratic Republic of Congo quickly come to mind. The United States is well known to accommodate Africa's elite and governments regardless of their path to and often conduct while in power, whether through coups, fraudulent elections, or corruption. It is particularly notorious for its association and support for Zaire's Mobutu Sese Seko, a relationship that tolerated unbridled corruption, rampant violence and retarded economic development in that country, which persists to date in the period after Mobutu. Furthermore, rarely are American corporate leaders penalized for inducing African government officials with pay offs to procure contracts or gain markets. Also, the level of corrupt practices in the area of business is rife and has posed great risk to Africa for decades, but it is only in the recent times—because it may impact United States' interests—that American policy-makers have begun to emphasize enforcement of transparency laws to discourage it. In the interim, business and corporate corruption is one of the fundamental reasons for aviation mishaps in Africa (improperly inspected, poorly serviced, older, un-airworthy aircrafts sold to African airlines through corrupt officials and corporate leaders). Also, numerous environmental and health problems are caused by the practice of dumping of toxic foods, chemicals, or the like, on and unsuspecting African public by corrupt officials in cahoots with corporate officials who readily ship banned chemicals and other goods to Africa. The United States has neither been attentive to these issues, nor has it been interested in leveraging its considerable influence in multi-lateral institutions to curtail or end the outflow of funds stolen by corrupt government and business officials out of Africa, thereby undermining development and stability in the process. The United States has not established any regime locally to curb or stop local bank officials from acting as bankers for corrupt African officials; therefore, the United States is perceived in Africa as indirectly complicit in this corrupt practice. Its silence for years in the face of the prevalence of United States banks accepting stolen funds from Africa has posited it as an enabler and denied it of moral, ethical authority in regards to addressing such issues. Evidence that the United States could help to stamp out or minimize the outflow of stolen funds from Africa is exemplified by the decision recently by its close counterpart, Britain, to shut its doors against stolen funds by cooperating with Nigeria's anti-corruption agency, the Economic and Financial Crimes Commission (EFCC). It aims to stem the tide of corruption by taking the position that, according to British High Commissioner to Nigeria, Richard Gozney, his country would not receive any funds acquired illegally either by public or private officials from any part of the country (*Nigerian Tribune*, October 11, 2006).

Another crucial priority cited in regard to the risks and challenges to African energy development is civil unrest. Goldwyn and Ebel indicate that civil unrest militates against oil sector development, especially onshore oil activities. In Nigeria, Sao Tome and elsewhere, the study points out, the reduction of oil production rose to the tune, in Nigeria, of about 100 to 200 thousand barrels per day with attendant significant financial losses for Nigeria. The point that it missed, however, is that the radicalism and economic sabotage in oil producing regions of Africa are, apart from the policies of local governments, fanned by the environmentally irresponsible practices of oil companies, which spoil the environment and sources of economic life of the inhabitants, thereby engendering armed demand for redress.

In regard to terrorism, United States policymakers postulate that failed states and weak states tend to be favorable grounds for the incubation of anti-United States groups that use terror to advance their causes; hence, it helps these states to patrol their land and maritime borders. Resultantly, the United States has concluded military agreements with the countries of Nigeria, Ghana, Gabon, and Senegal for joint or unilateral sea border patrols. It also attempts to support many African counties in areas of their national defense that may be beyond the economic ability of such states. The United States, however, fails to see the dearth of social, economic and political injustices as the real reasons for unrest in many African countries, and how resolving such injustices would lead to conditions that are less favorable to the nourishment of terrorists and terrorism.

In regard to oil price volatility, there is little or nothing that can effectively be done to regularize it, since it is subject to global market forces that are outside of the control of the United States. A fairly predictable and peaceful global environment, however, is able to produce predictably steady, lower and less volatile prices. This is the reason the view that the United States' policy should focus on finding ways to work with governments, organizations and communities in oil producing areas to bring about peace, sustainable development and capacity building is cogent.

The issue of HIV/AIDS is particularly difficult; the disease has had and is progressively having a devastating effect on communities across Africa, with dire consequences for productivity, economic progress, and social stability. The devastation of the workforce is particularly problematic. Although the United States has pledged $15 billion to help fight the disease, the prevalence of illiteracy, poverty, and traditional beliefs has coalesced to render this task very difficult. Although the money allocated to the effort to fight HIV/AIDS in Africa is laudable, it should be known that money alone would not curb the spread of the disease. Collateral effort to arrest the decrepit educational, economic, political and healthcare infrastructures, as well as the debunking those traditional myths, belief system and practices that lend themselves to the spread of the disease are equally important to affect its arrest. So, money is necessary but not sufficient; it is, therefore, important for the United States to engage Africa in partnership in a more far-reaching manner than what presently obtains, especially in the healthcare delivery sector, to bring about conditions under which monies allocated for controlling and finding a solution to the disease would be best applied. Essentially, only with improvements in education, economic growth and measures crafted to combat HIV/AIDS prove successful.

Furthermore, as an approach to bringing African States to comply with United States' goals for its energy security, Goldwyn and Ebel suggest that the United States should leverage its ability and position to help Africa to meet its needs in certain areas; these needs include the following: (1) reputation, (2) ability to grant or persuade others to grant debt relief, (3) marshal effort to bring about electricity investment, and (4) trade financing. In regard to reputation, the report suggests that African leaders have inordinate interest in "laundering" their image by associating with high-level leaders of the United States. It further suggests that this associational need can be leveraged to compel African leaders to improve the quality of governance and management of their countries, thereby bringing about greater stability through the promise of close association for good performance. In other words, high-level United States leaders would not be accessible to any African leader who does not meet the criteria for good governance, security and transparency set forth by the United States. Contrary to this assertion, however, many Africans view the United States as part of the problem of corruption in many regards and lacking the moral and ethical audacity to employ reputation and close association as corrective tools to compel African officials to behave or govern in accordance with the American prescription. The prevailing view is that the United States is complicit in the corruption of African leaders, as many such leaders find lodging for their ill-gotten wealth in United States banks, with little effort on the part of the United States government to persuade or compel the banking sector to reject such funds that emanate from dubious sources, as Britain did recently by promising to partner with Nigeria to ensure that no questionable funds from Nigerian citizens would be accepted by banks in the United Kingdom.

Another, leverage cited by the proposal is debt relief. The proposal urges that debt relief should be linked to satisfactory adherence to social and fiscal conditionalities imposed by the United States. In other words, African countries that abide by United States programs for national stability and transparency should be rewarded with debt relief. This is rather unfortunate. Predicating human needs and development assistance on the behavior of states, which is mostly outside the control of ordinary people, is odious, since ordinary people, not states, tend to suffer disproportionately from the consequences usually brought about by punitive sanctions imposed on grounds of debt incurred by the states. Debt relief, many believe, should not be predicated on political and social conditionalities; moreover, most of Africa's debt was fraudulently incurred in the first place with the full knowledge of the United States. Furthermore, the United States considers only Chad, Sao Tome and Principe, Angola and Cameroon, all oil producing countries, as nations to be eligible for debt relief. This criterion leaves out many truly needy countries that have no oil, which comprise most African countries; these include Sierra Leone, Burkina Faso, Togo, Guinea, Benin, to name some. This further underscores the assertion that the United States policy toward Africa is neither based on partnership nor interest in Africa's development, but in Africa's energy resources.

In the case of electricity investment, there is a chronic shortfall of electric power supply in Africa. The proposal correctly estimates that Africa will need $609 billion for electricity sector investment alone between 2010 and 2030. It is impossible for any African government to finance even a fraction of this cost without help from the international financial community. Electricity is vital to sustainable development; but, just as in the case of debt and trade financing, financial assistance in this critical sector should not be subjected to international politics or employed as a punitive measure, since it is essentially basic to human development, economic growth and social stability. Coercive measures and conditionalities of this nature are best limited to non-economic matters such as military hardware, training, visa restrictions for high government officials, etc; it should not include activities that punish the poor along with the state officials who often experience no hardship as a result. The United States should reevaluate the repercussions of such draconian approach to Africa's economic development. It breeds frustration and alienates friends. Rather than take this approach, it should find friendlier ways to help Africa rid itself of its problem governments without appearing to be against Africans; perhaps, by seeking to use creative ways to effect stability by instituting transparency, using non-governmental organizations (NGO's) to deliver development aid. This may produce development while minimizing financial graft and political corruption. This response now turns to the consideration of the proposal's policy recommendations.

Analysis of Policy Recommendations of the Proposal

In regard to policy recommendations, the proposal by Goldwyn and Ebel suggests that the United States Department of State should be reorganized to more effectively coordinate and manage a multi-sector policy between the President and the Secretary of State, and that a coordinator of ambassadorial rank should be appointed to manage linkages with senior African leaders. The proposal also points to the need to craft regional policies and programs to ensure economic and political stability in oil producing regions. It calls for the United States to devise a clear and transparent benchmark for regional behavior. Any leader who makes a commitment to meet the requirements of transparency and good governance set forth by the United States would be eligible for support programs. The programs for which committed nations would be eligible include: invitation to G-8 (Group of eight industrialized nations) appended bi-annual summits; benefit from United States sponsored peacekeeping training and international military education training (IMET); debt restructuring, rescheduling, relief or forgiveness; eligibility for power and other infrastructure development; capacity building program to train national officials in essential skills; eligibility for trade financing through the United States Export-Import (EXIM) Bank, the Trade Development Agency and their international equivalents; and, access to capital markets. This approach of rewarding compliant countries is resented and viewed by many in Africa as heavy handed and coercive. The conventional view is that ascribing these standards and preconditions as bases for helping Africa is resented, since it is the common people that suffer the consequences. This is tantamount to double jeopardy—the poor suffer from corrupt and poor governance by their leaders only to be penalized along with the same leaders, adducing punitive criteria that also hurt the poor more, as against perhaps freezing the individual accounts of government officials.

Furthermore, this posture and pre-assistance conditionality only serve to create animosity against the United States, thereby bringing about conditions that are bound to create preference for United States' competitors in the future, as well as an aversion for doing business with American companies. The United States is often viewed as having preference for sole decider status regarding acceptable reform effort rather than acting multilaterally and in partnership with Africa. The continent is important to United States' energy needs, as astutely articulated by Goldwyn and Ebel; they write insightfully that the profound challenges of the 21st Century warrant recognizing energy's central role in America's future and the need for much more ambitious and creative approaches to relating with Africa. Essentially, United States' energy security is best preserved by maintaining good relations between producing and consuming nations, strengthening trade ties and introducing greater cordiality in relating to key stakeholders, as well as winning hearts and minds in Africa. What works regarding energy security is engaging the world through partnership, shared commitments, interdependence and mutual respect. But, to date, numerous commentators and observers agree that the United States has taken only small steps to properly and creatively align its foreign policy towards Africa. Tension and contradictions that are likely to produce the effect of limiting the establishment of a new grand strategy remain in place.

The proposal also urges that the United States should undertake bilateral policies with the following African countries: Nigeria, Angola, Equatorial Guinea, Chad, Sao Tome and Principe, and Cameroon. The central focus of this proposal for bilateral relations with these select countries is to ensure political stability, transparency and good governance, elements of national attributes that would ensure that United States' interests are safeguarded in the respective countries. Ironically, these countries share the commonality of being oil producing countries. This is further evidence that, with respect to Africa, United States policymakers are essentially only interested in oil producing countries and in particular the evolution in those countries of socio-political and economic conditions perceived by the United States as necessary to guarantee its energy needs; hence, non-oil endowed countries are not considered as important for economic and political stability and social assistance (Kraxberger 2005:47).

Additionally, the proposal suggests that Americans should be educated on the importance and nature of the United States' energy stakes in Africa. This is meant to gain, through public diplomacy, the support of the American public for United States policies in Africa. Moreover, the United States, the proposal advances, should muster other international fora such as the United States—European Union Transatlantic Dialogue, Asia-Pacific Economic Cooperation (APEC), and the G-8 to foster conditions of mutual and general benefit in Africa's energy development, transparency and good democratic governance. Incidentally, the United States has not made any sustained attempt to marshal such transformational effort to correct Africa's many problems except sporadic responses to problems in oil producing states.

Analysis of Issues Omitted in the Proposal

Having touched on various areas of the proposal by Goldwyn and Ebel and expressed an African perspective relative to them, I shall now turn to identify and analyze other factors that the proposal either did not address or did not address adequately. They include the following: corporate responsibility on the part of United States oil companies, environmental factors, and readjustment of United States' foreign policy approach in Africa. These factors are crucial to assuring United States' energy security.

On the issue of "corporate responsibility," the proposal neglected to discuss the connection between energy security and the comportment of United States energy companies in Africa. In the interim, American companies would benefit significantly from image "laundering" and greater corporate responsibility. This would enhance Africa's perception of United States' motives and create an enabling environment for the security of its energy interests. People are invariably easier to persuade and work with when they like someone. Therefore, better corporate conduct, perhaps by contributing to the community in which they conduct business and ensuring that they do not contribute to pollution, would please the inhabitants and create a friendly atmosphere for business to thrive, and foster a sense of strategic partnership, rather than a feeling of exploitation and usury. Oil companies can achieve this by allocating some of their earnings for useful social programs and purposes meant to enhance the construction of health, academic, and social infrastructure for the local communities. And of equal importance is ensuring that pollution of the environment is avoided, attended by commitment to clean-up inadvertent oil spills and to reach mutually agreed upon just compensations when such spills occur.

It is clear that a great share of the cause of terrorism and radicalism associated with oil producing areas emanate from the degradation or damage of sources of local agricultural production and livelihood, usually occasioned by environmental pollution stemming from crude oil extraction and transportation activities. To illustrate this observation further, it is useful to cite the case of the on-going militancy in the oil producing delta region of Nigeria. This has reduced, by at least one-fourth, the productive capacity and earnings of Nigeria's oil industry. Many oil workers, especially expatriates, have also been seized as hostages by the militants; some have been killed, and the government has been engaged in sporadic fighting to dislodge the militants who have fought back with increasing tenacity and ferocity, inflicting severe casualties on the Nigeria armed forces. In the case of Côte d' Ivoire, pollution by an oil company actually brought down a government and imperiled the fragile peace in that country. The crisis began when "528 cubic meters (116,000 galloons) of toxic liquid unloaded from a ship called Proba Koala were dumped in 11 open-air sites in residential areas around the commercial capital, Abidjan ... the 'residue washings from ... gasoline cargo' were dangerous" (*The Economist*, September 16, 2006:58). Resultantly, people began to fall ill, and thousands took to the streets in protest.

Furthermore, many environmental groups are vehemently opposed to the activities of oil companies in Africa. It is common knowledge that attendant to oil drilling, extraction, and transportation is potential and often real environmental damage. For instance, natural gas flaring, which produces acid rain is a major environmental hazard, wrecking havoc on farm lands and fishing waters in such places as Nigeria, as well as other locales where oil exploitation is undertaken. Also common is the hazard posed by oil pipelines which often ruptures, producing oil or gasoline spills. These spills often contaminate ground water, posing a grave danger to communities of oil producing regions of Africa. Frequently, gasoline spills occur, as occurred in Jesse, Nigeria, in 1994, leading to an accidental fire that killed over 1,000 people who had been attempting to scoop up the liquid for sale. Furthermore, closely associated with crude oil exploitation is natural gas harvesting; the environmental damage associated with gas energy exploitation and its impact on the environment is well documented; in the article, "West African Gas Pipeline (WAGP) Project and its Impact on the Regions Development" (2005), Ifedi and Ndumbe illustrate the position of environmentalists regarding the effects of oil and gas exploration in the West Africa region. They write that the project has met with protestations from local and international environmental groups. The groups oppose the project on grounds of the attendant environmental problems that result from such explorations. Furthermore, take the issue of oil exploration and natural gas extraction, several local and international environmental "groups in Ghana, Nigeria, and Togo oppose the WAGP project. For example, Friends of the Earth, an environmental group in Ghana, argues that environmental impact assessments of the project were not given sufficient priority in feasibility studies" (Ifedi and Ndumbe 2005). Other groups in Nigeria argue that because more than 50,000 families in Nigeria, Ghana, Benin, and Togo could be displaced, the WAGP project should be abandoned.

Additionally, the groups in Nigeria claim that if the WAGP project is undertaken, it would exacerbate the devastation of fragile mangroves and wetland and increase erosion. This, they posit, is because inhabitants of such communities lose their lands—their main source of livelihood (Aderinokun, December 12, 2004). Noble Wadzeh, program coordinator of Friends of the Earth (FOE) in Ghana, argues that development is about the people; for development to be attained and sustained, the environment that provides the people with the means of livelihood and upon which they depend must be maintained and not destroyed. He adds that the environmental damage that would result from WAGP would be adverse to agricultural and fishing enterprises upon which the people of the oil producing region depend for their livelihood.

Apart from corporate responsibility and the environmental factor, which are quite intricately linked, another salient proposal omitted by Goldwyn and Ebel, which was discussed briefly in connection with other issues raised in the proposal, concerns the need to readjust the operational approach taken historically by United States policymakers and operatives in Africa. Traditionally, this approach is resented by Africans; if continued, it is bound to further exacerbate the existing alienation, thereby fostering preference for economic relations with other rising powers such as India and China, with important implications for United States' energy interests in the region. In Africa, it is common knowledge that the continent has been given a peripheral place in United States' foreign policy. Essentially, United States has paid little attention to Africa, often treating it with benign neglect. Eventually, it has engaged Africa only when some other foreign policy imperative compelled it to do so—the Cold War, decolonization, strategic resources, etc. Its relationship with Africa has traditionally been predicated upon events elsewhere, and has often comprised an attempt to position Africa to serve its interests, not help Africa as a strategic partner or build capacity for self-help and sustainable development there. In recent times, the United States is palpably interested in Africa due to its oil wealth.

James Dao alludes to this assertion in his statement that "Africa, the neglected stepchild of American diplomacy, is rising in strategic importance to Washington policy makers, and one word sums up the reason—oil (Dao September 19, 2002). In a similar vein, Paul E. Simons, Deputy Assistant Secretary for Economic and Business Affairs, United States Department of State, observes that "the fundamental objective of U.S. energy policy is to ensure that our economy has access to sufficient, affordable, and reliable energy supplies" (Simons August 1, 2006). The United States, therefore, should consider reframing its foreign policy paradigm relative to Africa; it should embark on a sea change in perspective and approach, if its energy interests in Africa are to remain assured in the long term. This readjustment has not occurred.

As has traditionally been the case, United States' interest in Africa is usually governed by events that are of little or no relevance or have no origin in Africa; and once the interest is met, the United States would usually abandon the region. It hardly established sustained long-term transformational partnership in Africa, to the detriment of the region. In recent times, as noted earlier, global energy concerns and terrorism are the rationale for United States' engagement in Africa. Hitherto, the United States supported decolonization in Africa to end European colonialism, but this made the United States effectively the legatee of colonialism. Following decolonization, the next salient impetus for United States' engagement in Africa was the Cold War; during this period, its attempt to contain the expansion of the Soviet Union outside of the latter's sphere of influence proved to be the decisive factor in its relation with Africa. Following the collapse of the Soviet Union and end of the Cold War, the United States, again, relegated Africa to the background in its foreign policy interests until after the September 11, 2001 terrorist attack against it and the radicalization of its sources of crude oil in the Middle-East, following United States' pre-emptive attack on Iraq. Uncertainty in the United States about the reliability of the Middle-East region compelled it to focus on African crude oil sources. It is, therefore, evident that the chief link between Africa and the United States in the post-Cold War era and the post-September 11, 2001 world is its increasing dependence on oil produced mainly in the unstable Middle Eastern region. Therefore, in the wake of the conclusion of the rivalry between the East and the West, the central feature of United States' interest in Africa has shifted decisively to maintenance of access to oil and war against its adversaries who employ terror tactics against it throughout the world. This shift is clearly expressed in statements by leading defense officials. According to General Alfred M. Gray, the United States Marine Corp commandant, the underdeveloped world's growing dissatisfaction over the gap between the rich and poor nations will create a fertile breeding ground for insurgencies that have the potential to jeopardize regional stability and America's access to vital economic resources (Volman 1993:2). Little or no attention is paid to non-oil pro-ducing countries. One outcome of this is that the United States attaches less importance to its relations with Africa, especially where there are no strategic resources or resources that it considers of value—especially oil, profitable invest-ment locations, places that are of geo-strategic importance and those that are via-ble consumer markets. The United States often takes into little or no consideration the pressing interests of Africa itself.

To win popular approval in Africa and ensure energy security, however, it behooves the United States to base its foreign policy on reciprocity and partner-ship, rather than domination; mutual well-being and cooperation, rather than competition. As the world's foremost super power and one that is in competition with major rising powers—India and China—in Africa, the United States would be best served by exercising equitable partnership rather than seeking imperial dominance or dictating to Africans on matters of policy, trade, social structure, and development. In other words, the United States should abandon the self-cen-tered, pontificating and self-referencing approach to Africa-United States rela-tions, which could undermine America's position as a desirable partner. There needs to be a sharp shift in United States' foreign policy direction away from browbeating others into line. This would serve well United States' national inter-ests and energy security and improve the prospects for sustainable political and economic development in Africa as well. As alluded to earlier, barring the occur-rence of a strategic shift in the fundamental basis and approach in its relations with Africa, the United States risks losing substantial grounds in Africa to com-petitors such as China, whose approach to business with Africa has been more measured and friendly.

Essentially, the United States faces a new context in Africa where a rising China and a new Asian bloc are shattering the final vestiges of its economic hege-mony (Bergstein March/April, 2004). Hence, it is important for United States policy-makers to take into consideration that "traditional policies and long stand-ing institutional approaches developed in the [1960s] and 1970s are inadequate to the challenge they face in Africa in the long term" (Morse and Jaffe 2004:11). Therefore, to assure its energy security and interests in Africa, the United States may do well to emulate the key elements of China's approach, which is worth dis-cussing at some length. A lengthy look at China's activities is useful; it would posit a comparative perspective as a way of revealing certain contrasts in approaches towards relations with Africa.

As in the case of United States relations with Africa, China's relations with Africa are multidimensional. In recent years, however, China's political, economic, and military relations with Africa have been subordinated to its quest to secure energy resources in the African continent. China's goodwill with African Countries can be traced back to anti-colonial struggles in the 1960s. Nonetheless, China's relations with Africa have shifted from holding a strong ideological bias in support of Communist regimes and Marxist insurgencies to being led by market and resource considerations. Today, the only ideological component to Sino-Africa relations is the One China principle, although there are even exceptions to this as seen in the growing Chinese energy interests in Chad, which still has diplomatic relations with Taiwan. African leaders are becoming more comfortable with China's approach to relations in the area of trade and development. The reason for this is astutely summed up by Chinese Premier Wen Jiabao on his recent visit to Luanda, Angola and talks with Angola's President Jose Eduardo dos Santos. Jiabao stated that China has adopted positions which respond to the development needs of African nations. China is prepared to work with Africa and engage in reciprocal co-operation without preconditions (*China Daily* August 1, 2006).

China currently derives a quarter of its oil imports from Africa, with oil interests in Algeria, Angola, Chad and the Sudan and increasing stakes in Equatorial Guinea, Gabon, and Nigeria. China's energy interests in Chad are of particular interest given that Chad still maintains diplomatic relations with Taiwan. China's growing energy partnership with the Sudan is one of a number of areas where Sino-United States energy interests diverge. China's National Petroleum Corporation (CNPC) established oil exploration rights in the Sudan in 1995. Two years later, the United States cut ties with the Sudan; China filled the vacuum, making the Sudan China's largest overseas production base. More than half of the Sudan's oil exports goes to China, accounting for five percent of China's total oil imports. CNPC owns a 40-percent stake in the Greater Nile Petroleum Operating Company (GNPOC) and pumps over 300,000 barrels per day in the Sudan. Another Chinese firm, Sinopec, is constructing a 1500-kilometer (932 miles) pipeline to Port Sudan on the Red Sea, where China's Petroleum Construction Group (CPCG) is building a tanker terminal.

African States are also drawn to China because of its non-ideological, non-interventionist approach, which contrasts with the Unites States' approach that places an emphasis on Western-style democracy, governance, human rights, and humanitarian intervention, other self-referencing conditions that are often construed as condescending and intrusive, consistent with Samuel Huntington's declaration that the United States, as the leader of a uni-polar world, was arrogant (Kagan, March/April, 2004:70). China has also appealed to Africa through numerous goodwill gestures. For example, the Chinese foreign minister has maintained a policy of making his first official trip to the African continent every year. For decades, China has also supported numerous infrastructure projects across Africa, as well as sending doctors and nurses to the continent, establishing scholarships for African students to study in Chinese universities, providing training for African businessmen and trade officials, and supplying funds to encourage Chinese businesses to invest in Africa. It also maintains dialogue with Africa through several bilateral and multilateral fora such as the Asia-Africa Summit and the China African Business Council, which was jointly established with the United Nations Development Programme in November of 2004 to support China's private sector investment in Cameroon, Ghana, Nigeria, Mozambique, South Africa, and Tanzania. In 2000, China initiated the China-Africa Cooperation Forum comprising 46 of the 53 African countries. Among its accomplishments are the unconditional cancellations of US$1.2 billion in debt for 31 African countries. China is also engaged in negotiations to create a free trade area with the Southern African Customs Union, as well as coordinating with African states in international organizations such as the World Trade Organization and United Nations.

On the economic front, Sino-Africa trade increased by 50 percent between 2002 and 2003 to US$18.5 billion, which was expected to grow to US$30 billion by 2006. At present, 700 Chinese companies operate in 49 African countries and eight African countries have been granted the status of "officially approved travel destinations" by China. Many of China's diplomatic initiatives in Africa are in direct conflict with American policy toward the region. For example, Beijing supplied US$1 billion in arms to both Ethiopia and Eritrea during their war from 1998 to 2000. Zimbabwe's President Robert Mugabe, whose regime has been isolated by the West, led by the United States due to its forced eviction of White farmers, has also turned to China for aid. Chinese investment in Zimbabwe amounted to US$600 million in 2004 and China has upgraded Zimbabwe's transportation infrastructure. China is also, having signed a contract to do so, engaged in an historic railway transport infrastructure improvement in Nigeria: "the federal government of Nigeria signed an $8.3b contract for the construction of a standard gauge railway line from Lagos to Kano with a Chinese firm, the China Civil Engineering Corporation. The line will link all the 36 capitals of Nigeria. The Chinese also recently granted a $2.5bn loan facility out of which a substantial amount will be used on the rail project. Over 50,000 Nigerians will be employed during the construction of the project (*The Punch* November 1, 2006:1).

With the Sudan supplying China 13 percent of its oil imports, attempts by the United States to persuade the Sudan to end the Darfur genocide brings it into direct confrontation with China's energy security policies. The United States and China, however, are not the only states vying for energy resources in Africa. Recently, Korea National Oil Corporation obtained a 65-percent oil and gas production right in two Nigerian offshore blocks, while India's Oil and Natural Gas Corporation, Videsh, obtained a 25-percent stake. South Korea and India are the world's fourth and sixth largest energy consumers, respectively. India and China both hold stakes in the Greater Nile Oil Project in the Sudan, with India having invested US$700 million in the Sudan's oil sector. China and India have also been engaged in direct competition for African energy resources, as seen in October 2004 when China outbid India to buy an interest in an offshore block in Angola.

Facing a plethora of internal crisis ranging from poverty to poor governance and civil war, Africa is likely to emerge as a volatile stage for Sino-United States energy competition. African states have been drawn to China by its non-interventionist, non-ideological approach in conducting its relations. This means that other big energy consumers such as China and India will compete with the United States for access to Countries that allow foreign investment in their energy sectors. Unless the United States changes its policy course, it will weaken its ability to influence those countries in Africa where China and India are making important inroads in economic and social areas dominated by dominated by the United States and the West (Bajpae 2005).

Conclusion

In their proposal and analysis of United States' energy needs and security and how to secure them in Africa, Goldwyn and Ebel provided keen and cogent insights into the issue and made recommendations. There, however, were analytical shortcomings and omissions in their report, especially when viewed from the African perspective. The proposals and recommendations ignore the historical contributions of the United States government and transnational corporations in the problems confronting Africa at the moment and fail to pay attention to the issues of the environment, corporate responsibility and the approach taken by the United States in its relation with Africa. The general thrusts of the proposal indicate that Africa would remain important in the United States' energy security calculus for the foreseeable future. But, the United States needs to foster strategic partnership with Africa and take an approach that is different from its historically benign neglect by looking at the continent as a whole not just the oil producing countries. This is important in light of the challenges posed by the new emerging competitors such as China and India. In this regard, the United States would be more successful in the future if it readjusts its diplomatic approach, becoming less pontificating, self-referencing and arrogant.

Also, energy security depends in large measure on the conduct of the United States' transnational oil companies. Their environmental record is essential to good relations with the local communities across Africa, so it is necessary for them to operate on strict guidelines meant to ensure that they follow environmental laws and keep from incessant pollution of the local environment, which alienates the local stakeholders, foments violence, and creates the very radical conditions that are inimical to United States' interests and energy security.

The United States, as a measure to curtail instability in the region, should leverage its considerable international clout to encourage the establishment of international regimes to combat fiscal corruption, which contributes so much to socio-political instability and makes it difficult for stable institutions to emerge. Without stable social, political and economic institutions, the likelihood of the stability is limited, and the security of United States' interests would be uncertain. In sum, it behooves the United States to adopt creative and carefully considered realistic strategies to help Africa succeed, if its interests and energy security are to be assured in Africa.

3

Peace-building and Conflict Resolution[1]

Mueni wa Muiu

Introduction

> Frictions between villages, especially within the same vicinage, were settled by
> arbitration through common palavers in a thoroughly decentralized manner.
> In these assemblies, "speakers" (*ngambi9/10*) for each matrilineage set out
> their positions, and decisions were reached by a consensus of the whole audi-
> ence (Vansina 2004:237).

Can there be an equitable partnership between Africa and the United States? Can
a lion become a vegetarian? In this chapter, I will analyze the United States'
peace-building and conflict-resolution efforts in Africa. To do so, I analyze European conceptions of Africa. How did European knowledge (which influenced
that of the United States) of Africa affect relations between the two? This is followed by a brief examination of the nature of African states and their role in
peace-building and conflict resolution. Whose Peace? What is the role of foreign
military bases? In this section, I will draw on examples from Mozambique, Sierra
Leone, Liberia and Tanzania to demonstrate that the conceptualization of
"peace" has different meanings depending on the actors involved. To the United
States, "peace" is part and parcel of a process of exploitation of Africa by Europe
which began during slavery. During that period, "peace" meant appeasing different African groups to ease the process of exploitation by creating plantations and
mission stations on African soil. This process continued during colonialism into

---

1. In this chapter, by Africa, I mean all the countries on the continent including its
    islands. "African" refers to anyone who considers Africa as his/her home.

the contemporary period, where "peace" means making way for foreign countries and companies to better exploit Africa's labor and resources. Such "peace" does not mean a cessation of conflict, nor does it mean that Africans have access to the wealth within their borders. It simply means that as long as Africans kill one another and die of disease and hunger, the United States has free access to Africa's mineral resources. This version of peace encourages ethnic conflict, moral decay and the creation of African leaders who are presented as "Peace loving" while they negotiate Africans' freedom away.

By 'peace,' I mean the end of both low-and high-intensity conflicts and the presence of justice. "Low-intensity" conflict means that although the community does not engage in armed conflict, fear is the norm because the state is incapable of providing security and protection from hunger, economic exploitation and war lords. Most communities organize their own security patrol to protect them-selves. In such a situation, lack of food, health care and shelter are forms of low-intensity conflict because the majority of the people face constant fear of disease and hunger. In such communities, the people do not control the resources within their borders. The degree of a country's "low"- or "high-intensity" conflict varies from one African country to another. In some cases, it is more obvious than in others. Except for Libya and Tunisia, most African countries (including South Africa) fall into the "low-intensity" category. "High-intensity" conflict refers to countries that are openly at war: for example, Sierra Leone, the Democratic Republic of Congo, Northern Uganda and the Sudan. Like low-intensity conflict countries, these countries do not control the resources within their borders.

Imagining Africa: European Construction of Africa

> There is a consistent Western cultural pattern throughout the duration of the African slave trade, namely the banishment of the blacks from humanity, for which the white race remains the only yardstick. Being removed from human-ity naturally leads to the extermination of the group. Such extermination can then take place without concern or objection, since the victims are supposed to belong to a different species (Plumelle-Uribe 2001:22).

From the 16th Century onwards, Europeans chose to create a new image of Africa and Africans in spite of the diplomatic/trade relations that Europe had with Africa. Africa's enormous wealth in natural and human resources—such as gold, prime agricultural land, and especially people who could be used as slave labor on European plantations—demanded that Europeans create an ideology that dehu-manized the African. Such an image allowed Europeans to exploit African labor and resources. Explorers, geographers, scientists, missionaries, and political, economic and military leaders engaged in the construction of the African as the "other."

Geographers also contributed to the characterization of Africans as "inferior." Quoting from a map of Africa published in Paris in 1761, Robin Hallett, in *The Penetration of Africa,* noted that Africa was characterized by burning sands and deserts where the scarcity of water forced animals and people to use the same resources. As a result, and in the heat of the moment, animals and humans engaged in intercourse which, according to Hallet, explained the monstrous creatures that were produced as a result. This image of Africans as creatures less than human reached its climax during the enlightenment. In a footnote to his essay entitled "Of National Character" that appeared in his *Essay and Treatises* (1768), Scottish philosopher David Hume argued that Africans were naturally inferior to White people. Africans never produced any art and science, and there was never a civilization of any other color than white. In his *Philosophy of History,* Georg Hegel, the German philosopher, after a short discussion of Africa (numbering eight pages out of a total of 358), noted that Africans lacked self-control and had not contributed to culture and world history. By the late 18th Century, African images were of great interest in European middle class circles where diverse ideas on Africa were presented. Middle-class European circles also debated the role of Africa as the antithesis of Europe ("the other"). These debates influenced European missionaries, explorers, geographers and scientists who later traveled to Africa.

Africa was also depicted as a passive object waiting to be reborn through various European forces. Reports about Africa depicted vast empty lands and wildlife ready to be taken (Magubane 1996, Barrow 1801-4, Achebe 1978, Benedict 1996). Africans' presence or claims to the resources within their communities were ignored. Africa came to represent all that Europe was not; for example, it was "uncivilized," ruled by "emotion" and "eroticism," rather than "reason" and "rationalism." European construction of Africans shaped imperial policy. A popular geographer of the early 19th Century, Hugh Murray, described Africa as a strange and mysterious place. The image was already forming of Africa as a place where "creatures" less than human survived in an order less than civilized. Social Darwinism added to the negation of Africans' humanity. Proponents of Social Darwinism in the academic world included William Graham Summer, a political science professor at Yale; Josiah Strong, a popular historian, lecturer, and congregational clergyman in the late 19th Century; John Burgess, William Dunning, U.B. Phillips, and several other prominent professors at Columbia University.

Social Darwinists believed that Africans' intellectual development was at the same level as that of animals and especially monkeys. By 1885, Strong visualized an Anglo-Saxons "move down Mexico ... over upon Africa and beyond. And can anyone doubt that the result of this competition of the races will be the 'survival of the fittest?'" In his *Our Country: Its Possible Future and Its Present Crisis,* Strong answered his own question:

> It seems to me that God, with infinite wisdom and skill,
> is training the Anglo-Saxons for an hour sure to come in
> the world's future ... the final competition of races, for
> which the Anglo-Saxon is being schooled....
> Whether the extinction of inferior races ... seems to the
> reader sad or otherwise, it certainly appears probable (in Harris 1987:23).

Endemic Violence: Europeans and Africa's Resources

> Civilization, civilization, pride of the Europeans and graveyard of innocents, you build your kingdom on cadavers. You are the force that prevails over the law, you are not a guiding light, but a wild fire (Ren Maran 1921).

> "Speak softly and carry a big stick" (Theodore Roosevelt, United States' President 1901-1909).

> The US programme is certainly imperialist in the most brutal sense of that word, but not "imperial" in the sense that Antonio Negri has given the term, since it does not aim to manage the societies of the planet ... to integrate them into a coherent capitalist system ... it aims only at looting their resources (Samir Amin 2003).

> If there is a country which has committed unspeakable atrocities, it is the United States of America ... They don't care for human beings (Nelson Mandela, South Africa's President 1994-1999).

> Could Africans be allowed to at least pretend to govern their continent? (Alec Erwin 2002).

An idea developed that since 'weaker' races could not survive, it was better to exterminate them to quicken the process. In Africa, the encounter with colonial powers meant only one thing: exterminate the African! Most people were not killed by guns but by germs that were introduced by Europeans. As a result, lands were emptied of their inhabitants. Weakened populations, calamities, famine and war made Africans easy prey for the colonial project, although they fought with all the weapons they had to retain their freedom. In 1850, Africans and Europeans were basically at the same military technological level. Both had small arms that could be reproduced in African villages. For example, the Dahomey kingdom that engaged in a long battle against the French reproduced these weapons. This elite corps was made up of women whose right breasts were removed for better marksmanship. The standard weapon was the muzzle flint musket rifle. The Prussians replaced the muzzle with a breech-loaded rifle called Dreyse, which was used by all Europeans. By 1869, Britain adopted the Martini-Henry. It was the first good weapon because it was swift and insensitive to wet conditions. The French introduced the Gras and the Prussians the Mauser which became the standard weapon for all Europeans. From then on, Europeans controlled military technology and made sure only technologically obsolete weapons reached the Africans. In 1885, machine-guns were introduced with the manufacture of the Hiram-Massim gun. It was capable of producing 11 bullets a second. It was also easier to carry. New methods of smelting iron, producing better weapons, were also introduced. By 1890, the rifle revolution was complete. In 1897, the Dum Dum bullet was manufactured in Calcutta. Its led core exploded in the body causing painful wounds. This bullet was not allowed among "civilized nations," except for wild game. In 1898, the British used the Dum Dum bullet to test it at the battle of Omdurman where 9,000 people were killed. From then on, the gunboat became a symbol of imperialism. Boats loaded with guns and navigating up and down major rivers such as the Congo and the Niger constantly and wantonly shot at the local people along the way. The killing was so widespread that the people believed "invisible" beings were killing them (Lindqvist 1996).

As a result of various factors (diseases, extermination, and military technology), only Ethiopia maintained its freedom against Europeans. Ethiopia's King Menelik did what most African leaders before him failed to do: he united his people in the face of European encroachment. He also used European powers against one another, which enabled him to purchase advanced weapons, thereby keeping abreast of military technology. On March 1, 1896, Ethiopia defeated Italy at the battle of Adowa, ending the latter's dream of a "Second Roman Empire." As a result, Menelik was able to set up a modern Ethiopian state.

In 1891 Cecil Rhodes noted the importance of foreign markets for capitalism to make profits when he wrote to a co-founder of the Round Table:

> Please remember the key of my idea discussed with you as a Society copied from the Jesuits as to organization, the practical solution a differential rate

(tariff) ... That the work, with America in the forefront, is devising tariffs to boycott your manufactures and that is the supreme question, for I believe that England with fair play should manufacture for the world and, being a Free Trader, I believe that until the world comes to its senses you should declare war—I mean a commercial war—with those who are trying to boycott your manufactures (White 1980:29-30).

Imperialism is the economic, cultural and political domination or control of one country or group of people by others in ways assumed to be at the expense of the latter. Based on Rosa Luxemburg,

capital cannot accumulate without the aid of non-capitalist organizations, nor ... can it tolerate their continued existence side by side with itself. Only the continuous and progressive disintegration of non-capitalist organizations makes accumulation of capital possible ... the relations between capitalism and non-capitalist modes of production start making their appearance on the international stage. Its predominant methods are colonial policy, an international loan system-a policy of spheres of interest-and war. Force, fraud, oppression, looting, are openly displayed without any attempt at concealment, and it requires an effort to discover within this tangle of political violence and contests of power the stern laws of the economic process (1923:452-3).

Luxemburg's analysis is still relevant for Africa in the 21st Century: international loans, military means and US allies in Africa continue to play a major role in maintaining control over the continent. This ties shape the type of "peace" that the United States and its allies promote in Africa. In the contemporary period, capitalism must still expand outside of its natural boundaries in industrializing capitalist countries in order to make super profit because its home market is insufficient. Excess population which could otherwise cause problems in industrialized nations finds an outlet through imperialism by settling in the colonies; the only area where capitalism can expand is in the non-capitalist areas of the world, namely the Third World/South (e.g., Africa, Asia, and the Middle East). Luxemburg emphasized the relationship between political domination, military occupation and external debt in capitalism by introducing the military-industrial complex.

Imperialism changes the status quo of the invaded country. It is arrogant because it is based on the belief that the dominating group is culturally and racially superior. Imperialism is totalitarian, since it rules every aspect of life: economic, political and social. It is imposed from above, which explains why it assumes that the majority of the people have no right to question it. Imperialism is based on violence. As seen from Joseph Conrad's *The Heart of Darkness,* if it was not for its liberal idealism, imperialism would be just robbery with violence. Imperialism is not static; it changes depending on the conditions facing it. Although Portugal had colonies in Africa before this period, 19th Century imperialism differed from previous periods in two ways: Seven European powers agreed to divide Africa between them. Next, these European powers directly occupied African countries for better exploitation and control. In essence, colonialism is the continuation of imperialism by other means. It is more efficient, direct occupation because it rationalizes imperialism. It tightens control over indigenous people. Imperialism is based on racism, which it redefines to suit the particular conditions it faces. Racism acts as its engine because it also informs the power relations existing between the conquerors and the conquered people; it justifies poverty in the sense that the conquerors are entitled to the wealth of the conquered people because the former is "superior." Without racism imperialism could be a failure. Albert Memmi argues that

> ... the colonizer resorts to racism ... racism encapsulates and symbolizes the essence of the relationship between colonizer and colonized ... a paternalist is a person who pretends to be generous, once racism and inequality have been established (2002:89, 94).

Colonialism was based on violence and corruption. For example, chiefs were given pots and pans, brandy, or jewelry in return for signing treaties. Cruelty informed all aspects of colonial rule. Catherine Coquery-Vidrovitch provides a detailed account of the mission of enquiry on alleged atrocities committed by the Concessionary Companies in the French Congo. Led by famed explorer Savorgnan de Brazza, the mission (April-September 1905) found that in Ubangi-Chari (Central African Republic), the *Société de la Lobaye*'s agents had, in the village of Nguakombo, rounded up 58 women and ten children as 'hostages' to force the men to produce their quota of natural rubber; 45 women and two children later died for lack of proper care. In Fort-Sibut (Krebedje), the mission found another concentration camp comprising 119 women and children taken hostage during a raid in Uhame-Nana. De Brazza concluded that in that particular region, taking women as hostages was a common practice to force the men to provide their quota of rubber, to submit to porter requisitions, or to pay their taxes in kind (Coquery-Vidrovitch 2001:171-7).

What was "civilization" to its victims? In colonial Kenya, the British put members of the Kikuyu ethnic group who were fighting for land and freedom in concentration camps. Between 300,000 and 400,000 people died as a result. Work camps where freedom fighters were held in inhumane conditions were set up throughout the country. Men were sexually assaulted "sodomized with bottles and rifle barrels, and castrated" (Elkins 2005:256, Collins 2001:306). Eggs and broken bottles were stuffed into women's vaginas. Women suffered on two levels: (1) as freedom fighters and (2) as a result of their gender:

> When they still could not get information from me they decided to put pepper inside my private parts. We were ordered to lie down in the open area inside the Ruthigit post. No one held us down, but guards stood over us with guns. We were ordered to separate our legs with our knees raised. Failure to comply invited ruthless beating. Then a bottle full of a mixture of pepper and water was inserted into my birth canal and the contents emptied, inside of me, it is impossible to imagine the torment. The burning could be felt everywhere, in the eyes, ears, nose, mouth, and all over. It happened that the previous day, the day we were arrested, a lady named Watiri had been given the same treatment, only her mixture had been made from pepper and petrol. It was fortunate that the vehicle had left by the time my mixture was being prepared. After this treatment I was later carried to where Watiri was still lying groaning in agony and vomiting (Elkins 2005:256).

Watiri died. Women were raped repeatedly by both African and British guards.

All colonial powers used capital punishment. For example, although the guillotine was banned in France, it was still used in the colonies. Imperialism masks itself under different guises. For example, in Africa it had a "mission" which was to "civilize" the people. This disguise masked its real purpose, which was extraction of raw materials, use of Africans as laborers as well as markets for European goods. Each country produced the goods needed by the colonial power; for example, in the case of East Africa, coffee, tea, peanuts, and sisal were the goods produced. West African countries produced cocoa, coffee, peanuts, and oil. Central Africa produced rubber and North Africa produced oil, as well as other natural resources. In South Africa, Britain used that country's minerals to improve its own standing in the world economy as well as to develop its national economy. Colonial powers used forced labor in all these countries. Ethnicity was privileged over national identity for better control.

The post-colonial state Africanized colonial structures. It accepted its role as a junior partner in an economic system that it did not control. The post-colonial state was incapable of conflict resolution because its colonial power maintained those rights. Furthermore, upon independence, African leaders used ethnic identity both to maintain control and to reward supporters. The post-colonial state also accepted its role as Europe's plantation, as it provided various European companies with the best land to produce coffee, cocoa, flowers, fruits or vegetables. Such a state was illegitimate in the view of the people because it was divorced from their needs and it used violence to control them. Hence, given the need for foreign countries and companies to "protect" these countries against the majority of the population seeking economic self-sufficiency, what democracy needs 'protection'? Which powers protected America's democracy during its inception?

Foreign military bases were encouraged to "protect" African countries. An infrequently discussed issue in African Studies is the presence of foreign military bases in the so-called "independent" countries of Africa. Indeed, the number of such bases has increased (rather than decreased) since the 1960s. In addition to the old French military bases in Senegal, Côte d'Ivoire, the Central African Republic and Gabon, the United States has set up new ones in Morocco, Botswana, Kenya, São Tomé & Principe, and has taken over Djibouti from the French. If these countries were truly independent, why would they allow military bases to be set up on their territories? Could one imagine a Brazilian military base in France, a Nigerian base in Germany, an Indian base in England, or a Chinese base in the United States? These military bases serve four main purposes, which are: (1) to protect economic interests, (2) to gather intelligence to repress any movement that calls for self-determination, (3) to protect puppet leaders against an uprising of their own people, and (4) to intimidate the people by presenting an all-powerful image of 'empire'—often re-named 'globalization' in contemporary Africa. Unfortunately, some Africans have been led to believe that the United States actually 'helps' them purely out of benevolence and good heart. Considering it takes out of the African countries-cum-super-markets by way of natural resources, raw materials, and cheap labor, United States' 'Aid' amounts to next to nothing. Africans do not want charity, pity or paternalism. They simply want to use their natural resources, raw materials, labor, which are theirs by right, and solve their conflicts whichever way they choose.

Peace Makers? From Colonialism to the Contemporary Period

Europeans who settled in the colonies were people who would otherwise cause problems in their own countries either through revolt, stealing, or murder. As a result, colonialism was not meant to create political institutions that protected citizens' rights because the colonial power's goal was to extract natural resources and to use these institutions for labor. Furthermore, Africans were not worthy of any rights unless being puppets of Western powers. According to Herman

Merivale, "the main reason [for 'the waste of human life'] is that 'civilization' out there is represented by 'the trader, the backwoodsman, the pirate, the bushranger;' to put it briefly, by whites who can do anything they like with no risk of criticism or control" (in Lindqvist 1996:123). There is nothing romantic about conquest, no morals to keep, nor lives to save. It is brutal and inhumane. Joseph Conrad notes:

> They were conquerors, and for that you want only brute force—nothing to boast of, when you have it, since your strength is just an accident arising from the weakness of others. They grabbed what they could get for the sake of what was to be got. It was just robbery with violence, aggravated murder on a great scale, and men going at it blind—as is very proper for those who tackle a darkness. The conquest of the earth, which mostly means the taking it away from those who have a different complexion or slightly flatter noses than ourselves, is not a pretty thing when you look into it too much. What redeems it is the idea only. An idea at the back of it; not a sentimental pretense but an idea; and unselfish belief in the idea—something you can set up, and bow down before, and offer a sacrifice to ... (1995:20).

The idea of exterminating groups that were not European developed. This idea had cost millions of lives long before Adolf Hitler. According to Sven Lindqvist,

> The air he [Adolf Hitler] and other Western people in his childhood breathed was soaked in the conviction that imperialism is a biologically necessary process, which, according to the laws of nature, leads to the inevitable destruction of the lower races. It was a conviction which had already cost millions of human lives before Hitler provided his highly personal application (1996:141).

After 1945, European imperialism changed to accommodate its critics and the United States which did not have any African colonies. The United States wanted access to Africa's resources and markets. Its companies would play a key role in shaping United States' involvement in African countries whether it was in oil, fruit, or the textile industry. Development corporations were created to grant loans to African countries which entrenched them further into the imperial yoke. Young Africans were given scholarships to study in American universities. As European countries prepared to grant freedom to their colonies, they also reached out to Africans who would protect their interests through various trade agreements. In most African countries, these moderate leaders became the first post-colonial political leaders. An unwritten law was in place: get your political flags, leave your resources for our use, and you shall have "peace." African countries that strayed from the "norm" such as Guinea (1958), Algeria, Mozambique, Angola, Congo (Lumumba) faced economic and political catastrophes. Another image of Africans developed: that by nature, they were violent people. Only an outside power would ensure "peace." In the contemporary period, the United States and its allies have replaced Britain and France as the major players in African conflicts. In this scenario, any group or leader that opposes United States' efforts becomes 'an enemy of peace' which for the United States means control over African resources. The United Nations acts as the United States' Trojan horse in its various "peace-building and conflict resolution" efforts in Africa. As Wayne Madison has argued elsewhere, United States' role in Africa has resulted in the escalation of ethnic identity and violence.

What kind of "peace" decrees that Africans' resources do not legitimately belong to them? How can one possibly call such a process "conflict resolution," except under the guise of a fallacious and paternalistic rhetoric? More to the point, what gives the United States' government—"the chosen few"—the right to decree that it holds in perpetuity the property title deed to all the African natural resources, and that Africans themselves have absolutely no rights or claims to these resources, which are obviously theirs by right? What kind of "civilization" allows the coercion, oppression, rape, brutality, mutilations, mayhem, murder and genocide of the days of slavery and colonialism to continue unabated at the dawn of the 21st Century? It is interesting to note in this regard that the practice of using porters and slave labor, and of cutting off people's arms, hands, legs and feet as an incentive to produce more rubber in King Léopold's Congo Free State (CFS) from the late 19th to the early 20th Century has being carried over to the present day by the combatants of Sierra Leone's Revolutionary United Front (RUF). According to Meredith, during the Sierra Leonean civil war, the RUF routinely conscripted civilians to work as slave labor in mines or as porters called "mules." The civilian "mules" were required to carry up to 100 kilos of equipment each. Not surprisingly (and just as in the days of the CFS), as one journalist observed, "the life span of a mule was not long." Furthermore, hacking off arms, hands, legs and feet of helpless villagers—men, women and children alike—as retribution for "aiding and abetting the enemy" became an RUF trademark (Meredith 2005:564-66). What kind of "peace" allows children—between the ages of 7 and 14—to be massively recruited as soldiers in various civil wars (notably Liberia, Sierra Leone, northern Uganda, southern Sudan and the Democratic Republic of Congo)? This practice is so widespread that the United Nations had to create a special position of Under Secretary-General for Children in Armed Conflicts (Olara Otunnu).

The perceptive analysis of the Congolese situation by the late Roman Catholic Archbishop of Bukavu, Archbishop Emmanuel Kataliko, applies, *pari passu*, to the whole African continent:

> Foreign powers, with the collaboration of some of our Congolese brothers, organize wars over control of the resources of our country. These resources, which should be used for our development, for the education of our children, to cure our illnesses, in short so that we can have a more decent human life, serve only to kill us. What is more, our country and our people have become the object of exploitation. All that has value is pillaged and taken to foreign countries or simply destroyed. Our taxes, which should be invested into the community, are embezzled (…) All this money, that comes from our labor, is directly taken by a small elite that comes from we don't know where … [and] means that some of our compatriots don't hesitate to sell their brothers for a dollar or ten or twenty (www.oikoumene.org).

Can there be peace without Africans controlling their economies? In what amounts to nothing less than a re-colonization of Africa, the United States, the United Nations and the World Bank arrogate themselves the power to take over the economic management, security and administration of a select number of African countries categorized as "failed states." In an article on Mozambique, David Plank explains the concept of "re-colonization": "the most likely successor to post-colonial sovereignty will be neo-colonial vassalage, in which Western powers assume direct and open-ended control over the administration, security, and economic policies of 'deteriorated' states under the banner of the U.N. and various donors" (in Saul 2005:100-1). In a speech given in Maputo in 1990, during the early stages of the formal negotiations process with Renamo, president Joachim Chissano of Mozambique lamented the fact that his country did not get any substantial aid in return for abandoning Marxism and Socialism under strong American pressure:

> The US said, 'Open yourself to … the World Bank, and IMF." What happened? … We are told now: "Marxism! You are devils. Change this policy." OK, Marxism is gone. "Open market economy." OK … We went to Reagan and I said, "I want money for the private sector to boost people who want to develop a bourgeoisie." Answer: $10 million, then $15 million more, then another $15 million. You tell me to do away with Marxism, the Soviet Union and the GDR [German Democratic Republic] and give me [only] $40 mil-

lion. OK, we have changed. Now they say, "If you don't go to a multi-party system, don't expect help from us" (in Saul 2005:101).

According to John Saul, "The key to this shift was … the re-colonization of Mozambique … the process still left a Mozambique dependent in its poverty and its vulnerability on the behest of the World Bank, the IMF, and the external aid community. And it left a leadership that had certainly lost touch with the aspirations of ordinary people" (2005:100). A Mozambican Member of Parliament (MP) explains how in 1995 Parliament actually met not in Maputo but in Paris, during the donor meeting. Another MP explains that unlike other countries and parliaments, "we accept that our budget is really set by donors at the annual Paris conference. We accept that our priority is to develop a donor-acceptable budget" (Saul 2005:105). In Liberia in 1987, in an attempt to clean up the country's chaotic finances, the United States appointed a team of 17 operational experts—the Opex Mission—to take over control of the Ministry of Finance, the Central Bank and other key government offices. However, as in the Blumenthal mission in Zaire, the Opex team's efforts to eliminate the numerous scams it identified and to establish new controls were constantly thwarted, and it decided to cut short its mission. In its final report published in May of 1989, it noted: "[President Samuel K.] Doe's Liberia was managed with far greater priority given to short-term political survival and deal-making than to any long-term recovery or nation-building efforts …" (Meredith 2005:91). Following the British intervention in May of 2000 to "restore law and order" in Sierra Leone, British personnel took up key posts in government, the Central Bank and the police and began the task of rebuilding a national army. In addition, the United Nations peacekeeping force was increased to 18,000, one of its largest operations in the world (Meredith 2005:91). Strangely, this evokes the situation prevailing in Tanganyika (later Tanzania) at the time of independence: "In 1961, the year of Tanganyika's independence, every senior civil servant in Dar-es-Salaam, every provincial commissioner and 55 out of 57 district commissioners were still British expatriates" (Meredith 2005:91). In September of 1992, senior managers of international non-governmental aid agencies operating in Somalia were advocating military intervention. As Philip Johnson, President of CARE-US, put it, "the international community, backed by UN troops, should move in and run Somalia, because it has no government at all" (Meredith 2005:474).

Under the present circumstances, even the best leaders would be unable to successfully undertake a process of institutional transformation designed to ameliorate the conditions facing the majority of the African people. One cannot build a house on a sinking foundation, or place the roof of a hut on wooden pillars eaten away by termites; the whole edifice would crumble. In indigenous political systems, people believed in themselves and in their leaders. They had the leaders they deserved. In colonial and post-colonial states, Africans do not have the leaders that they deserve. Even in South Africa, given another choice, South Africans would not have elected Nelson Mandela. The "Free Mandela" campaign and marketing strategy began in Western countries in the early 1980s once the Afrikaners discovered that they could safely "work" with Nelson Mandela. The same method that the British used with Jomo Kenyatta of Kenya—groom him for power while he is still in political detention—was effectively used by Afrikaners and Americans in the 1980s. As Meredith observes, "Mandela's secret talks with government officials had convinced them that he was a man with whom the white establishment could do business ... Like other white communities in Africa, they [white South Africans] had come to accept the old adage: give them parliament and keep the banks" (2005:435-6). Since they lack this type of historical knowledge, Africans and friends of Africa—duly influenced by an effective marketing campaign led by the Western media—were in awe of Nelson Mandela, whom they genuinely saw as the "shining light" of the "dark continent." Fully aware of the Afrikaners' appalling track record of excessive abuse of African labor under apartheid in South Africa, Nelson Mandela nevertheless encouraged Afrikaner farmers to settle in a number of African countries (notably Congo-Brazzaville, the Democratic Republic Congo, Kenya, Mozambique, Tanzania and Zambia), thereby "exporting" apartheid and encouraging conflict. Yet, it was under Nelson Mandela that the African National Congress negotiated away its economic, military and security rights, thereby hammering the last nail in the coffin of Africa's independence.

A Proposal for Peace and Conflict Resolution in Africa

Africans and United States interests are different. United States capitalism's goal is to make super profits. It is not interested in African people's dignity and welfare. In spite of its rhetoric, the United States has appropriated African resources for its own use at the expense of every African child, woman and man. To think that United States' efforts can result in peace in African countries remains just a dream and a distant one as such. There can never be any "equitable" partnership because for the United States, such a partnership would mean sole control over African resources, markets and labor. As long as these interests are in conflict, and the United States imposes its "peace" on Africans, conflict will continue. I reject the procedural and minimalist conception of liberal democracy (also called 'electoral democracy')—with its emphasis on multi-party elections, electoral competition, and civil and political liberties—as inappropriate in the African context (Abrahamsen 2000). The United States prefers this type of democracy because of its emphasis on free and fair elections rather than economic control. Such a democracy encourages low intensity conflict because it forces Africans to develop outside their culture. It also forces Africans to compete against international capita, which is better placed to reap the financial benefits of a liberal economy. Most Africans are forced to hassle in the informal economic sector because major American companies control the formal economy. Moral decay becomes the norm because the majority of the people are relegated to the margins of humanity. Liberal democracy assumes that beyond voting Africans have no say in their own development, even in resolving their own conflicts. Instead, I argue that African countries need popular democracy. By 'popular democracy,' I mean a type of democracy (i) in which people have effective decision-making power; (ii) that places emphasis on concrete political, social, and economic rights; (iii) that puts as much emphasis on collective rights as it does on individual rights; and (iv) a democracy of incorporation, that is as inclusive as possible (Ake 1996:132, Martin 1998:102-9).

In what follows, I outline what a true partnership would entail. The United States and Western countries have done enough for Africa. I restate Alec Erwin's questions: Could Africans be allowed to at least pretend to govern their continent? Can the United States stop forcing Africa onto the "peace treadmill"? Given the stakes involved, United States' allies and policies, conflict will continue. Unless the United States is willing to let Africans control their own destiny, there can never be any "peace-building." The best thing that the United States can do is to stop aiding its puppets while they murder African women and babies (Uganda, Ethiopia and Rwanda). "Peace" cannot be achieved without economic control over resources. Most people are forced to live on the verge of humanity because of policies drafted by the World Bank and the IMF. If the United States were interested in peace-building rather than conflict creation, it would not encourage policies that deny millions of Africans their humanity. The best path to peace would be for African countries to default on IMF loans en mass and use the funds for economic and social development especially to halt the progression of the AIDS epidemic (Ellerman 2004, Stiglitz 2002, Bond 2004). According to the United Nations Development Program's Mark Malloch Brown who worked as Public Relations Director for the World Bank, "it would be an absurdity for countries that are so dependent on financial assistance to poke the donors in the eye"; Mozambique's prime minister concurs: "If I stopped paying debt service, all my poverty-reduction money would stop from the World Bank and IMF. Fifty percent of our budget is from donors. I can not pay. The country would stop" (Bond 2004:209). United Nations Special AIDS Envoy Stephen Lewis retorted: "There are some donors who would be privately pleased, although they would never publicly take this stand" (Bond 2004:209). That post-colonial African states are unable to take a common stand against World Bank policies demonstrates their weaknesses and irrelevance in improving the conditions facing the majority of their people, let alone resolve conflict.

Whose Peace?

If sustainable peace and conflict resolution are to be in place in Africa, Africans must be at the center of that process. They must be involved in all levels, not as passive recipients of "advice," but as active participants because they alone will live with the results of the peace process. Can the present post-colonial states achieve this goal? No! Can the United States act as the engine for this process? No! Can the United Nations play the role of mediator? No, because the United Nations is the Trojan horse of United States' interests. Can United States' African allies such as the leaders of Ethiopia, Senegal, Rwanda, Uganda and South Africa act as mediators? No!

Fundi Wa Africa suggests that the continent be divided into five sub-regions for each part of Africa (North, West, Central,E, and South) under five presidents, with a federal system and a federal African army, using its history, culture, traditions and environment as the bases for governance. The new state of *Kimit* will include Algeria, Egypt, Tunisia, Libya, the Arab population in Mauritania, Morocco, Northern Sudan and Northern Chad. *Mali* will include Benin, Bukina Faso, Cape Verde, Côte d'Ivoire, Gambia, Ghana, Guinea, Guinea-Bissau, Liberia, Niger, Nigeria, Sierra Leone and Togo. The African population of southern Mauritania (Senegal river valley) will also be brought under Mali. *Kongo* will include Cameroon, Southern Chad, Congo-Brazzaville, Congo-Kinshasa, Central African Republic, Equatorial Guinea, Gabon, São Tomé & Principe, Uganda, Rwanda and Burundi. *Kush* will include southern Sudan, Ethiopia, Eritrea, Djibouti, Somalia/Somaliland, Kenya, Uganda, Tanzania (including Zanzibar), Seychelles and Comoros. *Zimbabwe* will include Angola, Botswana, Namibia, Malawi, Mozambique, Mauritius, Madagascar, Lesotho, South Africa, Swaziland and Zimbabwe (seethe following map). These states will eventually merge to constitute the new *Federation of African States*. Each sub-region will have a core state as the key power, according to population, size and natural resources endowment: Congo-Kinshasa, Egypt, Ethiopia, Nigeria, and South Africa (Muiu 2002).

Without political and economic unity—based on the people's interests and informed by indigenous institutions—among African states, there can neither be a united Africa nor an African Renaissance. This calls for Africans to get rid, once and for all, of their economic, technological and cultural *dependency syndrome* and to cease to be supplicants in international economic fora and institutions, going around with begging bowl in hand. In fact, Africans might just as well completely *forget* about the United States.

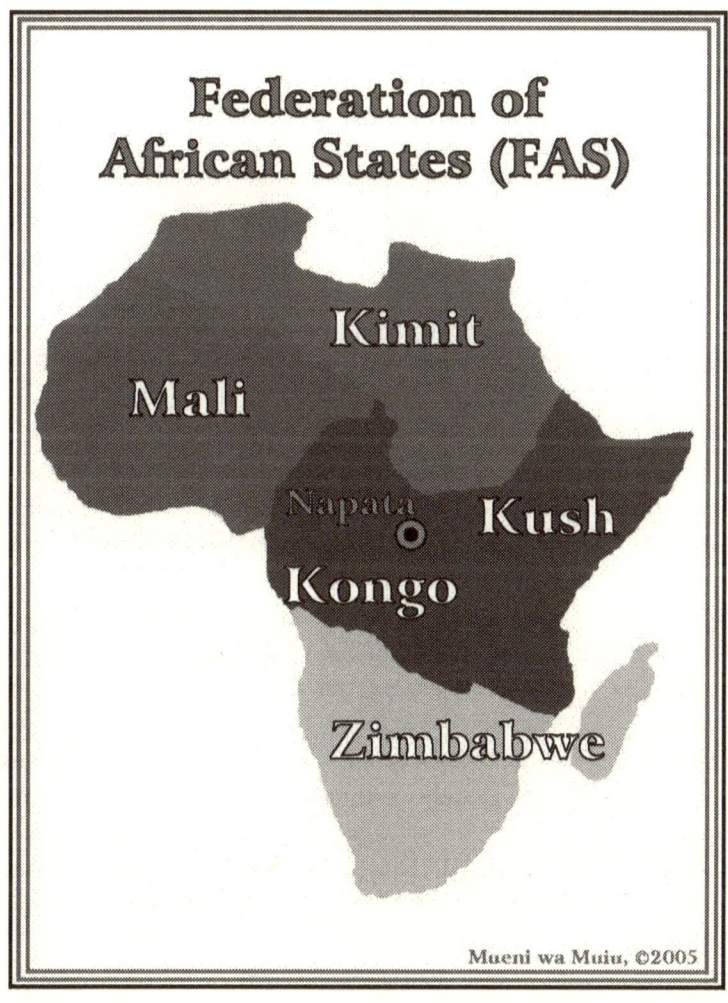

Federation of African States (FAS)

Kimit

Mali

Napata

Kush

Kongo

Zimbabwe

Mueni wa Muiu, ©2005

Conclusion

In this chapter, I have analyzed peace-building and conflict resolution based on *Fundi wa Africa* as a multidisciplinary approach. Why use history? *Fundi* uses a long-term historical as well as a multidisciplinary perspective not to create a 'victim's' historical account. It does so to present an exhaustive, panoramic view of the issues at stake in Africa's economic, political and social development, so that Africans can get out of conflict, hunger and poverty. The 'peace treadmill' is a process that recycles bankrupt ideas for the sole purpose of allowing the West, and specifically the United States, access to African resources, labor and markets. Used in this manner, history becomes a weapon. History helps us learn from the experiences of past generations—positive and negative, good and bad—without dismissing such events as "useless" or "primitive." History also becomes very important not as a "Golden Age when we were all queens and kings," but as a way of understanding the role of culture and tradition in political, economic and social development. It also sets a clear pattern: fragmentation of states, of institutions, of knowledge, of values and of a whole process of learning. Unless this process is understood, Africans will continue to accept models that apply cosmetic changes to a situation that calls for radical transformation. Is it possible to reform an institution based on slavery? Is it possible to reform a colonial state specifically designed to force African people into unpaid labor and military service, as well as to coerce, oppress, rape, brutalize, and murder? Can such a state's efforts result in peace that benefits the majority of Africans?

African people continue to blame their leaders for their venality and selfishness, characterized by greed, corruption, the instant gratification syndrome, and non-development. Leaders are only partially responsible for Africa's woes. After all if one inherits a house which has a leaky roof, one can be constantly mopping, yet the roof will continue to leak. Other Africans blame themselves, while still others turn against one another in deadly and fratricidal ethnic, factional or religious conflicts. As they keep on fighting, transnational corporations, mercenaries and all manners of warlords, adventurers and thieves mercilessly exploit their resources under the watchful eye of the United Nations which is responsible for maintaining "law and order" in these countries. Many states and corporations are only too glad to sell weapons to Africans. As long as Africans kill one another, business will continue as usual. All these policies aim at opening Africa further up for United States' exploitation, with the active support of some African leaders. Africans who refused to act as puppets—such as Barthélémy Boganda, Ouezzin Coulibaly, Ruben Um Nyobé, Patrice Lumumba, Sylvanus Olympio, Anton

Lembede, Robert Sobukwe, Steve Biko, Chris Hani, Oliver Tambo, Winnie Mandela, Frantz Fanon, Marien N'Gouabi, Thomas Sankara and Laurent-Désiré Kabila—have been systematically neutralized or eliminated by various means, including character assassination, strange diseases—various types of cancer, such as leukemia, 'heart attacks', AIDS etc.—, and outright murder. The message to the African leaders is clear: invest the state, occupy politico-bureaucratic positions, fight one another, starve and kill your populations while we 'help' you resolve conflicts and provide you with 'food aid' and 'peacekeeping missions,' but, by Golly, continue to let us take care of your mineral wealth, to which you have absolutely no rights. Understood? As one Western diplomat bluntly told a Tanzanian official in the early 1960s, "if you ever come between us and your resources, we shall kill you!"

To understand peace building and conflict resolution efforts in contemporary Africa, one must use history. When did Africa become a theatre of moral decay, starvation and violence? Are Africans by nature more conflict prone than other people? An examination of how Europeans knew Africa reveals the need for paternalism in order to justify their meddling in African affairs. As dependent people, Africans are not 'capable' of solving their own conflicts. They need the "superior" hand of the United States. Why the term "peace-building"? By using this term, one assumes that nothing exists on the ground that can act as a guide to conflict resolution (Vansina 2004:206-72). This ongoing belief that the United States knows better what is good for Africa shapes its approach to "peace." Following in the tradition of European imperialism, United States' interests in Africa include control over economic resources, markets, labor, and to create allies that "protect" these interests. The language has changed from the climax of empire; 'partnership' is more politically correct, but the goals are the same. United States' efforts are directed toward protecting those interests. As a result, any country, individual or group of people who challenge these interests become United States' "enemies" instantly. To the United States "peace" means protecting its interests. It has nothing to do with African dignity.

Unless Africans stop putting their faith in hopeless leaders and the United States, they will continue to be caught in the 'peace treadmill' where bankrupt ideas lead to more dispossession. The pertinent question to ask here is the following: Do Africans know what their national interest is? Are they Africans or Kenyans, Nigerians, South Africans, Kikuyus, Zulu, etc? If Africans do not know what their interests are, anyone can come in and take advantage of their resources. Furthermore, the African population is not a victim. It can choose to get rid of its leadership instead of taking refuge in alcohol, drugs, decadent Western cultural products, Christianity, Islam, or the so-called ideology of *Ubuntu*. Ultimately, it is the responsibility of the African people themselves to fight for their own freedom and to achieve peace that gives them economic control, food, health and freedom from all forms of suffering. Hence, there is an urgent need for a united Africa composed of informed citizens who will be in a better position to protect the continent's people and its resources.

4

Democratization

George Klay Kieh, Jr.

Introduction

Historically, the United States has claimed that the promotion of democracy around the world is one of the major contours of its foreign policy. This claim has, inter alia, been used to provide the rationale for various policy acts of the United States—the involvement in wars, intervention in the internal affairs of other states, the support for anti-government insurgencies, and the support for various regimes throughout the world. Carothers provides an excellent summation of the United States' claim as follows:

> For generations, American leaders have emphasized the promotion of democracy abroad as a key element of America's international role ... In the early 1960s, President John Kennedy embraced the idea of a noble campaign to foster democracy in the developing world ... In the 1990s, Presidents George Bush and Bill Clinton asserted that democracy promotion was a key organizing principle of U.S. foreign policy after the Cold War (1991:1).

Similarly, in the case of Africa, American policy makers have, and continue to claim recurrently, that the promotion of democracy is a major cornerstone of the United States' foreign policy towards the region. During the Cold War and its associated struggle with the Soviet Union for global domination, the United States tried to convince Africans that it was the "leader of the free world" and the Soviet Union was the "patron of totalitarianism." Accordingly, the United States, among other things, bombarded Africa with an avalanche of propaganda depicting the former's policy towards the latter as ostensibly designed to promote and protect human rights and other political freedoms. As the repository of evidence shows, however, American pro-democracy foreign policy rhetoric was not consistent with American praxis: On the one hand, while the United States professed to

61

be the "champion of democracy in Africa" in its official policy pronouncements, on the other hand, it played a pivotal role in providing the "economic, political and military oxygen" that sustained authoritarianism on the continent. Importantly, the contradiction between American policy rhetoric and praxis was so glaring and pervasive that pro-democracy movements in the various authoritarian American client states on the continent considered the United States as a major obstacle to the promotion of democratization on the continent. Eventually, even the United States was forced to admit that it was a "poor promoter of democracy" on the continent. For example, former President Clinton argued that "... our African policy had been sporadic and often destructive, and during the Cold War, we often picked our allies based on Cold War considerations, not on what the long-term interests of the human beings in all those African countries were, and what the long-term interests in our common bonds were" (Clinton 2006: 1).

With the end of the Cold War and its associated superpower rivalry, there was, and still is, the hope that the United States would match its perennial pro-democracy policy rhetoric with concrete actions in Africa. The sentiment was vividly captured by Michael Clough in his book, *Free At Last*. According to Clough, "With the end of the Cold War, the United States has an unprecedented opportunity to create a new policy toward Africa free from the constraints of East-West geopolitics" (1992:v).

Against this background, the purpose of this chapter is two-fold. First, it examines whether the foreign policy praxis of the United States has been, and is supportive of, the promotion of democratization on the continent. Second, the chapter discusses ways in which United States foreign policy on democratization in Africa can be rethought so as to help foster the development of an equitable partnership with Africa.

Methodology

Conceptually, by political democratization, I mean the process by which a polity establishes a system based on the promotion of, and the respect for, the political rights and freedoms of individuals; institutions are established to conduct the affairs of the polity in an accountable, transparent and inclusive manner; and rules are formulated within the context of constitutional architecture to govern all the activities take place within the polity. The chapter uses two samples—African states that are not allies of the United States, and ten African states that are considered pivotal allies of the United States—as the crucibles for assessing the relationship between United States' pro-democracy foreign policy rhetoric and practice in Africa. There are 43 countries in the former category, and ten countries in the latter—Algeria, Djibouti, Egypt, Eritrea, Ethiopia, Morocco, Nigeria, Rwanda, Tunisia, and Uganda.

The chapter uses secondary data. They were collected from Human Rights Watch's World Reports, 1990-2005; Freedom House's Freedom in the World, 1972-2002 and 2005. The data for the study were collected through the use of the archival method. Specifically, this involved the collection of the data from the various sources through the use of the library and the Internet.

The data were analyzed through the use of two indexes: the United States Foreign Policy Praxis Index (USFPPI) and the Political Democratization Index (PDI). The former is used to analyze American policy responses to major events related to political democratization in two categories of African states: (1) those states that are not allies of the United States (the majority of states totaling 43), and (2) those states that are American allies. The time frame covers the post-Cold War era (1990-2005). The latter is employed to assess the state of political democratization in the ten African states that are allies of the United States. The United States' Foreign Policy Praxis Index is calculated in three ways:

1. USSPD = PDS/TNPDE, where USSPD is the United States' support for political Democratization, PDS is the total number of pro-democracy (political) stances taken by the United States in a given year, and TNPDE is the total number of political democratization-related events for a particular year.

2. USOPD = OPD/TNPDE, where USOPD is the United States' opposition to or lack of support for political democratization, OPD is the total number of times the United States was opposed to the promotion of political democratization in a particular year, and TNPDE is the total number of political democratization-related events for a particular year.

3. NSUS = NA/TNPDE, where NSUS is no policy stance by the United States, NA is the total number of times the United States took no policy action on political democratization-related events in a given year, and TNDE is the total number of political democratization-related events for a particular year.

The Political Democratization Index (PDI) is determined based on the scores from Freedom House's Survey of World Freedoms for 1990, 1995, 2000, and 2005. The scores of 1.0-2.5 signify high progress toward political democratization, the scores of 3.0-5.0 indicate low progress, and the scores of 5.5-7.0 show the lack of progress towards political democratization. In short, in the jargon of Freedom House, the countries considered "free" have scores of 1.0-2.5, those that are deemed "partially free" have scores of 3.0-5.0, and those that are "not free" fall in the category of scores from 5.5-7.0.

The Cold War Era: A Background

The United States constructed the competition with the Soviet Union during the Cold War as an epic battle between the countries and forces of the so-called "free world" led by the United States and those of the "Iron Curtain" under the suzerainty of the Soviet Union. The explicit derivative was that the United States and its allies were committed to the noble ideals of, among other things, supporting the cause of democratization around the world. In other words, it was made to appear that American support for democratization around the world was not modulated by intervening factors. In the case of Africa, which had been subjected to the vagaries of colonial and imperial rule, the United States depicted itself as the quintessence of democracy in the world. Importantly, the United States undertook a systematic propaganda campaign through various media ostensibly designed to inculcate in the minds of Africans that the United States was the "Mecca of democracy in the world."

Interestingly, when the United States' pro-democratization rhetoric was juxtaposed with policy praxis, there was a clear and unambiguous disconnect between the two. This was particular evident in the cases where there were conflicts between the United States pro-democracy policy rhetoric and American national interests. In such cases, the United States' national interests took priority over issues of democratization. As Lancaster laments, "[The American value] of helping others achieve and protect their political rights [was]often compromised by the pursuit of other U.S. interests such as protecting autocratic regimes from communist threats, obtaining access to military facilities, or garnering votes on key issues in the United Nations" (1993:49). Several cases were instructive. The United States was the principal supporter of the racist apartheid regime in South Africa that committed countless violations of democratic principles, including discrimination and segregation, political exclusion of the majority Africans, state-sponsored violence against Africans and economies, and the commission of social crimes against Africans. In fact, the United States protected the racist regime from the sanctions of the international community. For example, on various occasions when the United Nations' Security Council sought to punish South Africa for its racist policies, the United States did not hesitate to use its veto power. Furthermore, the United States instructed its client regimes in

Africa—Liberia, Zaire, etc.—to establish relations with the apartheid regime. The action by the United States was designed to achieve two major objectives. First, it was designed to protect the repressive Pretoria regime from diplomatic isolation. Second, it was intended to convey the impression to the international community that apartheid was not as reprehensible as it was made to be.

In the case of Zaire (now the Democratic Republic of the Congo), the United States played a pivotal role in undermining and overthrowing the pro-people regime of Prime Minister Patrice Lumumba. His "major crime" was that he was unwilling to mortgage the interests of the Congolese People to the profit-seeking agendas of American multinational corporations and to the promotion of the American agenda for global domination. Eventually, Lumumba was murdered with American acquiescence and replaced by Joseph Mobutu (later Mobutu Sese Seko), a low-ranking military officer. Significantly, Mobutu was handpicked by the United States because Washington had made the determination that he would uncritically follow and pursue the foreign policy dictates of the United States even to the detriment of the development and welfare of Zaire. Throughout his 32-year reign, Mobutu was a faithful client of the United States. For example, he was the "point guard" of the United States' campaigns of destabilization in Angola and Mozambique. Fearing that Angola and Mozambique could provide alternative models (other than peripheral capitalism) of development in Africa, the United States supported warlordist militias in Angola and Mozambique to derail the two African states' transition from peripheral capitalism under Portuguese imperialism to socialism. In Angola, the United States supported the National Front for the Liberation of Angola (NFLA) led by Holden Roberto and the National Union for the Total Liberation of Angola (NUTLA) headed by Jonas Savimbi in the civil war against the government led by the Popular Movement for the Liberation of Angola (MPLA). Similarly, in Mozambique, the United States supported the Mozambican Resistance (FRELIMO) led by Afonso Dhlakama against the government led by FRELIMO. As the United States' principal surrogate in the heart of Africa, the Mobutu regime served as the major conduit for the funneling of money, arms and equipment to the insurgency groups in Angola and Mozambique. Also, Mobutu played a critical role in helping to undercut African solidarity in opposition to the United States' support for the racist apartheid regime of South Africa. In the economic realm, the Mobutu regime used the machinery of the state to foster the process of exploitation and accumulation by American multinational corporations, which were involved in plundering and pillaging Zaire's vast natural resources. As compensation, the

United States provided the Mobutu regime with financial and military support and defended the regime's horrendous record on democratization.

In the same vein, the United States supported the dictatorial regime of Siad Barre in Somalia through the provision of economic and military assistance. In exchange, the Barre regime provided the United States with strategic military bases in Somalia. As usual, the United States supported the regime's repressive policies. As Jackson correctly observes, "The unrepresentative and even undemocratic character of [pro-American regimes] [was] not an insurmountable obstacle to good relations with Washington" (1982:283). Even when it became apparent that the Barre regime's collapse was imminent, Washington remained supportive of the regime. For example, the Reagan and Bush Administrations continued providing the Barre regime with lethal military assistance amid the expression of concerns by various members of the United States Congress about vitriolic human rights abuses by the Barre regime.

In Liberia, the United States provided the political, economic and military resources that helped sustain the authoritarian regime of Master Sergeant Samuel Doe, who came to power in a bloody military coup d'etat in 1980. For example, during the nine years of Doe's murderous rule, the United States provided more than $500 million in economic and military aid (Liberia Research and Information Project 1988). Interestingly, when Doe rigged the 1985 presidential election, the Reagan Administration expressed its support for this blatant violation of democratic tenets (Kieh 1988). Chester Crocker, the United States' Assistant Secretary of State for African Affairs during the Reagan regime, summarized the United States' defense of its client as follows: "The elections portended well for the development of democracy in Liberia because of Doe's claim that he won only by a narrow, 51% elections victory—virtually unheard of in the rest of Africa where incumbent rulers normally claimed victories of 95-100%" (Crocker 1985:3). Significantly, the United States' unflinching support for the Doe dictatorship was against the backdrop that Doe was a very dutiful and faithful servant of American interests in Africa. For example, the Doe regime ensured that the OMEGA Navigation Station, the Voice of America transmitter site, the Central Intelligence Agency station, America's continuing access to the international airport and the various seaports were protected. Also, the Doe junta provided a conducive atmosphere for American businesses to plunder and pillage Liberia's natural resources—iron ore, rubber, gold, diamonds and forests, while the Liberian masses remained deprived and impoverished.

Finally, there is no doubt that during the Cold War era, democratization was subordinated to the economic and strategic interests of the United States. In other words, the United States' policy on democratization during the Cold War was guided by the Machiavellian dictum of "The ends justify the means" (Machiavelli 1994 ed.). That is, in the case in which democratization promoted the pursuance of the United States' national interests, it was supported. Conversely, when democratization clashed with the pursuance of American national interest, it was opposed by the United States.

The Post-Cold War Era

The end of the Cold War occasioned several consequences for Africa. First, the realignment of forces constrained some of Africa's "socialist states" such as Angola and Mozambique to institute an ideological shift from Marxism to capitalism. Clearly, in the new world order in which the United States had became the undisputed dominant power, the ruling parties in Angola and Mozambique made the determination that they no longer had a global power comparable to the United States to defend them against the inevitable recriminations from the United States, if they had retained their socialist systems. Second, several of the American client regimes lost their importance; hence, they were abandoned by Washington under the pretext of a new American policy anchored on the support for democratization. Against this background, regimes such as Mobutu's became vulnerable to internal pressures and consequent collapse. Third, fearing the prospects of losing power, some of Africa's quintessential authoritarian regimes opportunistically adapted to the so-called imperatives of the "third wave of democratization" by arresting, manipulating and controlling the process.

From the perspective of the United States, the end of the Cold War presented Washington with the daunting task of rethinking its policy on democratization toward Africa. The epicenter of the new challenge was the fact that in the absence of the Cold War, American foreign policy-makers felt that it would be quite difficult to justify the United States' continual support for authoritarianism on the continent.

Africa in General

Constrained by the lack of a coherent policy toward Africa in light of the changes propelled by the end of the Cold War, the United States initially made the determination to cynically disengage from Africa. The rationale was that in view of the end of the Cold War, Africa (with the exception of Egypt) was no longer central to America's national interests.

Table 1: The Index of the Praxis of United States Policy on Democratization Toward Non-Allied African States, 1990-2005

Year	U.S. Support for Democratization (%)	No Stance by The U.S. (%)
1990	0	100
1991	0	100
1992	80	20
1993	40	60
1994	30	70
1995	70	30
1996	90	10
1997	70	30
1998	50	50
1999	100	0
2000	100	0
2001	0	100
2002	0	100
2003	100	0
2004	100	0
2005	100	0

Source: Computed by the author from Human Rights Watch, World Reports 1990-2005 (New York: Human Rights Watch).

As Table 1 shows, from 1990 to 1991, the United States expressed no policy position on issues pertaining to democratization in African states that were not aligned with it. Interestingly, beginning in 1992, the United States became re-engaged in Africa. From 1993 to 1994, American support for democratization in Africa was quite low. Then from 1995 to 2000, American support for democratization on the continent began to experience sustained increases (see Table 1). By 2001, however, the United States returned to the strategy of expressing no stance on issues relating to democratization; this remained the dominant policy approach to democratization in Africa until 2002. Then by 2003, United States' support for democratization experienced a phenomenal increase. In all of the major issues related to democratization, the United States took pro-democracy policy positions; this approach was maintained through 2005. It is important to re-state, however, that the cases of democratization took place in African states that were not considered pivotal to American national interests. Accordingly, the United States had greater flexibility to support democratization. In effect, the fact that these were non-pivotal states gave the United States the opportunity to be critical of violations of democratic principles, including political rights and civil liberties (Human Rights Watch 1998).

Importantly, it should be observed that there was a particular category of states in the general cluster of the non-pivotal African states that constituted "special cases of non-pivotal states:" These were states that, although not pivotal to the pursuance of American national interests, had some economic and strategic value to the United States. For example, in 1993, the United States made the determination that it was no longer in its interest to continue supporting its long-time client warlord Jonas Savimbi. This was because American policy-makers came to the conclusion, after more than 20 years, that Savimbi did not have mass support in Angola. This was clearly reflected in Savimbi's very poor showing in Angolan Presidential Elections in 1992. Accordingly, the Clinton administration made the determination that with the end of the Cold War, the Savimbi-led UNITA had become a liability to the United States. Also, the fact that the MPLA-led government in Angola had abandoned its socialist path to development provided an opportunity for rapprochement. Importantly, given the fact that Angola has oil, the two countries could establish a "business relationship." Against this background, the United States established diplomatic relations with Angola in May of 1993. By 1996, the "business relationship" between the two countries was booming. This was reflected in the fact the U.S. bought more than half of Angola's exports (mostly oil), worth $5 billion (Human Rights Watch, 1998: 3). Also, the United States-led investments, with private capital, exceeded $4.3 billion in 1997(Human Rights Watch, 1998:3). The establishment of a "business relationship" with Angola had an impact on American policy on democratization toward the country: the United States turned a "blind eye" and remained silent on human rights abuses in Angola (Human Rights Watch 1998). Similarly, given the fact that since post-September 11, 2001, the Sudan has provided extensive support to the United States in the area of intelligence on Al Qaeda, the United States was measured in its criticism of human rights violations and other breaches of political democratization in the former for a period of about four years (2001-2005). Since the escalation of the Sudanese government-sponsored genocidal war in the Darfur Region, however, the United States has become much more critical of Sudan's policy on human rights in the region. It would be interesting to see how the recent policy shift on democratization by the United States toward the Sudan will affect the evolving "strategic relationship" between the two countries.

The United States' Allies in Africa

The real test of the United States' commitment to the promotion of democratization in Africa is the stances taken in matters affecting its allies in Africa—the states that are pivotal to the pursuance of American national interests. In this section of the chapter, the focus is on the praxis of United States policy on democratization in its allied states—Algeria, Djibouti, Egypt, Ethiopia, Eritrea, Morocco, Nigeria, Rwanda, Tunisia, and Uganda.

Algeria. Since it gained independence, Algeria has been an authoritarian state under the domination of a single political party. In 1990, amidst the so-called "third wave of democratization" in Africa, Algeria conducted its first multiparty elections at the local level. Interestingly, the Islamic Salvation Front (FIS), an Islamic-based political party, trounced the ruling National Liberation Front (FLN). The FIS won control of 32 of the 48 provinces (Human Rights Watch 1990). Surprisingly, the FLN-led government accepted the results. This action by the government raised hopes among Algerians that their country was bidding farewell to authoritarianism.

The 1992 legislative election was a major test of the prospects for democratization in the country. Interestingly, the Islamic Salvation Front won the majority of seats. In a major "about face," the government nullified the results of the elections, thereby thwarting the democratic will of the Algerian People as freely expressed in their votes. Although not an ally of Algeria at this time, the United States, however, encouraged the Algerian government in this action. In fact, one of the major options pursued by the United States was the encouragement of the Algerian military to intervene as a way of preventing the Islamic Salvation Front from taking control of the reigns of government. A month following the nullification of the results of the parliamentary election, the government declared a "state of emergency." Operating under the cloak of the "state of emergency," the government banned the Islamic Salvation Front and embarked upon a systematic campaign of vitriolic human rights abuses, particularly targeting the so-called supporters of the Islamic Salvation Front.

After the events of September 11, 2001, the United States "promoted" Algeria to a "pivotal state" in its "war on terror." Accordingly, Algeria became a major client of the United States in the prosecution of the "new Cold War" between the United States and "radical Islamic terrorist groups." One of the major highlights of the relationship was the signing of an agreement granting the United States the right to use the airfield at Tamanrasset in Southern Algeria for the deployment of United States P-3 Orion aerial surveillance aircraft (Volman 2006:7). In view of its strategic relationship with Algeria, the United States has become impervious to the continual wanton violation of political liberties and civil rights by the government. Basically, the United States does not take any stance on issues relating to democratization in Algeria. Instead, Washington has continued to emphasize Algeria's importance in the "global war on terror." For example, Francis X. Taylor, the Counter-terrorism Chief of the American State Department declared in 2003 that "Algeria is one of the most tenacious and faithful partners of the United States ... Algeria has cooperated with the [United States] in every domain" (Human Rights Watch 2003).

Djibouti. Like most African states, Djibouti had a one-party state from 1977 to 1992. In fact, the country's authoritarian system of governance and its attendant impact on the ethnic division between the majority Isaa and minority Afar ethnic groups plunged the country into civil war in 1991. The war was waged by an Afar-based insurgency group, the Front for the Restoration of Unity and Democracy (FRUD). Pressured by the effects of the civil war, the Gouled regime supervised the drafting and adoption of a new constitution, which has various provisions that were ostensibly designed to address the grievances of the minority Afar ethnic group. One of the provisions was the establishment of a multiparty system. Nonetheless, the constitution imposed a limitation of four political parties. Despite the steps aimed at liberalizing the political space, Djibouti remained an authoritarian state as evidenced by, among other things, the violation of basic human rights and the manipulation of the so-called democratization process by the regime.

Like Algeria, Djibouti became pivotal to United States' security interests after September 11, 2001. Given its strategic location in the Horn of Africa, the United States decided to forge a relationship with Djibouti in the prosecution of the "war on terror." The locus of the relationship is Djibouti's granting of permission to the United States to use Camp Lemonier as the headquarters of the Combined Joint Task Force-Horn of Africa, a multinational naval force led by the United States that monitors and interdicts possible terrorist activities in adjacent countries, especially in Somalia (Volman 2006: 7). Along with the head-quarters, almost 800 United States Special Operations Forces (SOF) troops have set-up base at Camp Lemonier (Volman 2006:7).

Characteristically, because of Djibouti's military-strategic importance to its foreign policy, the United States has failed to take policy stances supportive of democratization in the country. For example, the United States was very silent amidst charges that Djibouti's 2003 parliamentary election was plagued with fraud designed to keep the Union for a Presidential Majority, the ruling coalition, stranglehold on power.

Egypt. Since 1979, when the Sadat regime cemented its relations with the United States with the signing of the Camp David Peace Accords with Israel, Egypt became the United States' premier client state in Africa. The United States regards Egypt as a major strategic asset in the promotion of American interests in the volatile Middle Eastern region. Accordingly, for the duration of the Cold War, Egypt received billions of dollars in American foreign aid (second to Israel). Importantly, the United States refused to support the democratization efforts in Egypt by firmly supporting the autocratic regime of Sadat, and since 1981 the authoritarian regime of Hosni Mubarak.

Interestingly, despite the end of the Cold War and America's so-called new commitment to the "promotion of democratization in Africa," Egypt has remained a model of authoritarian governance on the continent. For example, this was vividly demonstrated in 2005, when the Mubarak regime instituted token political reforms, including the establishment of a multi-party system. In the end, the Mubarak regime manipulated the electoral process by, among other things, preventing credible candidates that could have posed major challenges to Mubarak's hold on the presidency from contesting. So, the charade of political liberalization was clearly designed to placate the regime's domestic critics and to help give credence to the United States' rhetorical support for democratization. The fact remains that the Mubarak regime has not wavered in its perennial viola-tion of civil rights and political liberties. Particularly, with American support, the Mubarak regime is continuing its suppression of Islamic groups, including the Muslim Brotherhood. This is an integral part of the prosecution of the United States' "war on terror."

Eritrea. When Eritrea won its independence in 1993, after decades of waging a war of national liberation against Ethiopia, the expectation was that the country would have become a model for reconstituting the state and for the pursuance of people-centered democratic development in Africa. Among other things, Eritrea laid the foundation for the construction of a democratic state by drafting and ratifying a democratic constitution through a process-led approach in which all of the country's various stakeholders participated. Regrettably, President Isayas Afwerki and his People's Front for Democracy and Justice failed to provide the requisite leadership for the building of a new and democratic country. Instead, a "police state" was established; since then, the regime has engaged in the wanton violation of political rights and freedoms. For example, no elections have been held; hence, the government is not accountable to the people. Also, no opposition political parties are allowed; consequently, the ruling People's Front for Democracy and Justice has unbridled monopoly over the totality of the country. Moreover, the regime has enacted various draconian laws designed to suppress freedom of speech, assembly and association. For example, one of the statutes requires that "No group larger than seven is allowed to assemble without government approval" (Human Rights Watch 2004: 1).

Interestingly, despite the wanton violation of democratic principles and ideals, the Afwerki regime has been a major client of the United States in the latter's campaign to "contain terrorism" in Somalia. So, from 1993 to 2001, the United States acquiesced in the commission of human rights abuses by the Eritrean regime.

Significantly, Eritrean-American relations became stained in 2001, when the Eritrean regime arrested and detained two local employees of the United States Embassy. In response, the United States implored Eritrea to release the two employees, but the Afwerki regime refused. Subsequently, in 2005, the conflict between the two allies escalated with the demand by the Eritrean regime that the United States Agency for International Development (USAID) end its operations in the country. In September of 2005, the United States made a symbolic denial of arms export license to Eritrea. This angered the Eritrean government because the arms are important for the prosecution of its seemingly unending war with Ethiopia, another American client state. Eritrea responded to the American action by accusing the United States Central Intelligence Agency of plotting to destabilize the country.

Interestingly, despite the tension between the two allies and the United States' pro-democracy stance, the strategic collaboration between the two countries is continuing. This is a clear indication that the promotion of democratization in Africa is secondary to the pursuance of America's national interests.

Ethiopia. The relationship between Ethiopia and the United States has gone through various cycles. During the reign of Emperor Haile Selassie, Ethiopia was a major client of the United States. After the overthrow and subsequent execution of the Emperor, however, the new regime under Mengistu Hailemariam adopted an anti-American posture. So, the United States "lost Ethiopia" to the Soviet Union in the two superpowers' competition during the Cold War.

After the overthrow of the Hailemariam regime, following a protracted civil war, Ethiopia again became an American client state in 1993. Interestingly, the new Ethiopian leader, Meles Zenawi, became a member of the United States' designed "club of the new African leaders."[1] Since he assumed power, Zenawi has governed Ethiopia with an "iron fist." This has been reflected in the violation of political rights and freedoms and the independence of the judiciary.

In spite of Ethiopia's sordid record on democratization, the United States has remained very supportive of the Zenawi regime. This is because the regime is an important "foot soldier" in the promotion of American interests in Somalia and the Sudan. For example, Ethiopia invaded Somalia at the behest of the United States to "contain Islamic terrorists" As Human Rights Watch notes, "Ethiopia is considered an essential partner of the United States in its 'war on terrorism,' and Washington has generally been unwilling to apply meaningful pressure on the Ethiopian government over its human rights record" (2005:2).

Morocco. Morocco's monarchical regime has long been known for its autocratic proclivities. For example, it took more than four decades before "free" parliamentary elections were held. Despite the holding of the elections and the adoption of other measures, however, Morocco firmly remains an autocratic state that is fundamentally resistant to democratic change, especially efforts to reform the monarchical system of governance.

---

1.   The "club of new African leaders," which was designed by the United States, consisted of Isayas Afwerki of Eritrea, Paul Kigame of Rwanda, Yoweri Musevini of Uganda and Meles Zenawi of Ethiopia. The "club" was designed to serve as the major front for the promotion of American interests in Africa, especially in the central sub-region and the Horn of Africa. Two major developments exposed the artificiality of the club. First, Eritrea and Ethiopia, two of the United States' major allies and members of the "club" went to war in 1998. To the dismay of the United States, it was unable to stop the war. Since then, the war has waxed and waned. Second, the horrendous records of the members of the "club" in the area of democratization has undermined the United States' propaganda that portrayed these four African leaders as the agents of democratic development.

Like Egypt, Morocco is an old ally of the United States. For example, during the Cold War, Morocco was supportive of American interests in North Africa. The dawn of the post-Cold War era has witnessed the further cementing of the relations between Washington and Rabat. For example, against the backdrop of the American "war on terror," Morocco has become a major partner in a strategic region of the world. Presently, Morocco has provides the United States with air-fields and ports for military-security and strategic purposes related to the "war on terror."

Nigeria. Nigeria has been, and remains, a major consideration in American policy calculus for several reasons. At the core is the fact that the country has oil, which is important to the industro-manufacturing complexes of the United States and its European allies and Japan. Another major reason is that the country's large population makes it attractive to American private investments. Also, Nigeria is the major sub-regional power in West Africa, a region that has become volatile since the 1980s.

With the exception of the brief tenure of Murtala Mohammed, the various regimes in Nigeria since the 1960s have been supportive of the promotion of American interests in Africa (with the exception of the wars of liberation in Africa on which the two countries usually differed). Nigerian-United States relations were at their lowest point during the regime of General Sani Abacha. This was due basically to the terrible human rights record of the regime, including the bru-tal murder execution-style of Ken Saro Wiwa and the other human rights activ-ists from Ogoni.

Since the ascendancy of Olusegun Obasanjo to power in 1999, Nigerian-United States relations have reached unprecedented heights in the political, eco-nomic and military spheres. For example, Nigeria has become one of the major "point guards" in the promotion of American political and strategic interests in West Africa and the African region as a whole. In the economic sphere, Nigeria is one of the major suppliers of oil to the United States. Central to the emergent alliance between the two countries has been the establishment of a framework of "regular consultation." In this vein, President Obasanjo has visited the United States on numerous occasions to "consult" with President Bush on various Afri-can and global issues.

In terms of its policy praxis on democratization, the United States has refused to criticize the Obasanjo regime for its authoritarian proclivities. For example, the Obasanjo regime has used the seizure of passports as a policy tool to cow human rights activists into submission. For example, in December of 2002, to the bafflement of Nigerian human rights organizations, the passports of three human rights activists were seized by the Obasanjo regime (Okome 2005:100). Characteristically, the United States government did not take a stance on this important matter relating to democratization. Also, in 2003, when the Obasanjo regime rigged the elections (Udogu 2005), the United States encouraged the opposition parties to accept the fraudulent results. Moreover, Nigerian security forces have carried out extra-judicial killings in the Niger region for the past four years (Human Rights Watch 2003:4). Again, the United States has remained silent on these matters. Even when President Obasanjo decided to orchestrate a "coup" against the Nigerian Constitution by tele-guiding efforts to amend the constitution so that he could seek a third term of office and beyond, after the expiration of his second and final term in May of 2007, as usual, the United States remained silent on this issue, which is critical to the survival of the democratization project in Nigeria and the stability of the county. The major concern of the Bush Administration has been the protection of the oil fields against angry and dejected Nigerians in the Delta region who are being robbed and deprived by an alliance among the Nigerian government, Shell and the other suzerains of international finance capital.

Rwanda. Rwanda's political history is littered with the sordid records of the repressive regimes of Gregoire Kayibanda and Juvenal Habyriamana. Both regimes used violence, terror and the strategy of "divide and rule" to foster the interests of the local ruling class and its external patrons. Significantly, the cycle of state-sponsored violence that has engulfed the country since independence reached its crescendo in 1994, with the commission of acts of genocide. During the pre-genocide era, the United States had very little relations with Rwanda.

In 1994, following the end of the genocide, the Rwandan Patriotic Front seized power, amid widespread expectations that the cultural, economic, political and social factors that contributed to the occurrence of the genocide, including the bankrupt "genocidal ideology" based on the "Hutu-Tutsi divide" would be addressed, and that the country would have the opportunity to make a new democratic beginning. Unfortunately, the Rwandan Patriotic Front-led regime under the leadership of Paul Kigame has returned the country to the era of authoritarianism. This is reflected in the fact, among other things, that fundamental democratic rights such as the freedoms of association, of the press, and of speech are being violated. In fact, those who dare to disagree with the Kigame regime and the ruling party are accused of propounding "genocidal ideology."

In terms of the praxis of American policy on democratization, the United States is quite supportive of the Kigame regime. This is because Rwanda is quite pivotal to the pursuance of American interests. For example, acting in America's interests, Rwanda joined Uganda in invading the Democratic Republic of the Congo and destabilizing the regime of Laurent Kabila. Given Kabila's socialist proclivities, he was seen as a threat to American interests. Accordingly, the United States used two of its client regimes to depose him. Also, Rwanda is playing a key role in the American "war on terror."

Tunisia. Since independence, Tunisia has been enveloped in a cocoon of authoritarian rule. Habib Bourgiba, the first president, ruled the country as his personal fiefdom for 31 years. During his reign, political competition was non-existent; and political rights and civil liberties were routinely violated in the interest of preserving the regime. In 1987, the aging President Bourgiba was deposed in a coup led by Zine el-Abidine. The coup, however, has not transformed the Tunisian political economy: the inequities in wealth, income and power backed by the brute force of the government remain in tact.

Like Algeria and Djibouti, Tunisia became pivotal to American interests after September 11, 2001. Tunisia has provided the United States access to its airfields and ports in the prosecution of the United States' "war on terror." Interestingly, like the other American client states, Tunisia's poor record on political democratization, especially the respect for human rights, is a source of embarrassment for the United States. Hence, on occasions, the Bush Administration has criticized Tunisia for its human rights record. Despite the denunciation of Tunisia's human rights violations, however, the United States has continued to collaborate with the former in the area of the war on terrorism (Human Rights Watch 2005:2). In essence, the United States has recurrently expressed concerns about the poor state of democratization on the one hand, but has praised Tunisia for its role in "stabilizing the region and combating terror" (Human Rights Watch 2005:2).

Uganda. Like other African states, Uganda is a classical case of the ways in which false starts and state failure can lead a country on the path to instability. When Milton Obote assumed the leadership of the country in 1962, after the gaining of independence from the British, it was expected that he would provide the requisite leadership for building an inclusive and democratic post-colonial state. During his nine-year reign, however, Obote was preoccupied with the maintenance of power and the private accumulation of wealth by him and his supporters. This provided the pretext for Idi Amin to stage a coup in 1971 and begin his reign as the "butcher of Africa." During the Amin regime, the state was the major threat to the safety and security of its citizens evidenced by the state's excessive reliance on the use of violence as the basis for mediating state-society relations. After Amin's removal from power, Uganda descended into the abyss of civil war and its associated chaos and instability.

In 1986, Yoweri Museveni and the National Resistance Movement came to power after years of civil war. Museveni put forward a progressive national agenda that was designed to build a new democratic Ugandan state. Museveni and company, however, soon abandoned the non-capitalist path to development and adopted the development blueprint designed by the Bretton Woods institutions. Clearly, this made him acceptable to the United States. Accordingly, Museveni cultivated a patron-client relationship with Washington. As Nabudere asserts, "… the U.S. saw in Museveni someone who could play the role of a regional power broker on behalf of the Anglo-American alliance" (2004:25). As expected, Museveni has served American interests in various ways. Uganda played a pivotal role in destabilizing the regime of Laurent Kabila, which was seen as a threat to United States' interests. Also, Uganda has played a critical role in helping Washington to contain the Sudan and "Islamic extremists" lodged in the Horn of Africa. For its part, the United States has failed to take issue with Museveni's poor record on democratization. For example, Museveni prevented others from organizing political parties for almost two decades, while his National Resistance Movement operated as the only political party and movement. Also, the Museveni regime is noted for its commission of various human rights violations—the muzzling of the press; the prevention of the exercise of the freedom of speech; and the harassment, arrest and detention of political opponents. Importantly, in 2005, Museveni orchestrated the illegal amendment of the Ugandan Constitution to allow him to seek a third term of office, in contravention of the Constitution. Even during the presidential campaign, Museveni used the power of the state to terrorize the opposition. In the end, Museveni dealt the prospects for democratization in Uganda a major setback by continuing to hang onto power, after two decades as president. Characteristically, the United States, the professed "champion of democracy," remained silent as Museveni systematically implemented the plan to establish his political dynasty in Uganda.

Table 2: The Index of the Praxis of United States Policy on Democratization Toward Its Allied States in Africa

Year	United States' Support for Dem. (%)	Opposition to Dem (%)	No Stance (%)
1990	0	0	100
1991	0	0	100
1992	0	0	100
1993	0	0	100
1994	0	10	90
1995	10	0	90
1996	0	0	90
1997	10	0	90
1998	0	10	90
1999	0	10	90
2000	0	10	90
2001	10	0	90
2002	10	0	90
2003	10	0	90
2004	10	0	90
2005	20	0	80

Source: Computed by the author from Human Rights Watch, World Reports 1990-2005 (New York: Human Rights Watch).

The Assessment of the Praxis of United States' Policy on Democratization

The results of the praxis of United States policy on democratization (political) in Africa show two patterns. The first pattern is that the United States showed support for political democratization in those African states in which it had no vital national interests (see Table 1). That is, in the majority of the states of Africa—those not pivotal to United States' interests, the United States had the flexibility of supporting democratization. On the other hand, the second pattern shows that the United States consistently took no stance the overwhelming majority of the time on issues concerning political democratization in the African states that were pivotal to its interests (see Table 2). In other words, when the imperatives of American national interests collided with the exigency of democratization, the United States accorded priority to its national interests.

Also, as Table 3 shows, in terms of political democratization, of the ten states pivotal to American interests, none is making significant progress. Only three—Ethiopia, Morocco and Nigeria—are making some progress toward political democratization. The remaining seven countries are making no progress toward political democratization. Overall, the United States is allied with authoritarian and quasi-authoritarian states in Africa.

Clearly, the findings show that there is no significant difference between United States' policy on political democratization during the Cold War and currently in the post-Cold War era. The fact is that the promotion of political democratization in Africa is secondary to the pursuance of American economic, political, military, security and strategic interests.

Table 3 The Political Democratization Index of African States Allied With the United States, 1990-2005

State	1990	1995	2000	2005
Algeria	5.0	1.0	5.5	5.0
Djibouti	5.5	4.5	4.5	5.0
Egypt	4.5	6.0	7.0	5.5
Eritrea	-	5.0	6.0	6.5
Ethiopia	7.0	4.5	5.0	5.0
Morocco	4.0	5.0	4.5	4.5
Nigeria	5.5	7.0	4.0	4.0
Rwanda	6.0	6.5	6.5	5.5
Tunisia	4.5	5.5	5.5	5.5
Uganda	5.5	4.5	5.5	4.5

Sources: Freedom House. Freedoms in the world.
www.freedomhouse.org/uploads/Chart18Files32.pdf
Freedom House, Freedoms in the World, 1992-2002, New Jersey: Piscatemy Transaction Publisher.

The subordinate status of the promotion of democratization in Africa in the pecking order of the United States' foreign policy priorities in Africa is vividly captured by the blunt comments of an American diplomat: "Foreign policy is about choosing, and in this case there is no question that the security interest of combating global terrorism with our allies ... is more important than the degree to which the peoples of these countries enjoy democratic forms of governance" (Cited in Schraeder 2004:283).

Rethinking United States Policy on Democratization: Towards an Equitable Partnership with Africa

The repository of evidence shows that United States' policy on democratization in Africa during the Cold War era was not designed to promote the building of democratic societies in Africa. This was because the United States was not committed to the promotion of democratization in Africa as a goal in the galaxy of its national interests. Instead, democratization in Africa was simply a tool for the promotion of United States' economic, political, military, security and strategic interests on continent. That is, democratization was supported by the United States only if it did not conflict with the national interests of the United States. The resultant was that United States' policy was by and large a hindrance to the promotion of democratization in Africa. This was evidenced by American support for some of the most repressive regimes on the continent.

With the end of the Cold War, there were high expectations among some Africans and Africanists that United States' policy on democratization in Africa would be, to paraphrase Michael Clough, "free at last" from the vagaries of the Cold War. Nonetheless, 15 years after the dawn of the post-Cold War era, it has become abundantly clear that the promotion of democratization in Africa is still not a priority of the United States. That is, the rhetoric notwithstanding, the praxis—especially in the cases of America's African allies—clearly indicates that the promotion of democratization on the continent is not part of the national interests of the United States.

Against this background, if the United States wants to make meaningful contributions to the genuine promotion of the democratization project on the continent, then the former must rethink its policy. Importantly, the process of rethinking must be done within a new framework of establishing an equitable partnership between the United States and Africa. Such an approach would be anchored on several interlocking poles. At the vortex, the United States must come to the realization that it is not the only country in the world that has interests. Instead, African and other Third World States have their own interests as well. Particularly, there are Africans who are genuinely interested in helping to build democratic societies on the continent. This issue is critical because United States' foreign policy toward Africa is premised on the overarching arrogant notion that Africans do not have interests; and if they do have interests, these are inconsequential vis-à-vis American interests. Hence, the central role of African states—especially those that are American allies, is to promote the national interests of the United States, even if it means jeopardizing their own interests. Accordingly, African states are mere instruments for the promotion of the interests of the United States. Significantly, the United States has to change this mindset and replace it with one that views Africa as a constellation of states with divergent national interests and agendas. So, the American approach should be based on the establishment of an equitable partnership that would involve, among other things, engaging the various African states in frank and sincere discussions about exploring ways in which the United States, on the one hand, and African states, on the other, can harmonize their respective national interests in ways that accrue mutual benefits. Addressing this epicenter of United States-African relations is the *sine qua non* for establishing equitable partnership in the realms of democratization and others.

Importantly, once the aforementioned framework based on equitable partnership has been established, then the promotion of democratization should become an essential element of the national interests of the United States. In practical policy terms, this would require that the United States treats the promotion of democratization in Africa as the *terra firma* for the achievement of its political, economic and strategic goals on the continent. This is critical because only democratic African states can provide the required accountable and transparent bases for the pursuance of mutually beneficial African and American interests on the continent. Conversely, as the empirical evidence shows, the tendency of the United States to pursue its interests in Africa through the establishment of patron-client relationships with various authoritarian regimes is shortsighted. Two major reasons account for this. First, authoritarian African regimes have no legitimacy; hence, developing clientelist relationships with them is a clear indication that American interests in Africa are antithetical to the promotion of democratization on the continent. Second, American interests in the continent would be ultimately jeopardized, because no matter the amount of time it takes these authoritarian regimes are bound to collapse. When this happens, democratic-minded Africans would develop animosity toward the United States because of its role in the asphyxiation of democratization on the continent.

Another major issue is that cognizance must be taken of the fact that democratization is a multifaceted phenomenon with cultural, ecological, economic, social and political dimensions. This is critical because the United States, even in its policy rhetoric, tends to view democratization in Africa as exclusively political—the foci are on the establishment of political rights and freedoms. The reality is that the promotion of political rights, freedoms, institutions, and the establishment of political rules and processes are not enough to establish democratic societies in Africa. Alternatively, the approach must be holistic—a synergy of the multiple dimensions of democratization.

Also, it is important to realize and accept the fact that there are various models of democratization and democracy and their associated pathways. Accordingly, the American liberal democratic model cannot be portrayed as the "only game in town." Alternatively, in the context of a new equitable partnership, African states should have the right to choose the democratic models—social democracy and liberal democracy and their variations and others—that are consistent with the objective realities and future trajectories of their respective societies. The major concern should be that the democratic model chosen by an African state is based on the general tenets that are common to all democratizing and democratic polities.

Conclusion

This chapter has attempted to address two major interrelated issues. First, it examined the praxis of United States' policy on political democratization in Africa. The findings indicate that the United States was not committed to the promotion of democratization in Africa during the Cold War era. In the current post-Cold War epoch, the praxis of American policy on democratization in Africa has remained the same. The overarching explanation is that the promotion of democratization in Africa is not part of the national interests of the United States. That is, the promotion of democratization in Africa is simply a tool for the achievement of the United States' central national interests in Africa. There are times, however, when the United States promotes democratization in Africa. But, there are two major preconditions. First, the African state concerned must not be an ally of the United States. In other words, once the authoritarian African state is not pivotal to United States' interests, it is then convenient for the United States to promote democratization. Second, and importantly, the promotion of democratization must not conflict with the national interest of the United States. The observation made by Antoine Glaser and Stephen Smith concerning the praxis of French Policy on democratization in Africa is applicable to American policy as well: "When confronted with the potentially conflicting goals of promoting democracy, ensuring development, and maintaining security, the leaders of Francophone Africa were expected to adopt the order of priorities: above all, security, followed by development and, finally, democratization" (Glaser and Smith, 1994:102).

Second, the chapter proffered suggestions for rethinking American policy within the framework of an equitable partnership with Africa. At the core, the United States must take cognizance of the fact that African states also have national interests. So, the appropriate approach would be for the United States and African states to work together within a framework of an equitable partnership and find ways in which their respective interests can be harmonized for their mutual benefits. Once this mindset is established, it will then provide the crucible in which African-United States relations would henceforth be conducted. In the area of democratization, the phenomenon should then become an integral part of American policy toward Africa. This is important because only democratic African states can provide the required legitimation for the mutually beneficial pursuance of American interests in the region. Also, democratization must be treated as a multifaceted construct with various dimensions—cultural, ecological, economic, political and social. It must no longer be viewed as exclusively political. Finally, as they democratize, African states should have the right to choose democratization models that are appropriate for their respective objective conditions.

5

Diplomacy and Peace Operations: The Case of the Democratic Republic of the Congo

Guy Martin

Introduction

Taking the Democratic Republic of the Congo[1] as a case in point, this chapter shows that the Africa policy of the George W. Bush Administration since 2000 is essentially aimed at mobilizing friends and allies world-wide in the global war on terrorism. Under the avowed aim of pursuing a global "War on Terror" after the tragic events of September 11, 2001, the United States seeks to build an international "coalition of the willing" against the main "enemy," which has taken the form of radical Islamic fundamentalist groups exemplified by al-Qaeda. In a scenario taken straight out of Samuel Huntington's *Clash of Civilizations* (1993), the new enemy of the United States and its Western allies in the post-Cold War world is no longer a defeated and now-defunct Communism, but "other" cultures, civilizations and religions which threaten the Western/Christian civiliza-

---

1. On 30 June 1960, the Belgian Congo became independent as the Republic of the Congo. In 1971, the country was renamed Zaïre by Mobutu. When Laurent-Désiré Kabila took over in 1997, he reverted back to the immediate post-independence name, re-baptizing the country the Democratic Republic of the Congo (DRC)—a name retained by his successor, his son Joseph Kabila—, distinct from the (former French) Republic of Congo, (or Congo-Brazzaville). While retaining the official denomination of Democratic Republic of the Congo, for simplicity's sake the name "Congo" will also be used in this chapter.

tion and way of life, specifically radical Islamic fundamentalism. I argue that such a confrontational and reckless foreign policy—which privileges conflict and war over cooperation and diplomacy and which informs United States' Africa policy—actually exacerbates ethnic, regional, factional and religious conflict throughout the world—as evidenced by the current Shiite-Sunni conflict in Iraq—instead of creating an environment conducive to diplomacy, peace and security. In essence, the current American foreign policy in general—and its policy towards Africa in particular—is merely a continuation of the age-old imperial strategy of *divide et impera* ("divide and rule") initiated at the end of the 19th Century by British imperialist Cecil Rhodes and pursued during the colonial era by various European powers, notably Britain and France (Martin 2002). After a brief overview of current United States' policy towards Africa, this chapter examines how this policy is actually implemented in the Democratic Republic of the Congo.

Africa United States Policy of the George W. Bush Administration Since 2000

While geopolitics determined United States' Africa policy during the Cold War era (1945-1989), and while economic interests prevailed during the immediate post-Cold War period (1990-2000), security concerns have taken precedence during the administration of George W. Bush (starting in 2000). After the tragic events of September 11, 2001, the world-wide struggle against international terrorism—in the form of Islamic fundamentalist groups such as al-Qaeda—has become the central focus and main objective of American foreign policy. Thus, the Pan-Sahel Initiative (PSI) is an informal military alliance including the United States and a number of countries from North Africa and the Sahel region of Africa, namely Mauritania, Mali, Niger and Chad, which have recently been joined by Algeria, Morocco, Tunisia and Senegal. United States Special Operations Forces regularly train West African forces from some of these countries, notably Mauritania, Mali, Niger and Chad. An initial sum of $7.5 million had been earmarked for the first phase of this project (2002-2004) while $125 million have been set aside for phase II (2004-2009) of the project (Source Watch 2006, Brown 2006). The United States has also, since May 2003, deployed 1,800 American troops in Djibouti, which constitute the Combined Joint Task Force (CJTF)-Horn of Africa. These troops are positioned primarily to wage war on al-Qaeda elements in Yemen, Somalia, Kenya, Sudan, Ethiopia, and Djibouti (Source Watch 2006). Under the aegis of the Department of Defense (DoD) and the National Defense University, an Africa Center for Strategic Studies (ACSS) has been created as one of five DoD regional centers for security studies. The aim of the ACSS is to promote democracy and good governance in African defense and security sectors, to counter ideological support for terrorism, and to develop networks among, and build trusting long-term relationships between African and American military and civilian defense leaders.

United States Policy in the Great Lakes Region of Africa under the Clinton and Bush Administrations, 1990 to the Present

Following the October 1993 United States' intervention in Somalia (20,715 troops, of which 18 were killed), and as per presidential directive PDD-25 of 1994 on Peace Operations, the United States decided to intervene in Africa only when American economic interests are at stake. The non-intervention of the United States in the Rwanda Genocide of April-June 1994 (which resulted in one million deaths) has been justified in part by this new policy. As part of this policy, the United States also developed new strategic alliances with various countries of the Horn and Great Lakes regions of Africa, notably Ethiopia, Eritrea, Uganda, Rwanda and the DRC. In particular, the United States praised Meles Zenawi of Ethiopia, Isaias Afewerki of Eritrea, Yoweri Museveni of Uganda, Paul Kagame of Rwanda and Joseph Kabila of the DRC as a the "new African leaders" worthy of American diplomatic and financial support.

The United States supported the joint Ugandan-Rwandan invasion of eastern Congo of 1996-1997, which led to the overthrow of the brutal dictatorship of Mobubu Sese Seko, who was replaced by the leader of the Congolese rebellion, Laurent-Désiré Kabila in May of 1997. In fact, United States Ambassador Dennis Hankins was posted to Goma (eastern Congo) in April of 1997 as liaison with L.D. Kabila. Then, in August of 1998, Kabila fell out with Rwanda and Uganda, which then—with United States' support—proceeded to invade the DRC, thereby starting the second Congo war. On January 16, 2001, almost 40 years to the day after the murder of Patrice Lumumba, Laurent-Désiré Kabila was assassinated and replaced, one day later, by his son, Joseph Kabila, who turned out to be a close, faithful and reliable ally of the West in general, and of the United States in particular. The American policy towards the Great Lakes region of Africa—which includes the DRC, Uganda, Rwanda and Burundi, was neatly summarized by Marina Ottawa: "The U.S. could intervene militarily to redraw the boundaries of Africa ... but ... it is preferable to let African civil wars develop and to allow Rwanda and Uganda to intervene militarily in the Congo. In this way, it is the African themselves who will divide up the Congo ... (June 8, 1999). In other words, what the United States is advocating is the further partition of

African countries, in a throw-back to the "divide and rule" and balkanization policies pursued by France in the late 1950s when it deliberately broke up the former Federations of French West and Equatorial Africa into smaller political units incapable of independent development. This statement also clearly demonstrates that the African states mentioned (Rwanda and Uganda) totally lack any kind of political autonomy and basically remain under strict (United States-dominated) neo-colonial rule. Indeed, these countries—the DRC included—are mere pawns in the "Great Game" currently being played by the major powers in Africa, in effect acting as proxies for the United States in Africa. Thus, it is no accident that the American Ambassador to the DRC, William L. Swing, is a virtual pro-consul in the Congo, acting both as chair of the International Committee for the Support of the Transition—a major advisory body to the Congolese government—and head of the United Nations Mission in the Congo (MONUC). A detailed political history of the Congo after independence reveals that a recurrent theme of Congolese-Western relations, from the first to the third Republic, is the deliberate instigation and exacerbation of ethnic or ethno-regional conflict by Western (particularly American) governments and firms in order to facilitate their access to, and exploitation of, Congolese natural resources. It is against the historical backdrop of the First (1960-1965) and Second (1965-1997) Republics that this chapter examines how United States' policy towards Africa has been implemented in the Congo under the Third Republic (1987-2007), and it also assesses the—mostly negative—impact of this policy on the Congolese people.

The Congo Under the First Republic, 1960-1965

During the independence ceremonies (June 30, 1960), an ominous incident occurred between Prime Minister Patrice Lumumba and King Baudouin of Belgium. To King Baudouin's paternalistic and patronizing speech which praised the accomplishments of his great-great uncle King Léopold II and basically told the Congolese not to destroy the valuable Belgian colonial inheritance bequeathed to them, Lumumba responded with an impromptu speech on the true meaning of independence for the Congolese people: "We should not forget that this independence has been won through a daily struggle; a struggle in which we did not spare our forces, our suffering, or our blood ... We shall make sure that the land of our ancestors truly benefits our people ... The independence of Congo is a major step towards the liberation of the whole African continent" (Braeckman, 2002:67-71). From the very beginning, Belgium, the other Western powers and their allies made every effort to politically neutralize Lumumba, viewed as an erratic and unpredictable leader, and as a dangerous 'Communist' willing to open the door to Soviet intervention, when in fact he was merely an African nationalist leader trying to create a unified nation-state and to achieve genuine economic independence for his country and his people in the spirit of Pan-Africanism. Thus, the Belgian-inspired *Loi Fondamentale* proved to be a constitutional straight-jacket; in particular, it failed to clearly define the respective areas of power and competence of the Prime Minister (Patrice Lumumba) and of the President (Joseph Kasa-Vubu), thereby opening the door to divergent legal interpretations and to political conflict. Furthermore, the massive exodus of Belgian colonial civil servants—only 1,600 out of 8,200 remained in Congo by August of 1960—rendered the Lumumba government powerless, as it was unable to implement key policy decisions (Merlier 1962:304-5). At the same time, the *Force Publique*—whose officer corps was almost entirely Belgian—remained firmly under Belgian military control. On July 5, 1960, the Belgian commander of the *Force Publique*, General Janssens, summoned the African non-commissioned officers of the army, wrote on the blackboard the phrase, "After Independence = Before Independence," and bluntly announced: "The *Force Publique* continues as before" (Quoted in Young 1965:316). In July-August of 1960, a mutiny of the *Force Publique* opened the door to a Belgian military intervention, followed by the secession of Katanga and South Kasai. Convened in Brussels in April-May of 1960, the economic Round Table negotiations between the Congolese leadership and the Belgian firms (notably *Société Générale*) and government resulted in a raw deal for the Congolese. All the Belgian state corporations (*Société Générale, Comité spécial du Katanga, Comité national du Kivu*) were disbanded (May-June of 1960) and replaced by a Development Fund controlled by Belgium. Thus, all the assets of these corporations were repatriated to Belgium, and the operation and management of the Fund remained firmly under Belgian control (Merlier 1962:290-93). With a top-heavy government of 36 ministers, which "amounted to a team of fantastically varied individuals, of different classes, different tribes, and different political leanings" (Kanza 1972:104), without effective control over the administration, the security forces (military and *Force Publique*) and the economy, and deprived of essential fiscal revenues and financial resources as a result of the secession of the mineral-rich provinces of Katanga and South Kasai, the Lumumba regime—which effectively inherited an empty shell and empty coffers in lieu of state—was definitely set up for failure.

Addressing Parliament on 15 July 1960, Lumumba succinctly and eloquently outlined his dilemma:

... three days after our inauguration, trouble started and we did not even have offices. How did you expect us to present a program of government in these circumstances? ... We are also demanding the repatriation to Congo of all our national assets—including our money and state corporate assets—still frozen in Belgium. We were told that these assets would be returned to us on 30 June [1960]; as you know, as of now we have received nothing (Lumunba in Bénot 1991:132-3).

The gold stock representing part of Congo's foreign exchange reserves was physically removed from Leopoldville to Brussels. In his address to Parliament on 7 September 1960, Lumumba explained the predicament of Congo's national bank and the issue of the money confiscated by the Belgians:

You must realize that on 30 June, when independence was proclaimed, our gold reserves reached a value of 3,764,000,000 [Belgian] francs, while by 15 August we only had 1,764,000,000—owing to a magical disappearance of 2 billion francs which Belgium had paid into [its] national bank in Brussels, supposedly in order to open a bank in Ruanda-Urundi (Kanza 1972:296).

It became increasingly evident that Lumumba stood in the way of a broad coalition of Western neo-colonial interests and had to be eliminated: "Lumumba became the last obstacle preventing Western governments and companies from making Congo their own neocolonial state ... As the political elimination of Lumumba had failed, it became clear that only physical elimination could neutralize him and clear the way for a conservative government" (Gondola 2002:123,125). The Belgian instigated an unconstitutional destitution of Lumumba by Kasa-Vubu on September 1960 marked the beginning of a long period of constitutional, institutional and political instability in the Congo (Braeckman 2002:34). On that date, Joseph-Désiré Mobutu staged his first military *coup d'état*, and replaced the government with a *Collège des Commissaires* (College of Commissioners) mostly made up of students. From then on, Lumumba was a marked man. On August 18, 1960, United States President Dwight D. Eisenhower formally authorized his assassination. CIA Director, Allen Dulles—who referred to Lumumba as a 'mad dog,' then sent several agents to central Africa to implement this directive, but none succeeded (Braeckman 2002:27-8, De Witte 2001:xiii-xiv). The Belgians, who strongly advocated Lumumba's 'final elimination' (Braeckman 2002:84), then took matters in their own hands and concocted a plan—managed by Minister of African Affairs d'Aspremont Lynden—whereby Lumumba would be captured and handed over to his sworn enemies, the Katangese. The plan for eliminating Lumumba was officially endorsed by the Belgian Government, and its financing was secretly authorized by the Belgian Parliament. Thus, 20 million Belgian francs (BF) were provided to Mobutu in order to allow him "to pay the soldiers' salaries and to consolidate his position," with the proviso that he should 'effectively neutralize' Lumumba. A further 500 million BF were disbursed for the benefit of the young Commissioners. Other beneficiaries of this Belgian largesse were Albert Kalondji (20 million BF) and minister of foreign affairs Justin Bomboko (five million BF) (Braeckman 2002:39-42). This helps explain and put in proper perspective the endemic state of venality and corruption that prevailed in Congo/Zaïre during the Mobutu regime. Finally, on December 2, 1960, Patrice Lumumba was captured as he was trying to escape to Kasai. On January 17, 1961, Lumumba and two of his ministers, Joseph Okito and Maurice Mpolo, were murdered by Belgian officers, in the presence of Katangese government officials (Moise Tshombe and Godefroid Munongo) (De Witte 2001, Braeckman 2002). Ludo De Witte unequivocally states: "It was Belgian advice, Belgian orders and finally Belgian hands that killed Lumumba on that 17 January 1961 … the Belgian government of Gaston Eyskens is directly responsible for the assassination of the Congolese prime minister" (2001:xxii). Apparently, the timing of Lumumba's assassination had more to do with American political transition than with internal politics in the Congo itself. As Madeleine Kalb explains,

> … one of the reasons for the hasty disposal of Lumumba may have been concern on the part of his enemies that the new Kennedy Administration would adopt a totally new policy … much of the sense of urgency in the first few weeks of January which led to the death of Lumumba came not from the internal situation in the Congo … but from fear of the impending change in Washington. The coincidence in dates is striking: Lumumba was flown to Katanga on January 17 and probably murdered immediately; the Kennedy Administration took office on January 20, three days later (1982:194,196).

The character of Congo's political system was substantially changed by the new constitution adopted in April of 1964 at Luluabourg. In particular, the fragmentation of the original six provincial units into 21 through a process of ethnic or local self-determination led to the weakening and decomposition of central authority (Young 1965). A major consequence of the Congo crisis was a sharp social and political division between the urban ruling elite and the urban and rural masses: i.e. between the politicians and the people, and the leaders and the led. Crawford Young aptly summarizes this situation:

In the Congo ... the extraordinary circumstances of independence have served to enlarge the gap between rulers and ruled and to produce a particularly sharp sense of alienation on the part of the mass ... Representative institutions became corporate guilds of parliamentarians. Parties lost touch with both rural and urban masses and now face an uncertain future. Leaders no longer had need of the led; the system was turned within itself. The sources of power were in the capital, not the countryside (1965:358,396).

The Congo under Mobutu: The Second Republic, 1965-1997

On November 24, 1965, Mobutu staged his second military coup and seized power by ousting Kasa-Vubu and Tshombe, thereby bringing to an ignominious end Congo's first Republic. Joseph-Désiré Mobutu was a sergeant in the *Force Publique* who dabbled in journalism and was initially close to Lumumba. Before independence, he was recruited by Belgian intelligence and by the CIA (Wrong 2001:206-7) and eventually became Lumumba's nemesis and arch-enemy. Indeed, he was personally involved in Lumumba's assassination. Thomas Kanza explains Mobutu's strategic position in Lumumba's entourage:

Joseph Mobutu was private secretary to the prime minister. Together with Jacques Lumbala, the second private secretary to the prime minister, he was the closest official collaborator that Lumumba had ... Both private secretaries had access to all the information, public or confidential, official or personal, that Lumumba was given ... He was Lumumba's guardian angel on all his trips to Belgium ... Mobutu succeeded in winning Lumumba's confidence to such a degree that Lumumba considered him his go-between in finding the support he would need from all parts of Europe when he became prime minister (1972:112-3).

During the four years of political chaos and instability that followed Lumumba's assassination (1961-1965), Mobutu—acting through the Binza group—was the king-maker and the real power behind the throne. Thus, the successive governments of Ileo (February-August 1961), Adoula (August 1961-June 1964), Tshombé (July 1964-October 1965) and Kimba (October-November 1965) were mere fronts for Mobutu's Binza group. The group—constituted in September of 1960 and composed (in addition to Mobutu himself) of Justin Bomboko, Damien Kandolo, Albert Ndele, and Victor Nendaka—was described by Kamitatu as an "association of the friends of Mobutu." The group was supported and financed by the CIA, which delegated Lawrence Devlin, former CIA chief of station in Léopoldville, to advise and financially aid it. So, in fact, the Adoula government (August 1961-June 1964) was effectively managed through the United States-supported Binza group (Kamitatu 1971:97-99, Young 1965:379-80). Mobutu eventually decided to directly assume power—with United States encouragement and CIA involvement—through the military coup of November 24, 1965.Yet as early as 1964, a guerilla war challenging his rule was initiated in Kwilu by various former associates of Lumumba, including Pierre Mulele, Gaston Soumialot and Laurent-Désiré Kabila.

Mobutu rapidly consolidated his power through a series of institutional reforms designed to firmly control the state. First, he created a rubber-stamped, powerless legislature. In March of 1967, Parliament was dissolved and a new one would not be constituted until 1970. Second, in order to curb the country's pervasive ethno-regional conflict, he progressively consolidated the 21 provinces into 12, then eight larger administrative units; the provinces became mere administrative divisions of a highly centralized state. In October of 1966, the abolition of the premiership led to an effective concentration of executive powers in the office of the President. Single state-party rule soon followed when Mobutu founded the *Mouvement Populaire de la Révolution* (MPR) in 1967. In 1974, the MPR became the nation's only political institution. Through tight centralized control, the progressive elimination of the *Binza Group*, and direct appointment of high-level party and state officials, Mobutu then proceeded—from late 1967 to 1970—to establish an increasingly authoritarian and personal rule, based on terror, political assassination and co-optation. In typical patrimonial fashion, all power derived from the presidency, and all decisions were made by Mobuto. This extreme centralization meant that all key state personnel depended on his continued favor to remain in office, fostering political insecurity among them: "Under the patrimonialism of Mobutu's regime, appointments to high offices were used to reward individuals who provided loyal service to their ruler. Strong centralization and expansion of the bureaucratic sector in Zaire under Mobutu allowed for the patrimonialization of public offices" (Gondola 2002:144-5). An extreme personalization of power and cult of personality resulted. Mobutu tried to provide an ideological foundation for his regime by developing the doctrine of "authenticity" in the early 1970s, which degenerated into the creed of *Mobutuism*—defined as the teachings, thoughts, and actions of the president—by 1974 (Schatzberg 1991:32-5). In January of 1967, the giant mining company, UMHK (*Union Minière du Haut-Katanga*), was transformed into a state corporation, the *Générale des carrières et des mines* (Gécamines). In November of 1973, Mobutu nationalized commerce and agriculture by turning foreign-owned stores and plantations over to individual Zairian "acquirers" (high-ranking politicians and bureaucrats), who quickly destroyed the firms they acquired, with dire consequences for the economy (the policy was reversed in late 1975 and completely abandoned in early 1976). Schatzberg describes what he calls the "dialectic of oppression" in Congo/ Zaire as follows:

> By the late 1970s the interactions of scarcity and insecurity had created a dialectic of oppression. Mubutu's policies … contributed to rising insecurity among officials whose tenure depended on the president's fickle favor … they used public office to create private wealth. Corruption flourished as never before … They … felt impelled to extract whatever they could, however they could, as quickly they could. Insecurity and scarcity thus fed on each other as the mighty extracted resources from those below them … This vicious chain of extraction weighed most heavily on those who could least afford it, prompting a national search for survival in the economy's burgeoning informal sector (1991:42-3).

Georges Nzongola-Ntalaja explains that through his nationalization project, Mobutu was pursuing two objectives, namely diversification of dependency, and strengthening the ruling elite's economic base:

> Thanks to his American connections, Mobutu became the instrument by which a U.S.-led international bourgeoisie sought to break the Belgian colonial monopoly to penetrate nearly all sectors of the Congolese economy … the basic goal of the Mobutu regime was simply to reinforce its bargaining power vis-à-vis foreign capital in order to provide the new ruling class with a relatively solid economic base (Nzongola-Ntalaja 2002:147-8).

Nzongola-Ntalaja also shows that this process of privatization of the state was a key factor in the collapse and eventual decay of the economy and of the state:

> For the money so diverted to private use could not be made available for productive investment in the country or for keeping up essential public services. The bulk of it went to foreign bank accounts and real estate holdings abroad. What remained in the country was used for the most part in conspicuous consumption (2002:150).

As the regime's legitimacy was eroded, Mobutu increasingly ruled through coercion. Thus, the army, the civil guard and party youth wing, and the political police (the *Agence Nationale de Documentation/*AND) were all used to control, coerce and terrorize the civilian population. Schatzberg describes this process as follows:

> The AND contributes to Mobutu's reign of terror by coercing and controlling the population through intimidation and fear ... Arbitrary arrest, imprisonment, and torture are the main devices the AND uses to exert control ... Mobutu's regime sustains a reign of terror, extortion, arbitrary arrest, detention without trial, and extrajudicial executions are all regular features of the state's interactions with its population (1991:44;6).

As Nzongola-Ntalaja rightly observes, "Nearly all of Mobutu's closest advisers worked in the security apparatus and used their positions as intelligence chief or security adviser to make themselves rich" (2002:160). Internal opposition to Mobutu's regime was both military and political. Some pockets of armed resistance dating from the armed rebellions of the mid-1960s subsisted, notably in the areas of Kivu and North Shaba (Katanga) controlled by the *Parti Révolutionnaire du Peuple* (PRP). Following a brief period of political liberalization in the late 1970s when the legislature was able to subject ministers to probing questioning (*interpellations*), 13 dissident legislators—led by Étienne Tshisekedi wa Mulumba—who had written the President a 52-page critical open letter formed, in 1982, a new political party, the *Union pour la Démocratie et le Progrès Social* (UDPS). The UDPS began to agitate for the political liberalization of the Mobutu regime and for democratic reforms, including competitive elections. External opposition and challenge to the Mobutu regime came from the South. The *Front de Libération Nationale du Congo* (FLNC) launched in March 1977 from bases in Angola its first invasion of Shaba (Shaba I). One month later, 1,500 troops from Morocco—provided with transport planes by France and with logistical support by the United States—repelled the invasion. In May of 1978, the FLNC again entered Shaba from Zambia, threatening the mines in Kolwezi and nearly toppling Mobutu's regime (Shaba II). This time, French and Belgian paratroopers, supported by United States' logistics, intervened and defeated the FLNC (Schatzberg 1991:54-8). The two Shaba invasions clearly showed that as long as Mobutu could count on active Western support, any armed opposition movement was unlikely to overthrow him. Mobutu's regime basically preserved Western economic and strategic interests. In the context of the Cold War, Mobutu himself was perceived as a staunch and faithful ally of the West in Africa. As such, his regime could count on Belgian, French and American military assistance whenever it was seriously threatened by internal opposition or external aggression. All three nations wanted guaranteed access to Zaire's mineral resources—especially, in the case of the United States, it wanted uranium, copper, industrial diamonds, and the cobalt and tantalum for its aerospace industry (Wrong 2001:203, Gondola 2002:120, Nzongola-Ntalaja 2002:29). Mobutu's patrimonial rule led to the obscene enrichment of himself and of his ruling clique. Thus, at the end of his regime in 1997, the personal fortune of Mobutu was equal to the country's total foreign debt, estimated at about $15 billion (Wrong 2001:202,295,303 and Braeckman 1999:325). Meanwhile, the Gross Domestic Product per capita stood at $590, and life expectancy at birth was a mere 49 years.

As a result of the end of the Cold War and the demise of the former Soviet Union, and under strong pressure from Western powers and donors, Mobutu reluctantly agreed to end one-party rule in April of 1990 and to initiate a process of democratization. In August of 1990, a Sovereign National Conference (CNS) was inaugurated in Kinshasa; it was suspended by Mobutu in January of 1992, but resumed its work in April of 1992 and, in August of that year, elected Éti-enne Tshisekedi wa Mulumba—leader of the UDPS—as Prime Minister. The CNS brought together 2,842 delegates representing all sectors of Congolese society, plus no less than 204 political parties. A provisional legislature of 435 councilors, the *Haut Conseil de la République* (HCR), was elected by the CNS to continue its work. The CNS finally concluded its work in December of 1992 without succeeding to unseat Mobutu, who had manipulated its participants and proceedings to stay in power. An active participant in this democratization process himself, Nzongola explains why it failed:

> In the face of an overwhelming popular desire for radical change, Mobutu and his entourage decided to pretend that they were in favor of democratic reforms, while doing everything possible to obstruct the democratization process ... As so many parties were being created, the regime found it useful to dilute the strength of the real opposition by setting up its own opposition parties. Financed by the regime, these artificial creations consisted of a few individuals who were mostly interested in money ... (2002:186,188).

Mobutu was eventually ousted from power by force by Laurent-Désiré Kabila in May of 1997, and he (Mobutu) died in exile in Morocco on September 7, 1997. Following the end of the Cold War, Mobutu's Congo had lost most of its strategic value to the West, which eventually abandoned him to his fate, something he had not envisaged. In the words of Atumba,

> President Mobutu continued, during the last years of his life, to rely—as he had done in the 1980s—on his 'friends' among the French right and the UNITED STATES Republicans, without realizing that after the fall of the

Berlin wall, he was no longer of strategic value to his 'Western friends' (1998:67).

A high-level United States delegation sent by President Bill Clinton and led by Ambassador Bill Richardson attempted, on April 29, 1997, to convince Mobutu to voluntarily relinquish power through an honorable, dignified and suitably compensated exit. Presented with what he viewed as an "ultimatum," Mobutu indicated that he would accept the deal, but needed time to draft his response. Mobutu then reneged on his word, but agreed to a face-to-face meeting with Kabila (Atumba 1998:295-306). Thus, following a mediation by President Nelson Mandela of South Africa, Mobutu subsequently met with Laurent-Désiré Kabila in Pointe-Noire (Congo-Brazzaville) on May 4, 1997 (the meeting was a total failure); and, again, on May 14, 1997 (when the meeting was sabotaged by the last-minute refusal of Kabila to attend) (Atumba 1998:306-322). By then Mobutu's fate was sealed; and, on May 18, 1997, he and his family hurriedly fled into exile in Togo, then Morocco. He died in exile in Morocco on September 7, 1997.

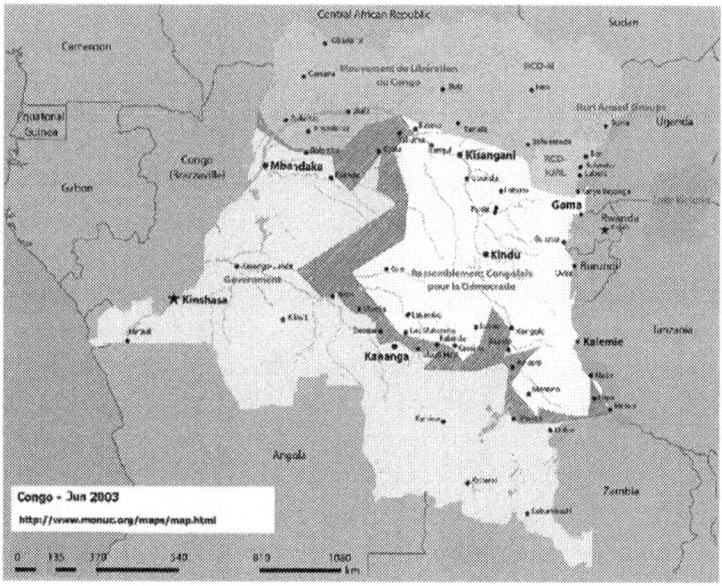

Map 1: Conflict in the Congo (as of June 2003), showing the areas controlled by the Government, the MLC and various RCD factions (RCD, RCD-KML & RCD-N)

The Congo's Third Republic, 1997-2007

Created in October 1996 under the leadership of Laurent-Désiré Kabila as a broad anti-Mobutu alliance, the AFDL (*Alliance des forces démocratiques pour la libération du Congo*) invaded Congo from the east with the backing of Rwanda and Uganda, took over the country in a few months, and took power in Kinshasa on May 17, 1997. How can the lightning speed with which the AFDL forces took over the country be explained? Michela Wrong recounts:

> ... the AFDL's lightning advance was not the result of massive logistical sup-
> port from Anglophone Western nations determined to destroy their former
> ally. Zaire's security system was collapsing like a maggot-eaten fruit. As village
> after village greeted the AFDL 'liberators', the campaign Rwanda and Uganda
> had launched to eliminate a border problem transformed itself into something
> else entirely: the takeover of a vast country ... never in the field of military his-
> tory had so much territory been captured by so few with such little effort
> (2001:253).

There is also evidence of direct United States' involvement in, and support of, the joint Rwanda-Uganda invasion in eastern Congo. In the months immediately preceding Kabila's rebellion, the United States had trained hundreds of Rwandan troops in everything from psychological operations to tactical special forces exer-cises. Rwanda's strong man, Paul Kagame, had trained at the United States Army Command and General Staff College at Fort Leavenworth, Texas and had visited Washington in August 1996, just six weeks before his country launched its inva-sion (French 2004:216). In addition, many United States Special Forces agents, as well as the United States military attaché, were spotted among the rebels in the combat zones (Atumba 1998:129-130). Furthermore, from their base on the island of Idjui (Kivu), United States Special Forces managed the rebels' entire communication system, and the AFDL's bold raid on Kitona was guided by American navy ships anchored in the port of Banane (Braeckman 1999:402-3). An American diplomat posted to Goma in April of 1997, Dennis Hankins, acted as liaison between Washington and Kabila (French 2004:211,216). During a *tête-à-tête* with the AFDL leader, Ambassador Bill Richardson, President Bill Clinton's personal envoy and representative to the United Nations, had these words of advice for Kabila:

> I told him that if he wanted a relationship with the United States, democracy,
> human rights and free-market economics were going to be important. I told
> him that he had taken a huge hit on the human rights issue, and that this was

going to be important for us. 'Clean up your act, because you'll be a pariah if this stuff continues.' I told him you're going to need us, and that's when the breakthrough came. We established a tie, and the ambassador [Daniel H. Simpson] even got his fax and phone numbers (French 2004:213).

Ambassador Richardson's allusion to human rights abuses—"this stuff"—refers to a United Nations' report about the disappearance of 100,000 Hutu from several makeshift camps that had come under attack from Kabila's army in the dense rain forest near Kisangani. Having already made common cause with Rwanda's Tutsi-led government, the United States made sure that no United Nations or Western investigation was launched into these alleged atrocities (French 2004:210,219).

Nonetheless, tensions soon arose between Kabila and his two allies. In July of 1998, Kabila removed Commander James Kabarebe from his post of chief of staff of the Congolese army and sent him back home to Rwanda, where he became chief of staff of the Rwandese army. Shortly thereafter, in August of 1998, Rwanda and Uganda, together attacked Congo in an attempt to overthrow Kabila. They were joined in this endeavor by various rebel movements, notably the *Mouvement pour la Libération du Congo* (MLC), led by Jean-Pierre Bemba, based in the Équateur province, and allied with Uganda; and the Congolese Rally for Democracy (*Rassemblement Congolais pour la Démocratie*/RCD), which broke up into two, then three factions in March of 1999, one of which, the RCD-Goma, was based in eastern Congo, supported by Rwanda and led by Jean-Pierre Ondekane (the others being the RCD-ML/*Mouvement de Libération*, and the RCD-National). Again, according to non-official sources in Kigali, there is strong evidence of United States' direct involvement in the military operations designed to overthrow Kabila, which were allegedly managed by United States Ambassador Robert Oakley, who was in Somalia in 1992-93 (Braeckman 1999:403).

Having declared the Kivu region a demographic and economic security buffer zone, the Rwandan (but also Ugandan and Zimbabwean) military proceeded to systematically exploit the natural resources of the regions under their control—particularly Ituri, Kivu and Maniema, both as a way to finance the war and as a means of personal enrichment. Geologists have determined that eastern *Orientale* Province (Ituri) and North and South Kivu (including Maniema) are regions of extraordinary, untapped mineral wealth which could, in the future, constitute the engine of Congo's economic development. Ituri contains gold deposits so rich that modern refining methods could produce six to seven kg. of pure gold per ton, while the rich Kilo-Moto (*Orientale* Province) gold reserves are estimated at between 3,000 and 6,000 tons. The whole Kivu region (including

Ituri and Maniema) is a treasure-trove of rare, strategic minerals essential to Western advanced-technology industries (aeronautics, space, electronics), such as copper, silver, cadmium, carbonatite, cassiterite, cobalt, columbite-pegmatite, columbo-tantalite (col-tan), beryl, lead, nickel, niobium, tantalum, tin, uranium, zinc, and wolfram (Braeckman 1999:161-3). In addition, huge oil deposits have recently been identified in Lake Albert, a few miles from Bunia (Ituri). Said to be equivalent to Angola's oil reserves, these deposits are under exploration by the British minor *Heritage Oil*, owned by Tony Buckingham, founder of the South Africa-based mercenary outfit *Executive Outcomes*: "we can easily imagine that ethnic conflict in Ituri will be resolved by private foreign militias who will ensure the maintenance of law and order around the oil fields" (Braeckman 1999:175-6).

A United Nations report on the illegal exploitation of natural resources in Congo notes that between September of 1998 and August of 1999, all the reserves of the areas of the DRC under occupation have been taken away: minerals, forest and agricultural products, and cattle. The Rwandese military and its RCD allies organized the mining and transfer to Kigali of 2,000 to 3,000 tons of cassiterite and of 1,000 to 1,500 tons of col-tan from Ituri and Kivu between November of 1998 and April of 1999. Rwanda's profits from col-tan exports from Ituri were estimated at $64 million in 2000 ($44 million in 2001); that same year, Rwanda's military budget amounted to $70 million. A United Nations panel estimated that in an 18-month period (from 1999 to 2000), Rwanda earned $250 million from Congo's col-tan. Rwanda's war economy—financed by the export of Congo's minerals—is managed by the *Congo Bureau* in Kigali, headed by a close associate of President Paul Kagame, James Kabarebe (army chief of staff), working closely with Colonel Dan Munyoza on-site in Congo (Braeckman 1999:197,244). The Ugandan military took over the rich Kilo-Moto gold mine in Ituri, producing on average an annual revenue of $100 million. Not surprisingly, Uganda's export of gold increased from $35 million in 1996 to $60 million in 1997 (Braeckman 2003:175,188-90). Similarly, Uganda's export of col-tan increased from 2.5 tons in 1997 to 70 tons in 1999 (Gondola 2002:177). It is interesting to note that at the time of its military intervention in Congo in 1998, Uganda benefited from a $2.2 billion loan from the IMF and World Bank—including an immediate disbursement of $830 million in 1999—generously authorized by the *Paris Club* of Western donors (Braeckman 1999:176,407). Uganda was also the first country to benefit from the *Highly Indebted Developing Countries Initiative* (HIDC); as a result, $650 million (out of a total debt of $3.6 billion) of its debt were cancelled (Braeckman 1999:176).

Jean-Claude Willame suggests that what we might be currently witnessing is a kind of return to the private chartered companies (*sociétés concessionaires*) of King Léopold's Congo Free State and their commercial outposts and *entrepôts*, under the protection not of the *Force Publique*, but of such foreign mercenary outfits as *Executive Outcomes*, *Sandline* and *Military Resources, Inc.*, abandoning the hinterland to a motley band of predators: smugglers, middlemen, warlords, and religious leaders, who routinely use violence as a means of wealth accumulation (Willame 1999:243).

On January 16, 2001, almost 40 years to the day after Lumumba, Laurent-Désiré Kabila was assassinated by one of his bodyguards (Rachidi Kasereka); and the next day, his son, Joseph Kabila, took over power and promptly indicated his readiness to work with the West by embarking on state visits to Europe and to the United States. Soon after assuming power, Kabila Jr. initiated an Inter-Congolese Dialogue culminating in the signature in April of 2002 in Sun City (South Africa), after seven months of negotiations, of a Peace Accord between the Congolese Government and the various rebel factions. As part of this Accord, Rwanda and Uganda agreed "in principle" to withdraw from Congo, initially scaling down their troops to about 20,000 each. In June of 2003, a Transitional Government of National Unity based on a power-sharing arrangement was put in place; it provides for a truth and reconciliation process, the integration of all military forces into a single army, and for general elections to be held in 2006. In October of 1999, a United Nations Mission in Congo (MONUC) was established, with 10,800 troops from 109 nations (including 2,500 from South Africa), headed by a former United States diplomat, William Lacy Swing. Acting as a peace monitoring force, MONUC is, interestingly, strategically deployed in all the mineral-rich areas of the country: eastern Congo, notably Ituri (Bunia), Maniema (Kindu), North and South Kivu, as well as in Katanga. In addition, MONUC has deployed 1,000 troops in Kinshasa as security detail to the Transitional Government. Yet conflict persists in the Congo in spite of the Peace Accord. On March 28, 2004, a coup attempt by Mobutist forces in Kinshasa was contained by loyalist troops. During that same month, 150 homes were burned down by rebels in Lutwegi (North Kivu); on April 12, 2004, 25 people were killed in the same town, prompting a United Nations' investigation. In Kazana (Ituri district), 34 people were killed by rebel troops on April 21, 2006 (IRIN 2004). Endemic ethnic conflict persists in various parts of the country, particularly in North Kivu (Ituri) and South Kivu between the Hima, Lendu and Nande, prompting the query: "in whose interest was it to drop a match?" Observing that ethnic conflict between the sedentary Lendu peasants and the nomadic

Hima pastoralists occurs in an area extremely rich in minerals and agricultural potential, Colette Braeckman suggests that this conflict eventually aims at de-populating Ituri so that multinational oil (Heritage Oil) and gold (Ashanti Gold-fields, Barrick Gold) companies may operate freely, and so that peasants from Uganda and Rwanda, or even whites farmers from Southern Africa or Israelis kibutzin, may settle there in future (Braeckman 2003:173,176-7). The lure of Congo's mineral resources actually sparked a falling out between Uganda and Rwanda. Thus, in August of 1999, there was a confrontation between the Rwan-dan forces and the Ugandan army for the control of the diamond-rich city of Kisangani (Orientale Province) (Gondola 2002:170-71).

Why would the Western powers in general, and the United States in particu-lar, after initially helping him to seize power and overthrow Mobutu in May of 1997, turn against Laurent-Désiré Kabila and decide to overthrow and physically 'eliminate' him, in a scenario eerily reminiscent of that which led to the assassina-tion of Patrice Lumumba on January 17, 1961? (Gondola 2002:173). In order to answer this question, one must remember that L.D. Kabila was, during 25 years, living in autarchy in the bush as leader of a Marxist revolutionary movement, the *Parti de la Révolution Populaire* (PRP), created in December of 1967 with a few associates. The PRP ruled over some 300,000 Babembe peasants organized in 350 families, living in total administrative and economic autarchy on the basis of a self-reliant communal system first centered on Hewa Bora, then moving in 1996 to Fizi-Baraka (Kivu) (Braeckman 1999:184-6). Politically, Kabila tried to progressively transform—through a democratic electoral process from below—the ADFL into a broad-based, people-centered political structure, the Committees for People's Power (*Comités du Pouvoir Populaire*/CPP). The attempt failed because the provisional CPPs were quickly infiltrated by the better-organized Mobutu loyalists, but also because—like Lumumba's MNC—Kabila did not have sufficient time to put the structure in place. In the economic sector, L.D. Kabila and his team presented at a donors conference in Brussels in Decem-ber of 1997 a minimal three-year development and reconstruction plan (*Plan tri-ennial minimum*) designed to put in place a "social market economy" (*économie sociale de marché*). The plan—requiring a $3 billion capital outlay—focused on re-building transport, water and electricity infrastructures, on kick-starting agri-cultural production, and on restructuring the industrial sector with a view to reducing unemployment. An uneasy mixture of populism and liberalism, the plan was rejected by the 'Friends of Congo' (Braeckman 2003:184, Martens 2002:243-5). But as Martens rightly notes, "The Plan had great political signifi-cance: it was the first time in Congo that the government had conceived a plan on its own, based on the most urgent needs of the rural and urban masses" (2002:245). Having learned from experience that he should rely essentially on his own capabilities, Kabila then initiated a state-based policy of economic independence.

On June 30, 1998, 38 years to the day since independence, the Congolese franc was successfully launched. Having reluctantly agreed to pay back the overdue amount on the foreign debt, Kabila refused to meet with a visiting IMF delegation in early August of 1998: the second war—financed by foreign firms—had already started. Kabila then proceeded to take a series of measures designed to tighten the state's control over the economy: centralization of the sale of diamonds, exclusion of foreigners from the diamonds sector (for mining, sales and marketing), and creation by decree of a Congolese commodity exchange entrusted with the marketing and sales of 70 percent of the production of minerals and precious stones. Predictably, such measures led to the massive smuggling of Congolese diamonds on the world market, via the capitals of neighboring countries. Thus, diamond revenues fell from $328.7 million in 1998 to $18.7 million in early 1999. Other populist measures, such as the creation of a National Bureau for Social Development (*Bureau national pour la promotion sociale*), of 'Popular Stores' (*magasins du peuple*)—designed to provide the ordinary people with affordable goods—and of small, import-substitution industrial units, were adopted, but also failed (Braeckman 2003:184-6). The Kabila regime, however, did achieve a measure of economic success in 1997: prices of basic foodstuffs stabilized, inflation was down to seven percent (against 741 percent the previous year), and state customs and excise revenues increased to $25 million (up from $8 million in 1996) (Martens 2002:232).

Of greater concern to Western economic interests were Kabila's attempts at achieving economic independence and at de-linking Congo from the dominant North-South trading networks. In as much as the goal of Western powers—through the convenient ideology of "African Renaissance"—is to better integrate Africa into the world economy, Kabila's policies were seen as going against the grain and as providing a 'bad example' to other African countries (Braeckman 2003:187). The United States in particular was concerned by Kabila's reneging on previously-concluded agreements with minor mining companies (Braeckman 2003:183, Willame 1999:79-93), on his insistence on demanding payment of taxes from foreign firms (which previously escaped their fiscal obligations through bribery), and on the decidedly socialist-populist and Pan-Africanist orientation of his regime. The last straw for the United States was probably an agreement that Kabila concluded on the occasion of a state visit to

China, whereby the Chinese Company of Non-ferrous Metals was granted a mining concession in Kolwezi for cobalt, a mineral of high strategic value to the United States' manufacturing of fighter jets (Braeckman 2003:328). Ludo Martens' analysis of the situation—while framed in Marxist terms—is quite perceptive:

> In early August 1998, the new Congo of Kabila is a country with extraordinary potential. From the point of view of the imperialist powers, this country is ruled by a new nationalist team which might initiate a process of autonomous, self-centered development focusing on the needs of the masses. Multinational firms might loose control over the fabulous wealth of this strategic country. This is the main reason why American imperialism has given the green light to the comprador bourgeoisies of Rwanda and Uganda to invade and take over Congo so as to overthrow its nationalist government. In order to achieve this objective, the Americans—known for their passionate advocacy of Human Rights—have sacrificed more than 3,500,000 Congolese lives to their thirst for profit (1999:157).

Joseph Kabila's eagerness to please the international community seems to confirm Martens' analysis. In May of 2001, a few months after coming to power, he initiated an IMF-supported economic stabilization program which included liberalization of oil prices and exchange rates, and adoption of fiscal and monetary policy discipline. As a result, the country has been able (since June of 2002) to get credit from the IMF and the World Bank, while bilateral donors have pledged to fund development and reconstruction projects. The Paris Club also granted the DRC *Highly Indebted Poor Country* status in July of 2003; this has helped alleviate the country's external debt burden and freed funds for economic development. In 2005, Gross Domestic Product (GDP) growth was over five percent, with an estimated total GDP of US $7.2 billion and per capita GDP of US $120 (Ngawi 2006a).

Actually drafted by South Africa, with Ugandan assistance and on United States' instructions, the Lusaka Agreement of July 2, 1999 was in fact a trap—or "merely the continuation of war by other means" (Gondola 2002:171)—that sealed the political fate of L.D. Kabila and of his regime. By recognizing Rwanda's right of pursuit of the *Interahamwe* (the perpetrators of the 1994 Genocide) in eastern Congo (Kivu and Maniema), the agreement effectively enlisted the cooperation of a broad sub-regional—Uganda, Burundi, Angola, Zimbabwe—and international—United Nations—coalition in support of Rwanda's and, to a lesser extent, Uganda's *lebensraum* policy which views eastern

Congo as their natural zone of influence and demographic and economic security buffer zone. Taking advantage of the endemic state of anarchy and of the power vacuum in this region, and supported by the United States, Rwanda and Uganda are encouraged to pursue their military occupation of eastern Congo which will eventually lead to some form of partition of Congo and re-drawing of the regional map to the benefit of the intervening powers and of the foreign multinational mining companies (Martens 1999:627-42). The following statement by Marina Ottaway before the Senate Subcommittee on Africa is quite revealing in this regard:

> There is no more state in the Congo and there is a power vacuum. It is therefore normal that Rwanda and Uganda intervene there militarily. When the state does not exist the principles of independence and sovereignty do not apply ... The United States could intervene militarily to redraw the boundaries of Africa and create new political entities but it could be costly. *It is preferable to let African civil wars develop* and *to allow Rwanda and Uganda to intervene militarily in the Congo*. In this way *it is the Africans themselves who will divide up Congo* and Central Africa will reach a new stability (June 8, 1999).

The "Pretoria Compromise" was signed in Pretoria (South Africa) on December 17, 2002 and ratified in Sun City (South Africa) on April 1, 2003. It adopted a transitional constitution with a President (Joseph Kabila) and four Vice-Presidents representing respectively the MLC, RDC, the (unarmed) civil society opposition groups, and the presidential faction. A final constitution was adopted on May 13, 2005. General elections, initially scheduled for June of 2005, were re-scheduled for July 30, 2006. A National Assembly of 500 members and a Senate of 120 members have also been put in place. All major decisions are to be adopted by consensus. In addition, five institutions designed to strengthen democracy have officially been set up, namely:

1. An Independent Electoral Commission

2. An Agency for Monitoring Human Rights

3. A "Truth and Reconciliation" Commission

4. An Anti-Corruption Commission

In addition, an international supervisory body, the International Committee for Support of the Transition [*Comité international qui accompagne la transition/ CIAT*], chaired by United States Ambassador William Lacy Swing, has been put in place. A United Nations Mission in Congo (MONUC) was set up on November 30, 1999. Also headed by William Swing, this force is composed of 16,700 military, 475 police and some civilian support staff. On October 23, 2005, the United Nations Security Council, through Resolution 1635, authorized a temporary increase of 300 military personnel for the period of the elections. The United Nations Secretary General has requested a 2,590-strong brigade for Katanga, but only 800 have been authorized so far. It is an understatement to say that the MONUC forces are vastly overstretched and thinly spread on the ground, and that their mandate, which precludes the use of force except in self-defense, is woefully inadequate. Only in response to the killing of MONUC troops in February of 2005 (12, including nine in Ituri), and another eight on January 23, 2006 in north-eastern Congo, has their mandate been strengthened. Persistent rivalry and conflict between the four factions represented in the present government of national unity has resulted in a stalemate and blocking of the political transition process, as the four factions neutralize one another. According to a recent report by the International Crisis Group (ICG),

> The main reason for the impasse, including postponement of elections, has been the reluctance of the former belligerents to give up power and assets for the national good. All have maintained parallel command structures in the army, the local administration and the intelligence services. Extensive embezzlement has resulted in inadequate and irregular payment of civil servants and soldiers, *making the state itself perhaps the largest security threat to the Congolese people* (2005:1).

In its pre-electoral assessment report, the ICG further notes that

> State institutions ... remain weak and corrupt ... Senior positions in the administration and state-run enterprises were shared between signatories, and state resources were siphoned off to fund election campaigns and private accounts. Between 60 and 80 per cent of customs revenues are estimated to be embezzled, a quarter of the national budget is not properly accounted for, and millions of dollars are misappropriated in the army and state-run companies ... Unpaid soldiers harass and intimidate civilians. Factions within the army and government continue to fight over mines and control of border crossings (2006:i).

Conflict continues unabated in eastern Congo (North and South Kivu, Ituri district of *Orientale* Province in the north-east and in (northern and central) Katanga between various armed groups, including the FDLR (*Forces démocra-*

tiques de libération du Rwanda/Democratic alliance for the liberation of Rwanda, a Hutu Rwandese opposition group), the Mai-Mai militias (created by the late Laurent-Désiré Kabila), the Allied democratic forces (ADF) and the Congolese national army. In what the ICG calls the "Congo's forgotten crisis" in northern and central Katanga (and in a scenario reminiscent to what Connor Cruise O'Brien already observed in 1963-64), the election campaign has reignited the old conflict between the Lubas of Katanga and the Lubas of Kasai. This conflict has created tensions manipulated by the politicians who, in 1992-1993 (and, again, in 1998), organized militias to fight a popular resistance force (the Mai Mai) and ethnically cleanse the province, which resulted in the killing of more than 5,000 Lubas of Kasai. The United Nations estimates that as a result of the latest wave of conflict, some 170,000 persons have been displaced within central Katanga alone, an area known as "the triangle of death" (IRIN 2006). In the run-up to the July 2006 elections, violence erupted again in eastern Congo, forcing tens of thousands of people to flee their homes yet again. The worst violence took place in the northeastern district of Ituri where militias continue to fight for territory. Some 38,000 internally displaced persons have taken refuge in Gety (Ituri Province) in the wake of recent fighting between militias and government troops. In Kotoni, near Bunia (Ituri), more than 14,300 displaced people are in need of food assistance (Africa Report 2006). The United Nations estimates that 9,500 of the 17,500 foreign combatants, mostly from Rwanda, in North and South Kivu provinces refused to disarm and to return home.

In spite of this chaotic situation, presidential and legislative elections were held on July 30, 2006. The elections, made possible by a new electoral law adopted in March of 2006 and financed by international donors to the tune of $458 million, drew 32 candidates for President and 9,709 candidates from some 210 political parties contesting in 189 constituencies and 11 provinces for the 500-seat National Assembly; this required 50,000 polling stations for some 25.7 million registered voters. An Independent Electoral Commission (IEC)—chaired by Reverend Apollinaire Malu-Malu and composed of an electoral staff of 260,000—was set up, and some 47,000 national and 1,500 international observers monitored the process. Among the top presidential contenders were the incumbent, Joseph Kabila, and two former rebel leaders, Jean-Pierre Bemba and Azarias Ruberwa. Also in the running were the children of former Presidents or Prime Ministers, including Patrice Guy Lumumba (son of Patrice Lumumba), Nzanga Mobutu (son of Mobutu Sese Seko), and M'poyo Kasavubu (daughter of Joseph Kasavubu). The incumbent president, Joseph Kabila, narrowly missed winning a majority, with 45 percent of the vote while Jean-Pierre Bemba, a businessman and ex-rebel leader, took second place with 20 percent. As a result, a run-off presidential election was held on October 29, 2006. Joseph Kabila—with 9,436,779 votes or 58.05 percent of the votes—was declared the winner while challenger Jean-Pierre Bemba received 6,819,822 votes, or 41.95 percent of the votes. On December 6, 2006, Joseph Kabila was officially sworn in as President at a ceremony in Kinshasa attended by a number of African heads of state, including Jose Eduardo dos Santos (Angola), Thabo Mbeki (South Africa), and Omar Bongo (Gabon). Jean-Pierre Bemba, who did not attend the inauguration, nevertheless accepted the role of opposition leader (Ntuli 2006, Ngawi 2006b, Masango 2006, Gettleman 2006).

South Africa's own IEC has taken the lead in providing electoral assistance to the DRC, including 300 information technology technicians and a 128-member observer mission headed by Safety and Security Minister Charles Nqakula. It is interesting to note in this regard that a 2,500-strong contingent of the South African National Defence Force (SANDF) has been operating for some time now in the DRC, alongside the United Nations' security forces, to ensure peace and security in the country. The South African Police Service (SAPS) is also helping with the training of the Congolese police. In addition, major South African multinational firms such as Eskom (electricity), Vodacom (telecommunications) and Mvelaphanda (mining) are already investing in the country (Tang and Dube 2006). Under the circumstances, the recent warning of the Catholic Bishop's Conference of the DRC that "in the current situation, all the conditions have not been met for a really transparent, free and democratic vote" and that "a combination of elements confirms the allegations of manipulations, deception, if not actual fraud" [a reference to the IEC's recent finding that nearly 1.5 million voters had disappeared from the poll register] is not surprising (allAfrica.com July 21, 2006). Neither is the fact that a main opposition party headed by Étienne Tshisekedi, the *Union pour la démocratie et le progrès social* (UDPS), called for a boycott of the elections. As one party official bluntly put it, "we do not want these biased elections" (IRIN 2006). In Kasai province (Étienne Tshisekedi's stronghold), voters' turnout did not exceed 20 percent; while in Kinshasa, UDPS voters—confused by the contradictory signals emanating from their leadership—massively voted for ex-rebel leader Jean-Pierre Bemba. Furthermore, there were reports of violence on Election Day in south-eastern Kasai, where 11 polling stations and voting material were set alight by UDPS militants. As a result, in Mbuji-Mayi, election officials had to re-open 174 of the 1,041 polling stations on July 31, 2006 (Ayad 2006). Final elections were reported on August 31, 2006.

Joseph Kabila was declared the winner, but opposition leaders still dispute the results.

The ICG's assessment of the situation was that "the national elections scheduled for 30 July 2006 risk creating a large class of disenfranchised politicians and former warlords tempted to take advantage of state weakness and launch new insurgencies" (2006:i). This assessment was confirmed by Human Rights Watch, which, two days before the elections, noted its concern over rebel army general Laurent Nkunda's threat to take action if minority groups were not included in the new administration (Inter Press Service 2006). The secretary general of the World Council of Churches (WCC) was much more skeptical in his evaluation of the situation:

> In this atmosphere the world has demanded a democratic election for president and parliament. It is almost as if by waving some magic wand called western democracy, the Congo is going to be saved when the partition is being forced by politicians playing the game of the western mineral corporations (WCC July, 2006).

It is interesting to note in this regard that the political transition process, the peace-keeping operation and peace-making process are all firmly controlled by the West, specifically by the United States in the person of their Ambassador William Lacy Swing. While the United States is the undisputed leader of the International Committee for the Support of the Transition, which acts as a major advisory body to the Congolese government and is chaired by Ambassador Swing, the European Union (EU) is another key actor in this process. In April of 2006, a United Nations Security Council resolution endorsed the deployment of a German-led EU reserve force to provide additional security during the elections. This 1,450-strong force named *Eufor-RDC*, which arrived in Congo on June 12, 2006, will also guard the Kinshasa airport—where 1,000 have been deployed, protect strategic installations, and support MONUC. A reinforcement contingent of 1,200 troops has been posted to Libreville (Deen 2006, Flipo 2006). Indeed, the current diplomatic dithering and multiplicity of competing actors and interests involved suggest that the conflict is likely to persist for some time to come, because "the war is useful to many of those involved. For the Western countries that supply weapons, neighboring countries such as Rwanda, Uganda, and Zimbabwe, and rebel factions and international corporations, their interests are better served by continuing to fuel the conflict" (Gondola 2002:179).

Conclusion

Forty-seven years after independence, Congo is still at war and is actually disintegrating under the combined forces of the external intervention of three African countries and of inter-Congolese factional rivalry. While the war in eastern and southern Congo goes on in spite of the July 1999 Lusaka Agreement and the April 2003 Sun City Peace Accord, ethnic conflict persists, widespread human rights abuses are occurring, and everyone (including Western firms) is pilfering the country's vast mineral resources. Furthermore, the Congo's predicament belies the argument of the "failed state" and "criminalization of the state" theorists, who vastly underestimate the responsibility of Western international, governmental and non-governmental agencies in this situation. As the Secretary General of the World Council of Churches rightly points out,

> It is fashionable these days to talk about the 'failed state' syndrome of Africa, the process of criminalization and the loss of legitimacy of political institutions. But the Congo belies this thesis. Theorists of the failed state underplay the extent of international business and western influence in the failures they lament. Globalization has sustained the wars in Congo and other African governments played their part (WCC July, 2006).

Meanwhile, the death toll from the war in the Congo continues to rise and is currently estimated at about five million since August of 1998 (equal to the population of Denmark, Finland or Norway) (Ntuli 2006), the country is—as per the United States plan revealed by Marina Ottaway—effectively partitioned into four autonomous regions, and the descent of Congo into chaos and anarchy continues. The United Nations estimates that every day, 1,200 people (half of them children) die in the Congo because of violence, disease—including trypanosomiasis (sleeping sickness), malaria, meningitis, measles and AIDS—and malnutrition. *Doctors Without Borders* estimates that for every violent death in eastern Congo, there are 62 non-violent deaths. And, as the ICG notes, the Congolese state itself has become the greatest security threat to its own people. All of which, sadly, evokes the cry of Kurtz to Marlow in Joseph Conrad's *Heart of Darkness*: "The horror! The horror!" (Conrad 1983:147,153).

This pessimistic assessment and somber picture certainly do not mean that there is no hope and no future for Congo and the Congolese people. Some observers, like Ludo Martens, advocate the creation of a federal state regrouping Congo, Rwanda and Burundi on the basis of a common popular project based on economic independence, autonomous, self-centered development and people's power (2002:167). There are, in our view, four preconditions to an exit strategy from conflict, chaos and political, economic and social decay in Congo. The first condition is the immediate cessation of all types of foreign interference and intervention in Congo, by African and Western countries, agencies, firms, mercenaries and individuals; the message should be: leave the Congolese alone, and let them sort out and solve their own problems. The second condition is that the Congolese people should be allowed to regain full control over their country, their land, their natural resources, their economy, and their destiny. The third condition is the emergence of a new leadership fully committed to a radical transformation of the state and genuinely work for the people. As Nzongola-Ntalaja correctly observes, "the politicians who arise to lead the [democratic] movement are for the most part self-centered seekers of political power and material benefits. They are not interested in transforming the state radically by democratizing it and increasing its capacity to serve the people" (2002:256). The fourth condition stands in contrast to Crawford Young's observation that "There is no alternative in the Congo to the administrative framework bequeathed by the colonial state … it … cannot be totally replaced by a political party or any other structure" (1965:598-9). On the contrary, my fourth condition is that the existing Congolese state—an unreformed colonial structure—should be destroyed, and an entirely new state based on Congolese values, traditions and culture, and genuinely in the service of the Congolese people, should be re-built in its place. Congo would then become the core state within the larger Kongo State in central Africa, one of the five constituent units of the proposed Federation of African States (FAS).

6

Security and Stability

Godwin Ohiwerei

Introduction

> The goal of the African Union is "A united and integrated Africa; an Africa imbued with the ideals of justice and peace; an interdependent and virile Africa determined to map for itself an ambitious strategy; an Africa underpinned by political, economic, social and cultural integration, which would restore to Pan-Africanism its full meaning; An Africa able to make the best of its human and material resources and keen to ensure progress and prosperity of its citizens by taking advantage of the opportunities offered by the globalized world; an Africa engaged in promoting its values in a world rich in its disparities. (Statement by H.E. Dr. Maxwell M. Mkwezalamba, Commissioner for Economic Affairs, African Union, on the occasion of the Opening of the African Union Private Sector Forum, 22 June, 2006, Banjul, The Gambia).

Africa is currently faced with a myriad of problems. The problems of stability and security strongly undermine the development of the nation states and therefore are instrumental in terms of the political, economic and social sluggishness of the various African states. For most of the 20th Century, European imposition on the African continent through colonization was blamed for the backwardness of the continent. But the question now is the following: What is responsible for the current problems of instability and insecurity in post-colonial Africa? There are various paradigms used to explain the current state of the continent, but few are offered in terms of effective mean for positive change. In essence, it will take Africans to provide the appropriate medicine for these problems.

To a greater extent, it can be said that the myriad of problems confronting Africa today relate to the question of security, defined here as an all encompassing concept that enables the people of Africa to live in peace and harmony and to have equal access to the resources and participate fully in the process of their governance. The most important element of security is internal security, which is the security of the people and the security of the state or the government. The security of the people is seen in terms of the satisfaction of the social, cultural, economic, political, human rights and the needs of the people.

External factors relate to threats of armed invasion from outside the country. The universal principle of non-interference in the internal affairs of the state and the concept of sovereignty make it difficult for African organizations to intervene in order to resolve such conflicts peacefully. Conflict between two African states has largely tended to be a result of disputes over borders. On some occasions, conflicts have also arisen as a result of disagreements over policies or other forms of rivalries. This chapter focuses more on issues of internal security. These issues seem to be more threatening than those of external factors affecting security. The breakdown of internal security tends to create the conditions for external threats.

Peacekeeping and peace making are conflict control mechanism designed to defuse tension and provide the peaceful environment that is conducive for the peacemaking process. Peacekeeping involves armed troops and unarmed observers on the ground, while peacemaking implies negotiations or mediation efforts at resolving the conflict/dispute using the governmental, political and diplomatic machinery (Africa Leadership Forum 1990). For this chapter, the discussion concentrates more on structural changes within the operating norms of state rather than peace keeping or peace making.

Insecurity and unstable governments in Africa have produced systemic socioeconomic retrogression and have rendered social conditions unbearable for the African people. Within the sub-Saharan regions, conflicts have diminished opportunities for productive cooperation within and between states and have created unpredictable and, therefore, unacceptable conditions for investment. Divestment and outflow of capital from Africa on insecurity and instability grounds have, in large measure, contributed to worsening economic conditions in the region. More importantly, conflicts have provided justification for inexcusable large military budgets, which are implemented in total disregard of the meager resources at the disposal of these governments, resources which are needed to meet the numerous basic necessities of the African people (Africa Leadership Forum 1990).

Developmental Impediments to Security and Stability

Impact of colonization and Globalization

There is question of comparing colonized states under the European influence with the post-colonial governments. Colonization seemed to work in terms of stability because the colonized state had the parent state to back it up. Once the colonial era officially ended, the leftover colonial state needed a different sort of glue to put it together. It is this glue that Africans are still struggling to find or create—a glue to hold the state together or stop the continent from falling into a state of anarchy. In piling up into one unit of state administration unrelated groups of persons, and splitting up organically related groups of persons, the Europeans left a wobbly inheritance for the continent (Menkiti 1999).

At a point in time that Africa is struggling to find answers to the problems of colonization, the continent is now besieged with globalization. Globalization, which is the growing integration of economies around the world, favors the developed countries more than the developing countries. Rapid growth and poverty reduction of emerging economies of China and India, that were poor 20 years ago, has been the positive examples for globalization among many failed or failing states. Globalization has generated significant international opposition over the concern that it has increased inequality and environmental degradation. Some view globalization as inevitable and irreversible. Others view it with hostility, even fear, believing that it increases inequality within and between nations, threatens employment and living standards, and thwarts social progress. Also, globalization tends to be negative on the weak states in that that it leads to the intensification of poverty and deprivation, the violation of basic human rights, and the undermining of national sovereignty

Globalization means that world trade and financial markets are becoming more integrated. Positive outcomes of globalization vary between countries and between continents. Generally, Asian economies seem to be benefiting from globalization, while African economies seem to have slow or negative growth. In sum, developing countries' experience in catching up with the advanced economies has been mixed. Some countries, especially in Asia, indicate that their per capita incomes have been moving quickly towards levels in the industrial countries since 1970. On the other hand, a larger number of developing countries have made only slow progress or have lost ground. In particular, per capita incomes in Africa have declined relative to the industrial countries and in some countries have declined in absolute terms.

A more recent effect of globalization on a weak state occurred in Côte d'Ivoire. While globalization brings wealth and opportunity to many people around the world, it brought horrible sickness and death to the slums of Abidjan, Côte d'Ivoire. The failing state of Côte d'Ivoire, due to civil war, was vulnerable, in that for a small fee, hazardous waste, shipped nearly halfway around the world, was steadily dumped around Abidjan. The waste, a fuming mix of petrochemicals and caustic soda, ended up in the slums of Abidjan. The waste started out in the Mediterranean and ended up in Africa. The Swiss trading company named Trafigura leased a tanker, filled it with hazardous waste material with the intension of dumping the waste in Amsterdam. Trafigura changed destination when confronted with a bill of $300,000 in Amsterdam. Instead, it proceeded for a cheaper venue in Africa where the waste was dumped in the city of Abidjan. The effect of the cheap disposal sickened 85,000 people and at least eight people died. For a company that had revenue of $28 billion in 2005, it is unconscionable to have balked in paying $300,000 for safe disposal in Amsterdam as previously planned (*New York Times* October 4, 2006).

An area of globalization that is considered to be positive for any country concerns the issue of migrant remittances in boosting national economic growth and household incomes. The fact is that migrant remittances should not be seen as a panacea for poverty reduction at local and national levels. Little attention is being paid to the effects on sustainable development, equity and long-term poverty reduction; and that, while remittances can relieve poverty selectively in the short-term, there is no evidence that they provide a solid foundation for sustainable development in the long-term (Paiewonsky and García 2006).

Governance

The end of the Cold War has pulled down the proxy cover for leadership and administrative inadequacies in Africa. The implication is a new set of challenges for African governments. While underdevelopment has multiple and complex causes, Africa's experiences with the adverse consequences of governance problems have been very clear, as the absence of good governance has proved to be particularly damaging to the corrective intervention role of governance. Programs initiated for poverty alleviation, for example, have been undermined by corruption and lack of public accountability (Africa Leadership Forum 1995).

The problem of corruption and lack of accountability is reflected in the total disregard by the leaders of Africa for the office they occupy. An important point to note is that most of the African states are very young and, according to Menkiti (1999), many Africans are actually older than their own countries. Menkiti asked whether one could imagine an American older than America or a French person older than France. The fact is that this sort of issue is not only imaginable but real in Africa. Menkiti further mentioned that when a critical observer of the states of Africa notes the failure of African governments, the failure of the loyalty and respect towards the modern African state, the matter of state infancy is important to keep in mind. Africa is an elder continent, and also a continent in which elderhood, on its own, carries the basis of respect. In a situation where an elder is more interested in gaining control, the elder may indirectly undermine its younger subjects. In this case, the leaders of Africa lack the respect for their countries because they see themselves as the elder and unwilling to subject themselves to the nation state.

African states are young because they were created by Europeans to serve European need and greed and also to destabilize the continent. Europeans destabilized the continent by making sure that they did not encourage homogenous states. Menkiti (1999) explained that in West Africa, large segments of the Yoruba population are included in Nigeria and segments of the same Yoruba population are included in what is now the Republic of Benin. Menkiti's conclusion is that it does not take a genius to understand that something is wrong when states are created with opposing or dissimilar groups. It is understandable when different groups are brought together in a multiethnic embrace, but it is not understandable when an ethnic group is divided between nation states for the sake of stability or security.

A further complication of stability and security in African politics is in the relationship between leaders and subjects. African politics is laddered with presidential grandiosity, political sycophancy, ostentatious corruption, violence, and coercive ceremonialism. Opposition is quickly crushed or seriously undermined. The absence of organized popular opposition and effective alternative to despotism is a common problem. What is rather unfortunate is that governance in Africa tends to reflect regimes in which the people tend to obey and the ruler pretend to believe in their obedience. This shows a pathological contradiction at the heart of African political subjectivity. That is, Africans criticize and ridicule the excesses and grandiosity of their rulers but the same Africans also expect and even demand such grandiosity. This behavior seems to positively relish rulers who indulge in excesses, amass illicit fortunes, and gorge themselves on scarce resources. Vacillating incoherently between these extremes, the governed systematically disempower or at least discredit both themselves and their political leaders (Karlstrom 2003).

The legislatures hardly offer a balance or counter the executive branches. The fact is that the legislatures serve as conduits for presidential interests and thereby fairly weak and marginalized in most African countries. Their autonomy, although guaranteed by constitutions, is often compromised by the executives through lobbing, financial inducements and sometimes intimidation. In most African countries, poor educational training and caliber of legislators circumscribe their ability to perform efficiently (United Nations 2005).

Majority Democracy

Majoritarianism is a political philosophy or agenda which asserts that a majority, which may be defined by religion, language, or some other identifying factor, of the population is entitled to a certain degree of primacy in society and has the right to make decisions that affect the society. This should not be confused with the concept of majoritarian electoral rule, which is simply an electoral system based on single-member constituencies. Under the democratic majoritarian political structure, the majority would not exclude any minority from participation in the democratic process. Majoritarianism is often referred to as "mob rule" or the tyranny of the majority. In Africa and in most developing countries, ethnic, tribal, or religious identity is strongly influential in the political system and in many cases creates a hostile division between the majority and the minority within the political structure. The tyranny of the majority is a dilemma facing a democracy when a minority's own interests are consistently blocked by an electoral majority. One of the most common ways of addressing the problem is through provisions in a constitution. As discussed earlier, in Africa, a constitution can also be undermined.

Majoritarianism is not accepted in Africa as a tradition. Dividing people arithmetically into a majority and a minority and saying that the minority must yield to the majority is not part of an African culture. This is why in those countries where this system has been instituted mostly by the Europeans, the majoritarian principle has been distorted, the significant opposition is seriously weakened, and the legislature is left without opposition. In-depth reform must be implemented if the majoritarian principle were to be accepted in Africa (Nzouankeu 1998).

Security and Rise of Private Armies

According to Shannon (2000), one of the most troubling problems in Africa is the loss of state control over the means of violence. A serious case of national insecurity was created as a result. This is a dangerous imposition on nascent states. Especially in developing societies, people are taking up arms and fighting under banners that look nothing like flags. Declining economic growth, corruption, greed, ethnic rivalries and the struggle for scarce goods create national insecurity. To an extent unprecedented in the modern era, war is being waged by entities other than nation states across physical and ideological boundaries. Although the forms of state conflicts vary within a country and across countries, their collective effect is manifest in an emerging global phenomenon. What can be observed is the erosion of state monopoly over the use of violence. The basic fact is that states lack the means to control insurgency. The implication of the lack of the state wing of law enforcement to control violence is that terrorists, mercenaries, guerrillas, warlords, militias, and other irregular armed forces are exacting a heavy toll on the populations, thereby emasculating national governments. The outcome is that state power and substance are declining world wide with great economic, social and human consequences. There is a serious problem when the power vested in the state is usurped by warlords or militias.

The inability of governments to control militias and warlords has resulted in some states in Africa contracting with private armies. The problem of relinquishing control to private armies will become pressing in the future, as the United Nations and European Countries or former colonial powers abdicate their responsibilities by issuing an African solution to African problem. At a point in time when the idea of accountability, governance and democracy as conflict management tools are seen as utopian, conflict management through military force may become more popular. Hired armies are now used to carry out assignments that regular armies would consider as morally repugnant and illegal (Dokubo 2000).

As earlier discussed, in the developing world, the end of Cold War has created a vacuum of power. Shannon (2000) point out that where the superpowers once competed for states and control, where a significant size of their military forces was retired, several professional soldiers have created security consultancy firms to fill the void. The emergence of a private actor with national capabilities carries dire implications for the integrity of the state in Africa. The threat is not just to developing economies generally, the threat is also to the country from where the private army originates. The most active of these firms in Africa are based in the United Kingdom and South Africa. The most prominent company, Pretoria based Executive Outcomes (EO), is perhaps the most competent mercenary outfit. Executive Outcomes is the most deadly and efficient force operating in sub-Saharan Africa today, with the exception of the South African army. Executive Outcome's staff of 40 officers and 200 troops is highly disciplined, extensively trained, and battle hardened. In the field, EO's hardware, which outclasses those of many nationals, includes Russian-made Mi-17 and Mi-24 helicopter gunships, a radio-intercept system, casualty evacuation aircraft, and fuel air explosives (the last weapon, which disperses fuel vapor over a one mile radius and ignites it, is considered the deadliest form of conventional bombing). EO owns two Boeing 727s for troop transport and two Russian Mig-23 fighter bombers. Executive Outcome was prominent in the war in Sierra Leone and as a matter of fact was partly responsible for the success of the government of Sierra Leone (the National Provisional Ruling Council) over the rebel army known as the Revolutionary United Front (RUF).The pay back to EO was that over the next 22 months, the NPRC signed three separate contracts with EO for a total of $35 million. Although officially hired for training services, EO's contingent of 250 troops actually engaged in most of the government offensive, for which the Sierra Leone military lent only a support role commensurate with their lean capabilities (Shannon 2000).

Taublee's (2002) perception of the growing reliance on private military firms supports the general belief that private armies are exploitative. He states that despite the negative perceptions of past experience, various African regimes have resorted to private companies to provide the internal stability essential to economic activity and the rebuilding for critical elements of the supporting infrastructure. It is important to note that the close association between European governments, private military companies and companies that wish to exploit strategic mineral or oilfields has elicited new concerns about a resurgence of neo-colonialism as well as questions about the future of the traditional sovereign states as the appropriate and effective form of political organization. Companies like Executive Outcomes, which actively engaged in combat operations for its employers, and Military Professional Resources Incorporated (MPRI), which presumably offers only training and advice, represent the new face of neo-colonialism. Private Military Companies (PMCs) and Private Security Companies (PSCs) are organized and chartered as corporations intended to conduct business as permanent, continuing concerns.

A critical understanding of the threat posed by private armies is their capacity to visit death and destruction on their opponents than in their ability to position themselves as more credible guarantors of stability. Mercenary organizations and their business associates have taken advantage not only of the insecurity in Africa, but also of the willingness to get involved in African crises. As long as the international community and the industrialized countries remain militarily detached from Africa and allow states to falter, there will be a market for private security forces (Dokubo 2000).

In many weak states, one can state that globalization has led to fragmentation and not integration. Taublee (2002) makes the point that the current landscape resembles late medieval Europe with supernational, national and subnational actors and processes vying against one another (military security and economic welfare). Resort to private companies in these circumstances constitute a symptom and not a cause. Recently, a new dimension to policing or stabilizing developing states is an all female police unit that is shortly to be deployed alongside United Nations peacekeepers in Liberia. In Liberia, they will form part of a specialized unit, the Formed Police Unit (FPU), which in the past has been used as a rapid reaction force. This will be used to control riots and crowds and also train local police forces (Majumber 2006).

Suggested Solutions

Proportional Representation

The preceding structural problems described in terms of dis-stabled states call for some restructuring towards a more stable and secure state. One of the factors to consider is the need to move from winner-take-all form of voting (majoritarian democracy) to proportional representation. Proportional representation deals with a system where representatives are elected from multi-seat districts in proportion to the number of votes they receive. What this means is that political parties or candidates will have the percent of legislative seats that reflects their public support. This is in contrast to the United States of America where the tyranny of the majority exists or a system where the winner-take-all is applied. The United States' form of representation is a system where the losing candidates and their votes are wasted, even if a candidate garners 49.9% of the vote. This leaves significant blocs of voters unrepresented. The consequence of this is that voters do not vote for a candidate that they like but rather the one who realistically stands the best chance of winning, or voters do not vote at all knowing that the candidate in whom they are interested will not win (www.fairvote.org).

Proportional representation opens up the system to everyone who cannot win through the process of representation. This applies especially to minorities. Proportional representation gives voters more choices at the polls, allowing more voters to participate. In most African countries, voters have very little choice, since most races are based on a winner-take-all policy. Voters see this process as non-competitive; hence, many voters do not vote for perceived losers. Proportional representation has a positive effect on campaign spending. Due to the fact that candidates need fewer votes to win, they do not have to spend as much money to win votes. With proportional representation, voters have more choices at the polls; as a result, more voters will cast votes for a winner. Voters have the opportunity to listen to a range of political perspectives and policy options, and then vote for the candidate or party that best represents how they feel. Voters, therefore, have an opportunity to cast their votes for their hopes, instead of their fears.

Transparency

The problem of corruption in Africa continues to impede economic and political growth. The lack of accountability, unethical behavior and corrupt practices have become entrenched, and even institutionalized. Corruption is a norm of behavior in its own right across Africa to the extent that the issue has now become a matter of major concern.

When a government is the direct beneficiary of a centrally controlled major revenue stream and is not reliant on any form of accountability in the management of revenues, those who rule the state have unique opportunities for self-enrichment and corruption. For most African leaders, achieving political power often becomes the primary avenue for achieving wealth, the incentive to seize power and to hold on to it indefinitely is great.

This dynamic has a corrosive effect on governance and, ultimately, respect for human rights is undermined. Instead of the government bringing prosperity to the nation, rule of law and transparency, the government rather reinforces or exacerbates undemocratic rule—the leaders thereby entrench and enrich themselves without any corresponding accountability (Human Rights Watch 2003).

The question of how to solve the problem constitutes a major debate among political intellectuals in Africa. Aderinwale (1995) suggests that the crucial safe guard of standards of public ethics and accountability in Africa has to fall on the ability of average citizens, people's organization and the media to hold public institutions accountable for their acts and also to ensure that public institutions fulfill their functions and responsibilities properly and effectively. Aderinwale (1995) points out that the independence of institutions such as the media, the judiciary and other organizations that play the role of regulating the operation of public policies should be established and safeguarded. He warns that leaders in Africa should not only demonstrate their commitment to transparency and human rights, but must also ensure a mechanism that would serve as instruments in the right against corruption. He also states that the core organs of government must submit themselves to these mechanisms, irrespective of their positions or involvement. That is, public office holders must declare their assets before assuming office. Such declaration must be given wide publicity. A mechanism must also be created that encourages any member of the public to challenge the declaration of assets, if such an individual has data that contradict the declaration.

Empowering Women

Nations that marginalize half of their populations cannot function and thrive as full democracies, nor can countries that ignore women as vital sources or resource be competitive in today's world. Since 60% of children in Africa who do not attend school are girls, many are faced with limited economic and political opportunity. It is the opportunity of a basic education that can help them transform their lives (Dobriansky 2006). The Estimate is that one-sixth of the world's population is illiterate and two-thirds of the illiterate are women. The result is that girls continue to lag behind boys in basic literacy, thereby perpetuating a cycle of inequality and poverty that impedes developing countries from moving forward. In much of the developing countries, girls represent an untapped resource and a hope for the future if the necessary intervention were to be made. Educating girls is a crucial component of building a foundation for democracy, and a prerequisite for creating and sustaining free, open and prosperous societies.

Slayter and Sodikoff (2001) state that to promote economic development and attain the Millennium Development Goal 3 (MDG3) in terms of the overarching poverty reduction and gender equality, the global community must renew its attention to women's economic empowerment and thereby increase investment in women. They stress that gains in women's economic opportunities lag behind those in women's capabilities. The relationship between opportunities and capabilities are important because of the argument that women are not capable or that norms and values prevent women from participating. The discrimination against women in the work force has a serious negative impact on their families because most of the families in Africa have one source of income. Males generally dominate the work place. This is inefficient, since increased women's labor force participation and earnings are associated with reduced poverty and faster growth. Women will benefit from their economic empowerment, but so too will men, children and society as a whole. Women's lack of economic empowerment, on the one hand, not only imperils growth and poverty reduction, it has a host of other negative impacts including unfavorable education and health outcomes, on the other hand.

Moreover, women's economic empowerment will help in children's education, health and general social welfare. The fact that women will be less dependent on men or their husbands will reduce the terrible social and economic effects of the loss of the head of household. In sum, the case for expanding women's economic opportunities is becoming increasingly evident; this is nothing more than smart economics (Slayter & Sodikoff 2001).

Can prospects for improving livelihood, security and building sustainable environments in Africa be increased if women have greater influence in decision-making about how to manage resources? Anecdotal evidence suggests that this question should be answered in the affirmative. Yet, few development agencies perform systematic evaluations with gender-disaggregated data, despite nearly two decades of development literature describing the pitfalls of failing to do so. There are some steps to take in fostering women's empowerment, such as the increased access to business services for women entrepreneurs, the provision of quality day-care services and reduce their cost, the increased access to credit and financial services, the provision of business set-up grants, the reform of laws restricting women's right to inherit or own land, the introduction of legislation promoting women's employment, the increase of women's access to existing training programs.

Children's Welfare

A growing problem in Africa is the marginalization of children and the disregard for their safety and security. According to Hope (2005), children in Africa face harsh risks and are often subjected to hostile environments that severely limit their emotional, mental, physical and social growth and development. That, in turn, significantly limits their prospects for childhood survival, increases their chance for having to enter into employment voluntarily or forcibly, and makes them susceptible to poverty. Children do not voluntarily subject themselves to employment or hard labor when they have a better alternative. They subject themselves to employment because of poverty and as a means of helping their families. Hope's explanation was that as poverty deepens in Africa, more and more children at younger ages have been engaging in paid economic activities. The loss of adult economic support and supervision as a result of conflict and diseases such as HIV/AIDS has contributed significantly to the increase in the number of children at work in Africa. In many African countries, there is a declining capacity of both immediate and extended families to support the children. Consequently, children with jobs make a major contribution to household livelihood security.

In order to understand the serious predicament of children in Africa as compared to other regions in the world, Africa is the only area where the proportion of children at risk of poverty, disease, malnutrition, orphanhood, mortality, sexual and labor exploitation has been increasing over the past several decades. During the past four decades, sub-Saharan Africa has consistently had the highest rates of children dying each year. By 2002, the mean mortality rate in the region for children under the age of 5 was 174 per 1,000 live births, compared to 97 in South Asia, 90 in the developing countries and 158 in the least developed countries. In 2002, child mortality rates were 25 times higher in sub-Saharan Africa than in the industrialized countries compared to 18 times higher in 1990 and seven times higher in 1960. By magnitude of child mortality rate in descending order, the 30 countries with the highest rates in the world are all in sub-Saharan Africa. In 2002, children comprised almost 45 percent of the 650 million total population living in Africa. Approximately 45-50 percent of these can be regarded as poor based on national poverty lines and census data on household (Hope 2005).

Another serious issue is that among the emerging characteristics of child labor in Africa, there is child trafficking, which is the recruitment, abduction, transportation, transfer, harbouring, or receipt of a child for sexual exploitation, forced labor, or slavery. Child trafficking appears to be much more prevalent in West and Central Africa with common routes from West Africa to the Middle East and Europe. Trafficking in humans begins contemporary form of slavery. Trafficked children are sent to other countries for domestic service, or put to work on plantations, in petty trade, as beggars, in soliciting and as commercial sex providers (Hope 2005).

Child trafficking is not unique to Africa. It is a global problem. The International Labour Organization, a United Nations agency, estimates that 1.2 million children are sold into servitude every year in an illicit trade that generates as much as $10 billion annually. Children are more vulnerable in Asia, Latin America and Africa. Africa's children, the world's poorest, account for one-sixth of the trade. It is suggested that nearly 12,000 trafficked children toil in the cocoa fields of Ivory Coast. The children cleared fields with machetes, apply pesticides and slice open cocoa pods for beans (*New York Times* October 29, 2006).

Lower fertility and slower population growth temporarily increase the relative size of the workforce. With fewer dependent children and older dependents relative to a larger, healthier working-age population, countries can make additional investments that can spur economic growth and help reduce poverty. If jobs are generated for the working population, this demographic bonus can result in higher productivity, savings and growth. In East Asia, where poverty has dropped dramatically, this demographic bonus is estimated to account for about one-third of the region's unprecedented economic growth from 1965 to 1990. In the poorest countries, where fertility remains high, the demographic window will not open for some time, but investments in reproductive health services can hasten its arrival and ensure future dividends.

Conclusion

Africa, like other continents, exists in a world in which political and economic strength counts, where might is right, and not one which operates simply on morality. For Africa to be heard and make a positive impact, it must seriously consider the conditions or structures that can sustain economic and political growth. This means that must be stable and secure. The challenge to the various governments and peoples of Africa is to create an Africa which is noticed for its strengths and not for its misery and weakness. A strong Africa must be one which is economically integrated, financially stable, politically united, and has a distinct culture and set of values.

Elements that can help foster the preceding goals are rooted in good governance. The conditions under which good governance can thrive are embodied in the following: pluralism, freedom of expression and association and protection of human rights, independent judiciary, political accountability, periodic election of leadership, independence of civil service and promotion of literacy. Also critical are elements related to genuine democracy, compliance with human rights treaties, and multiparty democracy. In addition, good governance creates an environment where a capable workforce and viable economy lead to a capable state where peace, security and stability have the potential to thrive.

Nzouankeu (1998) states that programs have been developed over the decades to help promote good governance. The discussion of good governance in developing or emerging economies is not a recent phenomenon. The United Nations and the Organization of African Unity (OAU) recognized that good governance, like democracy, peace, security and stability, is an essential factor in economic and social development. For example, in June 1995, the Cairo Agenda for Action, adopted by the Organization of African Unity (OAU), recognized this truism. Other initiatives include the one that was launched by the United Nations in 1996 known as the System-wide Special Initiative on Africa. This was launched in order to provide support for the United Nations' New Agenda for the Development of Africa (UN-NADAF). Within that framework, the United Nations Development Programme (UNDP) created a subsidiary program, the Special Initiative on Governance in Africa (SIGA), to promote good governance by developing sound institutions, increasing the role of civil society, and encouraging transparency, responsibility and effective results. The fact is that we are not short of initiatives; the issue has been how to successfully implement these programs. This was the reason why it was earlier suggested that the types of democracy, representation and legislative assemblies are critical to the success of creating good governance and capable states.

It is no longer disputed that good governance is a major factor for the maintenance of peace, social stability and security. It is also true that good governance can strengthen the legitimacy and authority of governments by eliminating, or controlling, the conflicts which are undermining many of them. Also, good governance is linked to development because it enables countries to develop faster and in a more sustainable manner (Nzouankeu 1998). In the case of Africa, good governance is a rarity. The low representation of good governance among African regimes directly impacts issues of stability and security.

The creation of capable states is one of the most fundamental challenges in contemporary Africa. A capable state is one in which peace, security and stability are guaranteed and sustained. Without these attributes, there will be no long-term development. A capable state creates an enabling political and legal environment for economic growth, and promotes the equitable distribution of the fruits of growth. The capable state interjects policies that deliberately attack poverty and promote education, health and social safety nets. The capable state also builds an enabling environment for the private sector to generate economic growth, jobs and income (Amoako 2005). Most African states lack the social and economic order necessary for this kind of development.

The process of creating a strong Africa must also involve a strategy to make education an important factor and to develop the continent's human resources by placing special emphasis on quality education in critical areas such as science and technology. A strong Africa will only come about through hard work.

Economic development and transformation will be impossible in Africa without sustained policies for human resource development and utilization. Therefore, Africa must accord high priority to human resource development and utilization. The focus of such policies should be the training of a critical mass of top quality high-level manpower required for the continent's long-term development and transformation. The training as well as retention of this caliber of persons has been severely hampered by the economic crisis of the 1980s and the structural adjustment programmes (SAP) implemented by African countries. The fall of real income of university staff as a result of the massive devaluation of currency and inflation has escalated the "brain drain" from Africa. There is an urgent need to rehabilitate Africa's higher educational institutions. It is essential to create an enabling environment for creative thinking, teaching, and research through appropriate policies while also endow the institutions with adequate resources that could enable them to fulfill the strategic role they are supposed to play. Indeed, it is incumbent upon Africans to solve their problems.

7

Combating HIV/AIDS

Doyin Coker-Kolo and Oluseyi Kuforiji

Introduction

In the battle against Apartheid, we scored a tremendous victory in the face of considerable evil. The solidarity of people from around the world.... strengthened us at some of our darkest moments. Now as we enter another battle-the battle against HIV/AIDS we need the same solidarity, the same passion, the same commitment and energy.

—South African Archbishop Emeritus Desmond Tutu (Global AIDS Alliance 2002:1).

As Bishop Desmond Tutu predicted, the HIV/AIDS crises in Africa have received a great deal of attention and commitment worldwide. Many initiatives have been proposed, some good and some bad. At times, some of the good ideas have been badly implemented and some initiatives have died a quick death because not enough was done to institutionalize them. The reasons for the inconsistencies are not difficult to explain; Africa is a continent of great diversity and the issues facing it are complex. Sometimes those proposing solutions to African problems fail to recognize the complex nature of these problems and the need for a multifaceted approach in resolving them.

This chapter reviews and critiques the United States' most recent policy in addressing the HIV/AIDS crises in Africa contained in the report titled "Rising U.S. Stakes in Africa: Seven Proposals to Strengthen U.S.-African Policy" edited by Kansteiner and Morrison (2004). Chapter seven of this report titled "Continuing U.S. Leadership to combat HIV/AIDS in Africa and globally" was written by Todd Summers. The current chapter examines the veracity of United States' claim to provide continuing leadership in the global fight against HIV/

AIDS. The chapter is divided into three major sections. An overview of the prevalence of the HIV/AIDS pandemic is first presented. This section uses statistical data to explain the prevalence of the disease; it also examines the root causes (for example, poverty and gender discrimination) and discusses its global impacts. This is an attempt to lay the foundation for a comparison between the magnitude of the problem and the existing efforts to address it. The second section is a critique of the report "Continuing U.S. Leadership to combat HIV/AIDS in Africa and globally." It focuses on the leadership, commitment, collaboration and coherence of efforts provided by the United States in addressing the HIV/AIDS pandemic in Africa. The section seeks to answer the following questions: How credible is the United States' claim to leadership, and how productive and sustainable is it? Finally, the chapter proposes some alternative solutions to the United States' approach based on research about strategies that have proven to be culturally and pragmatically appropriate for the African continent.

The prevalence of HIV/AIDS in sub-Saharan African is well documented in various literature (scholarly and others) and well covered in electronic media all over the world (Rotberg 1988, Mendel 2005, Bage 2004, White 2004, Wangila & Akukwe 2006, CNN 2006). While there may not be an agreement on the origin of the HIV virus or the best approach to stop its spread, there is a firm consensus that the numbers of victims and potential victims of HIV/AIDS in the world are on the rise and Africa is getting the worst of it. African countries are fast becoming the "highly infected nations." The situation is so dire that Todd Summer (in Kansteiner and Morrison 2004:138) calls Africa the "epicenter" of the AIDS epidemic. Campaigns to stop the spread of the disease have been intense and the participants many, but the path to a lasting solution is unclear. Twenty five years after the disease was discovered in Africa, the pandemic has not let up; instead, is still gathering strength (Wangila & Akukwe 2006). Consequently, it is necessary to forget the rhetoric and instead engage in concrete actions that can yield effective and sustainable efforts to minimize the prevalence until a cure is found. As Nelson Mandela strongly suggests, "This is a war. We must not continue to be debating, to be arguing, when people are dying" (Global AIDS Alliance 2002:1).

Bage (2004) suggests that the campaigns made against the pandemic are widespread but not specialized and intensive enough to meet the challenge. He also argues for the need to first confront the social and economic weaknesses that lie at the heart of the epidemic. These social weaknesses include limited economic opportunities, gender problems and the material inadequacies of rural communities. Bage also posits that we cannot succeed in changing the dynamics of the epidemic until the impact of these factors is reduced. As we understand these facts about the precursors to HIV/AIDS, it is also imperative to mobilize local, regional and international governments, the United Nations and non-governmental organizations (NGOs) to unite in the fight. The focus on combating Africa's social crises is an essential complement to activities that specifically address the disease.

While HIV/AIDS is a global epidemic, it is an issue of disastrous proportion for most countries in sub-Saharan Africa. There are many reasons for this assessment. One is the increasing prevalence of the pandemic. Even though Africa is only home to 10% of the world population, about two-thirds of HIV victims (64%) in the world reside in the region and 77% of all women infected with the disease are Africans. South and South East Asia come second with 15%. According to a 2004 figure, the total number of people living with HIV in the world was approximately 40 million (United Nations 2004 Global Report on the AIDS Epidemic). In the same year, it was reported that about 26 million of those infected with HIV/AIDS were living in Africa. Africa has an HIV prevalence rate in the general population of 7.4%. The prevalence of a disease is a measure of the proportion of people in a population affected with a particular disease at a given time. It was also reported that in 2005, approximately 2.7 million new infections occurred in sub-Saharan Africa and an estimated two million people in the region died from the disease. The total death of children and adults from HIV/AIDS in the world in 2005 was estimated at 3.6 million. Additionally, more than 12 million children under the age of 17 have been orphaned by AIDS in Africa. (UNAIDS 2005, Walton 2006).

The epidemic is not homogeneous within the sub-Saharan region, as some countries are more afflicted than others. Even at the country level, there are wide variations in infection levels between different areas. As shown in the following statistics, different countries have different rates of HIV prevalence, but the situation is grim for all African countries in general. The lowest rates are recorded in Somalia and Sudan (less than 1%) and highest in Southern African countries: Botswana (24.1%), Lesotho (23.2%), Swaziland (33.4%), Zimbabwe (20.1%), Zambia and South Africa (between 15-29%). In East Africa (Uganda, Kenyan and Tanzania), the rate exceeds 6%. Most West African countries have variable rates, with the highest in that region found in Côte d'Ivoire and Gabon (7.1 and 7.9%, respectively). In Nigeria, the most populous country in the continent, the news is that the rate of HIV is fast increasing and around 2.9 million people (3.9% of the population) now live with the disease (Graham 2006).

These statistics, as grim as they seem, only tell a part of the story. The death toll resulting from the epidemic will continue to rise because an increasing number of people with HIV/AIDS in Africa do not have access to testing and treatment. Moreover, when someone has contracted HIV, it takes from eight to ten years for the disease to develop. Hence, there are people that are asymptomatic of the disease, thereby appearing healthy but pass it on to unsuspecting partners. This means that if action is not taken, the epidemic's impact on African societies will be felt most strongly in the course of the next ten years and beyond. White (2004) suggests that in 2003, there were 3.2 million people who newly contracted the HIV virus in Africa and that by 2010, 20 percent of children in some parts of the region will become parentless. Its social and economic consequences are already widely felt, not only in the health sector but also in education, industry, agriculture, transport, human resources, and the economy in general. Bage sums up the dismal situation this way:

> Sub-Saharan Africa faces a triple challenge of colossal proportions which are:
>
> - Providing health care, support and solidarity to a growing population of people with HIV-related illness, and providing them with treatment.
>
> - Reducing the annual toll of new infections by enabling individuals to protect themselves and others.
>
> - Coping with the cumulative impact of over 20 million AIDS deaths on orphans and other survivors, on communities, and on national development (2004:2).

To make matters worse, there is a sense that the AIDS victims have been abandoned by the international community whose focus has shifted to other crises like refugees and terrorism. There is also some sense in some communities that the AIDS situation is under control giving its reduction in countries like Rwanda, Senegal and Uganda (WorldReport 2004). Some also believe that the increasing availability of funds from private and international donors has led to a wider access to treatment. For instance, the Kansteiner and Morrison (2004) report discusses not just United States' policy about the HIV/AIDS but also American financial contributions to the fight against the pandemic. The American President Emergency Fund for AIDS relief (PEPFAR) earmarked $15 billion for the program. This contribution was touted as the largest in United States' history. But given the grim statistics presented earlier, and the resulting effects of HIV/AIDS on Africans to be discussed, the question one is tempted to ask is the following: What long-term difference has such funding made? Besides, the promised funding was not only cut, much of the funds appropriated remains to be seen by the promised recipients.

The Effect of HIV/AIDS on Women and Children

It is a well known fact that HIV/AIDS is mainly a heterosexual disease. Nonetheless, there is a gender difference in the rate of infection, with women being on the higher end of those infected. Across sub-Saharan Africa, more women are infected with HIV than men, with 13 women living with HIV for every 10 infected men, and the gap continues to widen. Additionally, women are being infected with HIV at earlier ages than men. The difference in infection levels between women and men is most pronounced among young people (aged 15-24 years). In this age group, there are 36 women living with HIV for every 10 men (Wilkepedia Free Encyclopedia Online 2006).

What factors account for the disparity among men and women in the contraction and prevalence of the disease? Some observers have suggested traditional values, prostitution, lack of education and lack of economic independence. Since Africa is a patriarchal society, women are more subordinate to men and their wishes. For instance, a married woman could not refuse to have sex with her husband even when she suspects that he has HIV/AIDS. She cannot force him to get tested or to use a condom to protect herself from getting infected. In fact, most African men resist the use of condom (White 2004). Another factor is the practice of early marriage by which girls between the ages of 10-13 years are married off to much older men. These adolescents usually do not have a career or any source of economic independence, making them less likely to challenge the authority of their husbands. To make matters worse, a woman who contracts the disease is ostracized by her husband's family because she becomes unproductive (that is, she can no longer trade or work on the farm). There is more stigma on a woman that is infected than on her male counterpart. Added to the seriousness of the situation is the likelihood of an infected pregnant woman passing on the disease to her baby.

The Role of Poverty and Poor Social Conditions

Although there are many factors contributing to the spread of HIV/AIDS, it is still largely recognized as a disease of poverty, mostly affecting people who are marginalized and suffering economic hardships (Bage 2004). The rapid spread and persistence of the disease mirrors the social conditions that make Africa's poor vulnerable. Lack of access to education and communication means that people cannot gain an understanding of HIV/AIDS and the dangers it poses. A low level of public services leaves families and communities without support in confronting the crisis. Poor people in rural areas, particularly women, are the largest and weakest segment of Africa's population. They have fewer economic opportunities and limited access to education, information and public services such as health care. As a result, these people are the hardest hit by HIV/AIDS and their families and communities become even poorer and more vulnerable. They exhaust their already meager resources in caring for the sick and are permanently weakened by the loss of their most active family members.

Poverty in Africa is due to years of colonial rule, the economic dip of the 1980s and the effect of foreign debts. For example, in July of 2000, the Export-Import Bank of the United States offered loans of one billion dollar per year for five years to sub-Saharan countries to purchase HIV/AIDS medication and services from American Pharmaceutical Companies (Warren 2000). Since repaying these loans was going to place an additional economic burden upon countries, many of which are already highly indebted nations, some countries like South Africa rejected the offer. This is also reminiscent of the effects of International Monetary Funds (IMF) loans on countries in sub-Saharan Africa in the 1980s and 1990s. Most of these countries have had to cut back on essential social services because of the structural adjustment programs under which they were placed by the IMF as conditions for the debts they owed. By pushing poor people in Third World countries even deeper into poverty, the international community may be increasing their vulnerability to HIV infection and reinforcing conditions where the scourge of AIDS can flourish (The World Development Movement 1999).

The deepening poverty across the African continent has caused an increase in people's susceptibility to not just the HIV/AIDS pandemic but to other diseases as well. Poor living conditions, lack of basic infrastructure, unclean drinking water, inadequate sanitation, and erratic electricity and health services have made it difficult for early recovery even where testing and treatment are present. Poverty has also led to a breakdown in family relationships, so that sick people are becoming ostracized. AIDS orphans are considered liabilities and are abandoned. In a featured story aired by CNN on September 23, 2006, the reporter, Christiane Amanpour, interviewed some grandmothers called the "unsung heroes of Africa," who are now raising their grandchildren because both parents have died of AIDS. In all of these stories, these families live under deplorable conditions. They lack basic amenities and adequate nutrition. There was the case of one grandmother taking care of four grandchildren who earns a living by selling plastic bags picked from dumpsters. The story got even worse after the children in her care were tested and two out of the four were found to be infected with the deadly disease. According to the CNN story, there are between 50,000 to 80,000 AIDS orphans in Nairobi, Kenya alone. Many of them only get food to eat when they are at school. In some families, the grandparents are left with nothing to eat after feeding the children with the limited food available. In one village, the men send their wives to prostitute in order to get food and then dispose of them when they get infected as a result of the prostitution (Amanpour 2006).

Dealing with HIV/AIDS as a disease may be a scientific challenge, but dealing with the social and economic factors that favor its spread is not an impossible task. The issues and solutions involved in dealing with the poverty underlying the HIV/AIDS epidemic are as well known as those involved in dealing with malaria and water-borne diseases—the other deadly diseases in Africa that are driven by socio-economic forces. It is imperative to understand these facts about HIV/AIDS and mobilize governments, the United Nations and donors to focus on combating Africa's social crises as an essential complement to activities that specifically address the disease.

The Implications for Sustainable Economic and Social Development

HIV/AIDS is most commonly thought of as a disease wreaking havoc on human lives. Since it typically strikes individuals during their most productive years, however, governments and businesses are increasingly realizing that AIDS can cripple the economic development of entire countries and regions. With its prevalence in Africa, the disease poses great challenges to all sectors of the economy from the farmland to the classroom and, of course, the boardroom. HIV is having a disastrous effect on already fragile economies of countries in Africa. With many African countries recovering from wars or natural disasters like droughts, HIV/AIDS is able to destroy what gains have been made in the past decade (White 2004). The disturbing consequences of death from AIDS on households, employment, schools and health facilities are alarming and of important consideration. Many studies suggest that the AIDS pandemic is unraveling many years of development gains and setting them backward (Bage 2004, Human Development 2001, Kelly 2001).

At a macro level, the economic toll is significant. A number of countries have lost as much as ten percent of their labor forces, a figure that can be much higher in urban areas. Employers, schools, factories and hospitals have to train other staff to replace those at the workplace that become too ill to work. Migrant workers often acquire the disease much more readily than the general population.

Armed forces in countries around the region also test positive for HIV at a higher rate that the general population because of their tendency to engage in high risk behavior (White 2004). The vast majority of people living with HIV/AIDS in Africa are between the ages of 15 and 49, the prime of their working lives. For many companies, AIDS has become a bottom-line business issue. Its effect on family income and employment cannot be underestimated. Many families are losing their income earners. In some cases, income earners are forced to stay at home to care for relatives who are ill from AIDS. The HIV/AIDS pandemic also has serious consequences for life expectancy in Africa. Although life expectancies in many sub-Saharan countries are some of the lowest comparatively in the world, they even drop lower when HIV/AIDS is factored into the equation (White 2004). Average life expectancy in sub-Saharan Africa is now 47 years, when it could have been 62 without AIDS. Many of those dying have surviving partners who are themselves infected and in need of care. They leave behind children grieving and struggling to survive without a parent's care thereby exacerbating the social impact of the disease. In the early 1980s, barely two percent of African children were orphaned, but more recent estimates put the proportion to be as high as 17 percent in some countries (White 2004).

While these statistics paint an alarming picture, the AIDS toll in many African countries is not easily quantified. It is hard to put a dollar figure on the indirect cost to the family of a sick person in terms of losses of income and time spent caring for the sick at home, or the effect on the employer in terms of labor productivity decline. There are cases where children, especially girls, are being pulled out of school, severely limiting their life chances and placing them at risk in the future; the movement of orphans and widows to urban areas in search of income may lead them to resort to high risk behavior out of economic necessity. Also, an indirect cost of the crisis is the physical and psychological exhaustion of women (especially grandmothers) left behind to care for orphans and the sick (CNN 2006).

Combating HIV/AIDS: An African Response to United States Policy—A Critique

The report by Todd Summers in "The Rising Stakes" discusses the largest international health initiative directed at a single disease undertaken by the United States government. It consists of recommendations for implementing President Bush's 2003 Emergency Plan for AIDS Relief (PEPFAR), the latest in the United States' policy in addressing the AIDS pandemic. In its introduction, the policy is described as "increasing U.S. engagement on the global HIV/AIDS epidemic by committing new resources, increasing political commitment, legislative and public support" (Kansteiner and Morrison 2004:136). President Bush in this new initiative announced a $15 billion, five-year plan to fight HIV/AIDS in Africa and the Caribbean. Nineteen out of the 25 countries benefiting from the initiative are in Africa. The money is to help purchase antiretroviral drugs, train health care workers and workers caring for the orphans of AIDS. It also makes provision for education on abstinence for teenagers who engage in high risk behaviors (White 2004). This initiative represents a gigantic leap in America's bid to assume a leadership role in the fight against the HIV/AIDS pandemic.

This will not be the first time that the United States government has offered assistance to combat a health crisis in Africa, but it would be the first initiative that is directed specifically to AIDS with a huge financial, legislative and presidential backing. It will also be the first time that the beneficiaries of the initiative are mostly African countries. Earlier efforts include the United States' contribution to African development through the Global Fund to Fight AIDS, Tuberculosis and Malaria in 2002. There was also the Millennium Challenge Corporation (MCC), which was established by the United States in 2004. President Bush requested $3 billion in MCC funding for the fiscal year ending in October 1, 2003 and has pledged to increase funding to $5 billion in the future. (Walton 2006). This historic action and generous financial commitment by the United States is a bold act of leadership and a quantum leap in the response against HIV/AIDS, and the United States should be commended for its moral action. The question, however, is why has this effort yet to translate into greater success in eradicating the AIDS pandemic, or slowing down its spread? The authors of this paper submit that while the intent of this current effort by the United States may be noble, there are serious problems with the credibility of its motive, the coherence of the leadership and the sustainability of the plan.

There were two specific recommendations contained in the report. Part one is a request to the Secretary of State (which at the time was General Colin Powell) to continue to use his personal influence and engagement in the fight against HIV/AIDs epidemic. It stresses the need for the Secretary to provide visibility on the issue, to engage other countries' leaders in the fight, to attend high visibility conferences that focus on the issue, and to seek partnership with other governmental agencies. In part two of the recommendations, the position of the duties of the coordinator for the program is outlined. This is the gem of the policy. This coordinator is expected to sort out all the complexities in establishing the necessary partnerships and mechanisms for implementing the policy and to do so without conflict and duplication of efforts with existing organizations. The report is quick to admit the chaos that already exists in the workings of the different agencies. It also expresses the fear about bureaucratic practices, mismanagement of funds and time, and irreconcilable differences in motives that may arise between the different non-governmental agencies and the United States government in dealing with the HIV/AIDS issue. It expresses hope that the coordinator's office will be able to resolve these differences through research, training, open communication, consultation, and the availability of resources provided for the program. Such concerns are well founded and, as this chapter will further present, the United States' timing, underlying motive and level of commitment in joining the fight have been questioned in many quarters.

Timing and Motive

It has been more than 20 years since HIV/AIDS began spreading across Africa and medical researchers first identified the behavioral prescriptions to avoid AIDS. The question is why the United States is just now intervening directly? Even though the policy was titled "Continuing US Leadership to Combat HIV/AIDS in Africa and globally," critics suggest that the policy was too little too late, was self-serving (to protect United States Military serving overseas from AIDS) and, in some cases, a cultural misfit. Gellman suggests that in 1987, United States' Intelligence Organizations declared the AIDS issue "an unfit subject of intelligence and its impact on US interests would be benign" (200:2). President Bush is said to have been skeptical of the severity of the situation and found it hard to commit resources to fight the battle. It was not until the fight against AIDS was linked to the fight against terrorism that the President decided to get involved in the matter. For instance, a large portion of the report is devoted to the linkage of the fight against HIV/AIDS to national security. It urges the coordinator to work with the Department of Defense and the National Security Council to "conduct a serious and comprehensive analysis of the implications of HIV/AIDS on U.S. national security interests" (Gellman 2000:141). The National Security Council had already issued a report that made a case for considering major infections, especially HIV/AIDS, as a national security issue for the United States. It suggests that United States' peacekeeping forces within the United Nations stationed overseas, especially in Africa, may be susceptible to getting infected from their interaction with African military officers or their activities in the continent. It also alludes to the potential for the destabilization of the political and economic spheres of African countries by millions of children orphaned by the disease and those disfranchised through lack of economic opportunities. These disenfranchised children may become ready ploys in the hands of terrorists. Moreover, the report advices that the United States and the Coordinator should regularly assess the prevalence of HIV among African military personnel (Kansteiner and Morrison 2004:142). The fear is that AIDS is decimating the African military, and this will put a strain on American and allied forces stationed overseas when African countries are unable to meet their quota. Many of the non-governmental agencies whose motives are purely humanitarian may have issues with the directions in which the American government is taking the HIV/AIDS situation and the motive in joining the fight against the pandemic. The defense agenda is problematic and should have been separated from the humanitarian effort in order for PEPFAR to have any credibility.

Moreover, there seems to be a new found understanding of how vital Africa is economically, and this shift to a strategic view of Africa requires a shift in United States' policies, programs, human skills and finances. Critics suggest that United States' assistance tends to have a selfish motive, not a humanitarian effort, tied to America's interest in oil in Africa, the emergence of West and Central Africa as key oil suppliers and its interest in trade. Critics also point out that the United States wants to strengthen Africa's capital markets and financial sector for its own selfish interests. Thus, the HIV/AIDS issue needs to be addressed on its own merit and not tied to other issues (Wangila and Akukwe 2006).

Lack of Credibility of the Claim to Continuing Leadership

The announcement by President Bush in 2003 to commit $15 billion to the fight of AIDS in Africa and the Caribbean was said to be a surprise to many in political circles (Stolberg and Stevenson 2003). The plan was grandiose in nature, the implementation strategy complex, and the leadership convoluted. First, the line up of the major executors of the initiative constitutes people that are so highly placed in the government that their availability on the issue of HIV/AIDS may be in question According to the policy, the activism of the Secretary of State (then Colin Powell), National Security Adviser and high ranking officials was meant to set the tone for addressing the HIV/AIDS crisis. The leadership needs to be re-examined, and there is a need for another advocate at the senior level in Bush's cabinet. Current Secretary of State Condoleeza Rice has not shown enough interest and same level of commitment expressed by previous Secretary of State Colin Powell under whom the policy was created and who supported the effort to develop the report under examination. The initiative was based on the personal credibility and interest of the former Secretary of State. One wonders, with the administration's focus on the war on terror in Afghanistan and Iraq, if the same level of commitment is still in place (Stolberg and Stevenson 2003:140).

Furthermore, whatever commitment there is has not been translated into success on the grounds. Wangila and Akukwe suggest that there is a mismatch between the rhetoric on HIV prevention and AIDS relief and the situation on the grounds (2006:1). In fact, they go as far as to consider this incongruence as the biggest crisis in the AIDS situation. They suggest that most international policies are orchestrated by the media, focused more on workshop and conferences instead of on developing and implementing comprehensive relief programs for the victims of HIV/AIDS and their families. Furthermore, the policy was touted as a global effort in which the United States would partner with other governments, international organizations, nongovernmental organizations, religious groups, civil societies and affected communities (Wangila and Akukwe 2006:137). Not only would partnership be explored externally, but internally as well through a multi-sectorial approach. Additionally, there were plans to involve a host of agencies including the USAID, Department of Health and Human Services, the Department of Defense, Department of Labor, and Center for Disease and Control, etc. Having too many key agencies involved may lead to a case of "too many cooks spoiling the broth." The complexity in the partnership could delay the flow of information and services to the grassroots level in the affected countries.

Lack of Coherence in Policy Implementation

Another inconsistency noted in the policy has to do with the lack of coherence with the mechanism put in place for its funding and implementation. It is a good policy on paper, but it lacks clear definition in some areas. There are two issues of concern here: one is the lack of freedom for the coordinator in charge of implementing the policy, the other is whether or not the right agency is the one appointed to take charge. The guidelines for implementation were set by the Congress, which was at the time controlled by President Bush's Republican Party. For instance, the funding distribution was legislated by Congress, which required that PEPFAR money should be divided in the following way: 55% for the treatment of individuals with HIV/AIDS, which is to be spent on the purchase and distribution of antiretroviral drugs; 15% for the palliative care of individuals with HIV/AIDS, 20 % for HIV/AIDS prevention, and 10 % for helping orphans and vulnerable children (Avert.org, 2006). Congress also directed that one-third of the money earmarked for the prevention be spent on promoting abstinence. The amount of money given to the program each year, however, is not necessarily what the President or the coordinator asks for but what the Congress approves. So the coordinator does not have control over what eventually gets done.

As mentioned earlier, the Department of State through the office of the new coordinator for global HIV/AIDS activities is charged with implementing the policy. Putting the program under the purview of the Department of State makes PEPFAR seem more of a political commitment rather than a "public health" commitment. Why place a health issue under the auspices of the State Department instead of the Department of Health and Human Resources which has the resources and expertise to deal with it? Why not put the job primarily in the hands of the department that normally deals with healthcare and have others channel their ideas through this main organ? Apart from the lack of coherence, focus and credibility with the leadership, the proposed implementation strategy is also faulty. The call for partnership might be hard to achieve when there are disagreements on the motives and the strategies.

Lack of Coherence in the Funding and Distribution of Resources

This section will address the funding for PEPFAR, the focus of the policy, and the progress being made towards its goals. There are many issues to consider. The first is the funding issue. The President in announcing the initiative pledged $15 billion over a five-year period. Nonetheless, not all this money is new money. Of the total $15 billion, $9 billion is extra funding, $5 billion is to continue the existing bilateral agreements, and $1billion is money proposed to be provided to the Global Fund to fight AIDS, Tuberculosis and Malaria (Avert.org, 2006). Also, not all the money requested will be provided; it all depends on how much money Congress appropriates. For instance, in FY 2005, Congress appropriated less money than the total budget for global HIV/AIDS ($2,598 million instead of $2,701 million). Part of the money ($1,374 million) was for running the United States' global Coordinator's Office, and $347 million was earmarked for the Global Fund. In essence, the attainment of the goals of treatment and prevention is predicated on the level of availability of the so-called generous donation.

The goal of providing treatment is dependent not just on how much money is earmarked per fiscal year but also on the availability of antiviral drugs that are affordable, so that many of the victims can be reached. The point was made by Avert.org (2006) that FEPFAR can only use the drugs that are approved by Federal Drugs Administration (FDA), but the African countries only trust the approval of the World Health Organization (WHO). Unfortunately, when there is disagreement between the FDA and the WHO in approving a drug (and this has happened with some generic drugs), treatment is stalled for thousands of people.

Another problem that has been cited is the implementation of the prevention part of the policy. In the first place, critics suggest that the limiting of HIV prevention money to 20% of the total PEPFAR money may be problematic (Noble 2006, Avert 2006). This may hinder the amount and type of education provided, the strategy for testing, the purchase of needle for drug users, and the distribution of condoms. Moreover, one-third of the total money earmarked for prevention at any given year is supposed to go to abstinence-till-marriage programs. This is based on the United States' "ABC model." "A" stands for abstinence, "B" stands for be faithful to a partner," and "C" for the correct use of condom." This plan looks good on the surface, but the problem occurs with how it is being enforced. Avert.org reports that the policy only provides condoms for groups that are engaged in "high risk behaviors." These are the prostitutes, the sexually active discordant couples (in which one partner is known to have HIV), and substance abuse users (2006:7). Condoms are not mentioned as a strategy for helping young people in general, even though these are the people that are the most vulnerable. Worst still, there are allegations that PEPFAR refuses funding to organizations that promote condom use beyond the high risk group. The European Union criticized this as partial or incomplete messages on HIV which are not grounded in evidence and have limited effectiveness (Avert 2006:7). PEPFAR's coordinator, Dr. Mark Dybul, has denied this excessive focus on abstinence and the refusal of funds to organizations with general condom distributing policy.

Conclusion and Recommendations

The preceding discussion concerning the prevalence of the HIV/AIDS pandemic in Africa and the summary and critique of chapter seven of the "Rising Stakes" report lay the foundation for the following recommendations in this chapter. We posit that the overview given here is just the tip of the iceberg concerning the complexities that affect the various dichotomies in the fight against HIV/AIDS. The evaluation of the United States' effort, although critical, should not be perceived as minimizing the effect that American resources and efforts through PEPFAR have had and will continue to have on the fight against HIV/AIDS in Africa. The magnitude of the HIV/AIDS pandemic and the rapidity at which the disease continues to spread, plus its direct and indirect impact on the political, social and economic lives of people in Africa, however, makes us skeptical of the effectiveness of current initiatives. Future direction dictates a strategy that aligns with the culture, characteristics and needs of Africans. We find the current effort inadequate because of its emphasis on treatment over prevention, because of its questionable motive, and because of the un-sustainability of the funding. We would, therefore, like to propose the following recommendations.

Make War on Poverty the Number One Priority

We suggest that some of the funding be earmarked to address the social and economic needs of the affected countries. As Bage (2004) suggested, and we agree, we cannot succeed in changing the dynamics of the epidemic and the fight against it if the social and economic weaknesses at the heart of the epidemic are not reduced. Dealing with the social crisis should go beyond providing food and water to focusing on capacity development, creation of economic opportunities, access to education, improved infrastructure, and a re-examination of social adjustment programs. The forgiveness of foreign loans should continue, so that African countries could have money to invest on social programs. Part of the problems being faced by African countries that drain their resources is the structural adjustment programs with which they are forced to comply due to the terms of the loans. If the international community can forgive the debts with the condition that the money that would have been repaid is spent on rebuilding the economies and social infrastructure of the African countries, instead of scaling back, the problem with poverty will be minimized. Life in general will improve for most Africans, even the ones that have the HIV virus, if there are better economic opportunities and social infrastructure.

We also appeal to the United States government to increase its contribution to the African Global Fund and use its influence to encourage other Western countries to increase their quotas. Part of the money in the Global Fund should be earmarked for promoting literacy and other forms of education, especially for women and those in the rural areas. This should be backed up with increase in the budget allocations of African countries themselves to the social programs. Piot, Feachem, Jong-wook and Wolfensohn (2004) noted that there has been a dramatic decrease, in per capita terms, of national and external resources devoted to helping Africa's rural poor build better lives. Moreover, much of the assistance has failed to develop the continent's strengths, especially in the rural areas. Some of the problems rest with the African counties themselves. During the Special Summit of the African Union on HIV/AIDS, Tuberculosis and Malaria (ATM) held in Abuja, Nigeria, the Nigerian President, Olusegun Obasanjo opined that "many African countries are still dependent on foreign funding, and funding sources are often neither predictable nor sustainable. Accountability and capacity utilization of funds secured remain major challenges. In spite of various continental and national initiatives to reduce poverty, poverty still remains pervasive on the continent, negating our efforts to fight these diseases" (AllAfrica, Inc. 2006:2). In essence, African governments need to have sustainable economies, increase capacity building, reduce poverty and corruption in order to fight the war against HIV/AIDS and other diseases. Public expenditure has been the focus of assistance; yet in rural Africa, households and communities primarily take care of themselves. Programs focusing specifically on HIV/AIDS must reach out to strengthen the capacity of families and communities. Rural development must also be strengthened and focused on the heart of the problem: poor men and women need the opportunities and capacities to build better and safer lives, rooted in enduring social and economic change (Bage 2004).

Emphasize Prevention and Education

The next recommendation deals with the need for increased emphasis on prevention, which should include education, testing, counseling and mentoring. Even though the amount of money announced for the program seems large, we now know that only 20 percent is allocated to prevention programs. Also, not all the money is new money and not all the new money asked for will be obtained (Avert.org 2006). There has to be a stronger commitment to funding the program. Currently, there is a mismatch between the extreme urgency of the situation on the ground and the pace of the effort by the international community, especially that of the United States (Wangila and Akukwe 2006).

There is a need to focus on free access to formal and non-formal education especially, for women and marginalized children, and to promote school-community linkages for better prevention, identification and treatment of the disease. The emphasis on abstinence may not be enough to address the reduction of the rate of infection among young people, most of whom are already sexually active and have the tendency to experiment with at risk behavior, including the use of drugs. There should not be a restriction on who is allowed to have condoms and no mixed messages about its importance in preventing the transmission of HIV.

Education and prevention should also involve testing and counseling. As Noble opines, "HIV counseling and testing is particularly important as a starting point for access to other HIV/AIDS related services. If a person does not know that they are infected, they cannot get any treatment or care" (2006:2). In most cases, people are already seriously ill before they are diagnosed, and this limits their choices for treatment as well as the cost-effectiveness of the treatment. In addition to counseling, it is important to raise awareness about the effectiveness of treatment and to reduce the stigma and discrimination associated with the disease. Some victims will not get treated because of the fear of being ostracized, in addition to battles with depression or alcoholism. Some have a fatalistic attitude that they are going to die anyway, so why worry. Moreover, young women should be provided with mentors who will educate them about the disease and encourage them not to succumb to early marriage or pressure to sleep with men who are infected. As far as the military is concerned, part of the prevention money could be spent on developing and implementing a "public health Crash Program on AIDS" for the American troops going to Africa, as well as for the African medical doctors that will be involved in the AIDS programs.

Take Cognizance of Cultural Differences

The policy for prevention is based on a United States model which may not be culturally visible in Africa. This policy models Bush's conservative position of emphasizing the "A-B-C" ("Abstinence, being faithful to one partner, and careful use of Condom") model. This model has only been found to be partially success-ful in Uganda. As indicated earlier, the policy is also shortsighted for not address-ing the root of the problem, which is women's lack of power in sexual relationships, the absence of counseling, inadequate health care and the irrele-vance of condom to most African men, especially after being intoxicated (White 2004). Additionally, the policy fails to address the reality of AIDS in Africa, not only in terms of poverty as an underlying factor, but also cultural values: for example, the role of traditional leaders, traditional beliefs about life and death, the relationship between men and women, and the increasing number of orphans. Partnership with African educators to design and implement informa-tion resources that are culturally appropriate will help to rectify this oversight.

Use a Multi-Sectorial Approach that is All Inclusive

Furthermore, the American policy argues for a multi sectorial approach with other governments, international organizations, non-governmental organizations, faith-based groups, and civil society. It does not touch upon collaborations with the victims or their representatives. This is the same untargeted approach that Bage (2004) condemned as ineffective. In addition to members of the interna-tional community, PEPFAR should work with local leaders who are usually the advocates for the victims and who have the believability to successfully carry out the message of prevention to the people. The plan must be decentralized and reli-ant on community-based programming. Regional organizations will form the bedrock for planning, resources mobilization and distribution. Civil society will assist with implementation and capacity building.

In order to bring the HIV/AIDS program closer to the victims, we recommend that the United States creates five regional centers in Africa to coordinate its HIV/AIDS programs. The proposed five regional offices should be: West Africa-U.S. HIV/AIDS Center, Central Africa-U.S. HIV/AIDS Center, East Africa-U.S. HIV/AIDS Center, South Africa-U.S. HIV/AIDS Center, and North Africa-U.S.HIV/AIDS Center. The United States should utilize the services of the Regional Economic Unions in these five identified regions to conduct need assessment research and disseminate information. The officials of the African Economic Union know and understand the needs and cultures of their people more so than the United States officials. Culturally, morally, and socially speaking, the Africans with the HIV/AIDS will relate better with their own native public health officials. To the extent that over 90% of the Africans living in the rural areas are not literate in English, it would be better and more cost-effective for the United States to employ the services of African public health officials.

To effectively carry out the suggested partnership, the American government would require the following:

a.   A very sound logistic head office that will coordinate the affairs of all the five HIV/AIDS Regional Centers in Africa. This logistic office could be located in Washington or Africa but should report directly to the Secretary for Health and Human Services, because we believe that HIV/AIDS problems are both health and social issues that must be handled by HHS.

b.   The logistic office will be responsible for monitoring and evaluating the performances of all five HIV/AIDS regional offices.

c.   The logistic office will administratively be responsible for the conduct, structure and performance of all the regional offices.

The HIV/AIDS pandemic in Africa is a serious problem. Surely, some advances have been made, but there need to be an agreement on priorities and a better coordination of all efforts. Effective and sustainable solutions would require collaboration among all local, national, regional and international stakeholders, and a swift movement from commitment to action. Research points to the fact that social issues relating to poverty and gender discrimination are major clogs in the wheel of progress in the efforts to reduce the AIDS pandemic. These issues need to be addressed simultaneously with any initiative aimed at combating the HIV/AIDS diseases. Additionally, there is a need to have a system in place for continuous evaluation and to hold all agencies accountable, including the governments of the African countries.

8

Higher Education

Ishmael I. Munene

Introduction

What strikes you most when you examine the report, *Rising U.S. Stakes in Africa: Seven Proposals to Strengthen U.S.-Africa Policy*, by the Africa Policy Advocacy group and authorized by the United States Congress in 2004? It may not be apparent; but to an educationist, the stark reality is too telling: education, and higher education for that matter, is ominously absent as a sphere of significance in strengthening Africa-United Sates relations. Was this by design or default, by commission or omission? It may not be easy to tell, but it is intriguing that such an important area of human endeavor could be excluded from such an important policy document that lays out the key areas of collaboration between Africa and the United States government. This exclusion does raise important issues about the existing partnership between Africa and America in the arena of higher education.

In the absence of proposals for strengthening Africa-United States higher education partnership, it behooves us to shift our focus on the structure and nature of current United States government support in the development of African higher education. In doing so, I shall explore the articulated, directly or otherwise, government policies and the character of multilateral and bilateral support directed towards African higher education. This should enable us to delineate a concise picture of the forces that inform the policy decisions in supporting the continent's higher educational development.

It goes without saying that the United States has been a major supporter of African higher education. Since the independence explosion in the 1960s, when Africans began to emerge from the yoke of European colonialism, America has expended a considerable amount of its financial treasure in support of the continent's higher education. The financial commitments to African higher education have not been without ideological undertones that have permeated much of the developed world. An examination of the United States' financial assistance to Africa's higher education indicates that ideology and self-interest have provided the anchor upon which aid decisions have been made. From human capital approach immediately after independence to rate-of-return analysis in the early 1990s, the current aid regime is influenced by tenets of globalization and the attendant market values as articulated by the World Bank and the International Monetary Fund (IMF). This prevailing aid approach has had considerable impact both at institutional and individual levels within academia.

Era of Optimism: The Development University and Development Assistance

Why should higher education be considered an important sector in the strengthening of Africa-United States relations? An answer to this question forces us to explore the role of higher education in national development. The debate over the role of higher education in national development has been settled; countries with the highest levels of university graduates also enjoy the highest levels of economic development. The contrast is equally true. Thus, America, the wealthiest nation on earth, has the highest number of university graduates alongside the most number of higher education institutions. The opposite is true of Africa, which is the poorest continent and has the least number of university graduates. These contrasting correlations are not by coincidence but rather indicate an empirical link between higher education and national development. The contributions of higher education to economic growth are seen in socio-economic terms with public and private benefits including the increase in income, greater tax revenues, as well as savings and investments. It does also spur entrepreneurial activities, civil society development, improved health, reduction in population, improvement in technology, and strengthening of democratic governance. Therefore, any United States' assistance to Africa's development efforts needs to incorporate a sizeable support for the continent's higher education development.

Upon attainment of independence in the 1960s, African nations placed considerable faith in the power of higher education in the eradication of poverty and other impediments towards national development. The 1962 UNESCO and United Nations Economic Commission (UNEC) for Africa Conference on Higher Educational in Africa held in Tananarive, Madagascar concluded that in addition to teaching and research, higher education was to contribute to social, cultural and economic development. It was to be the "source of high-level manpower to sustain newly-won independence" (Yesufu 1973:82). And so began the era of the one state one development university. Throughout the 1970s and 1980s, universities were engaged in national development efforts such as increasing food production, advising on poverty, housing development, and ethnic integration activities. These human capital benefits were the *raison d'etre* for the considerable injection of foreign aid in African higher education from the 1960s to 1980s. Education became an important focal point of development aid; indeed, it occupied the largest share. This period was the "golden age" of university development, as Eisemon and Kourouma noted:

> Educational expansion was the keystone of economic planning, of social policy and strategies for fostering political development in Africa and Asian countries in the 1960s and 1970s. This was the golden age of foreign educational assistance and coincided with expansion of higher educational systems in most of the donor countries (1994:276).

Bilateral agencies made commitments amounting to $100 million or more to tertiary level education. Among the prominent donors were Australia, Canada, France, Italy, the Netherlands, Norway, Spain, Sweden, Switzerland, the United Kingdom and the United States (ILon 2003). A positive outcome of this mode of development assistance is that it allowed African nations to participate in the planning of their higher education development. In other words, they identified the role of higher education and set out its priorities within the national development plans.

It is worth noting that the United States shared the prevailing universal view that African higher education was the key to the continent's emancipation from poverty and underdevelopment. In essence, both African nations and America had a shared view on the priorities for higher education in the continent based on an instrumental perspective of higher education's role in socio-economic development. Higher education was to be the agent of radical transformation of society, socially and economically. Financial assistance from America, it follows, was to play a critical role in institutional capacity building. This was achieved through Fulbright scholarships for advanced graduate studies along with general grants to support institutional infrastructural development.

Building on this view that higher education is the engine to spur economic growth and development, it would seem logical to expect the sector to continue receiving unprecedented attention by Africa's development partners, including the United States, even in the current dispensation. Yet, historical trends indicate that this has not been the case, as support for African education is a story of waxing and waning of resources and commitments (ILon 2003). Underlying these contrasting trends in commitment and support is the shifting ideological prisms through which the role of higher education in the continent has been conceptualized. It is a shifting ideological strand in which African nations have not been particularly active in shaping.

Era of Pessimism and Despair: The Development University Failure and Development Assistance Decline

One of the ideological signposts of the current African-United States higher education partnership was in the change of thinking about the role of African higher education that began in the early 1990s. In a move spearheaded by the World Bank, African national universities were seen as a failure (see for instance World Bank 1994 and 1988). It was a state of failure that undercut the high hopes that had been accorded the universities as engines of national development and agents of emancipation from poverty. The failure was epitomized in what emerged as the defining characteristics of the national universities in the early 1990s:

- small, Western-oriented, elite institutions which could not meet the growing demand for more higher educational opportunities by the burgeoning population;

- free on-campus residence for all students which necessitated the construction of expensive housing including public-supported board services;

- free tuition for all without means testing to determine ability to pay;

- unsuitable curricular manifested by massive graduate unemployment amidst manpower shortages in the critical scientific, technological and medical fields;

- infrastructural decay due to inadequate facilities maintenance occasioned by the tight fiscal restraints by the national governments;

- intensive politicization of the universities as they acted as the "opposition" to the one-party national regimes. This eroded institutional autonomy and academic freedom; and

- rate of return analysis which demonstrated that higher education had the lowest societal returns in contrast to basic and secondary education. Basic education had the highest rate of returns.

The net effect of this assessment was to cast serious doubts about the viability of African higher education as a focus of investment by international donors, bilateral and multilateral. It did, however, shift focus to basic education as a more socially beneficial area of investment. Due to its influential stature, and due to the fact that it is headed by an American appointed by the United States government, the World Bank set the tone and pace of policy direction for wealthy partners like the United States to pursue funding higher education in Africa as this edict indicates:

> Basic education will continue to receive the highest priority in the Bank's education lending to countries that have not yet achieved universal literacy and adequate access, equity and quality at that level ... As basic education system develops in coverage and effectiveness, more attention will be devoted to the upper-secondary and higher levels. Bank lending for higher education will support countries' efforts to adopt policy reforms that allow the subsector to operate more efficiently and at a lower public cost. Countries prepared to adopt a higher education policy framework that stresses a differentiated institutional structure and diversified resource base, with greater emphasis on private providers and private funding, will continue to receive priority (World Bank 1995).

This dim view of African higher education was further reinforced by the 1990 World Conference on Education for All (WCEFA), held in Jomtien, Thailand, sponsored by the World Bank, the IMF, the United Nations Educational, Scientific and Cultural Organization (UNESCO), and the United States Agency for International Development (USAID, among other donors. The Jomtien conference shifted focus from higher education to basic education among donor nations. The conference relied on both human capital theory as well as rate of return analysis to underscore the economic value of basic education. While it had a role to play, African higher education was deemed inefficient, incompetent and inequitable. The conference recommended that government funding be directed towards basic education and measures be taken to encourage privatization to fill the gaps in higher education finance.

Two important observations are apparent with this changing reality of assistance to higher education in Africa. First, priorities were now being set by international donor partners including the United States. While previously African nations would set priorities in higher education and then seek donor support, in the current dispensation, they had to align their needs to priorities set by external partners. Higher education ceased being a donor priority as had been previously. Second, their crucial role in national development notwithstanding, African universities were starved important financial resources for their development as "... most [donor] agencies and African governments disengaged from the sector in the 1980s and early 90s on the argument that rates of social return in basic education are much higher than in higher education. Denied of funds, African higher education was brought to near collapse," observed the Secretary-General of the Association of African Universities Narciso Matos (Matos 1998:5). The dawn of pessimism and despair in African higher education had set in.

Globalization: Markets, Privatization and the University

Globalization and the attendant notions of marketization and privatization have become the new kids on the block in higher education development, operations and management. It is, therefore, not farfetched to speculate that they have had tremendous implications for bilateral and multilateral aid. Due to the significance of these tenets of the Western, neo-liberal agenda, it is imperative that we examine what they entail and their ramifications for development cooperation between African higher education and the United States. The nexus between education and globalization in Western, industrial countries began in the 1980s, but it only commenced forcefully in African higher education in the early 1990's. It is by no coincidence that the accelerated promotion of the tenets of globalization by the World Bank and IMF came on the hills of the 1990 World Conference on Education For All (WCEFA) which deemphasized higher education as a priority funding sector.

Globalization is viewed as a process through which time and space are compressed and people think in global terms. It is what happens when people, ideas and goods move across nations and regions at an accelerated speed. It is also viewed as a process that combines a market ideology with a corresponding set of practices drawn from the corporate world. The globalized political economy has been the catalyst of enormous transformation in public higher education, the most striking being the accelerated movement of institutions into the marketplace.

Prior to the 1980s, from Africa to Asia, America to Australia, as well as in Europe, public higher education had a social mission, and faculty and institutions eschewed involvement in the market. Since then, states have enacted policies through which they have steered public institutions into the market. Such policies have included decreased funding leading to partnerships with business and industry focusing on innovative product development, marketing of education and business services, accumulation of power by state officials to shape programs and curricular and to standardize and routinize faculty work while costs are transferred to students, official encouragement of contract research and increased managerialism to manage it (Slaughter and Larry 1997), and recasting state-university relations in contractual terms. Simply put, public higher education has acquired an economic mission and its effectiveness is assessed by the success in the marketplace.

The infusion of market principles into higher education is informed by the link between economic growth, poverty and markets mediated by knowledge economy (read higher education). Knowledge has a market value in the global political economy. In the industrial West, universities have been identified as the cog in the wheel of international competitiveness among nations. Universities are part of the agency for creating national wealth by increasing a country's global market share through product development and increase in high paying, high technology jobs. Creating a global market, however, means less money for welfare programs and education functions but more money for building corporate competitiveness (Slaughter and Larry 1997). For higher education, this has meant funding geared for programs that complement multinational corporation involvement in the global economy. These include technology, health, business training and development of intellectual property rights. It is this juxtaposition of knowledge and the market that is central to the linking of aid to poverty reduction in Africa; through foreign aid to African higher education, the continent will be brought into the knowledge economy which will stimulate not only its own growth but also in the productivity knowledge of advanced industrial nations.

Without the active involvement and encouragement of global institutions the neo-liberal ideology of globalization would hardly have been successful. The World Bank, the IMF and the Organization for Economic Cooperation and Development (OECD) have encouraged Third World higher education institutions to adopt the American model and diversify their revenue bases as well as institute market-oriented academic programs. As we have already seen, the World Bank, through its financial clout, has been successful in imposing structural adjustment programs that has led to increased privatization of higher education in much of Africa today. In addressing the global character of the new knowledge and the disadvantage poor nations face, the World Bank's Task Force on Higher Education observed the following:

> Countries that are only weakly connected to the rapidly emerging global knowledge system will find themselves increasingly at a disadvantage. The gap between industrial and developing countries par capita incomes and standards of living will widen unless the corresponding gaps in knowledge and access to knowledge are successfully addressed. Compared with investment in the production of goods, investment in the production of new knowledge yields potentially higher economic returns but entails higher risks.... The winner-

takes-all character of investment in knowledge demands a high level of existing knowledge and skills even to enter the fray. Few developing countries possess this knowledge (Task Force on Higher Education and Society 2000).

It is this ideological bent, linking knowledge, market and poverty, that has been a powerful influence in the nature and structure of United States' support for higher education development in Africa.

Show Me the Money: Trends in USA Aid to African Higher Education

How has globalization and the attendant market values manifested themselves in the United States' support for African higher education? An answer to this question requires us to examine America's support for African higher education in the last few years. This will allow us to see the trends in such funding and raise important issues germane to equity in the partnership. I will first briefly examine the nature of the support by looking at the overall trends in development assistance. This will be followed by close scrutiny of two key projects for specific in depth analysis to be followed later on by a critical analysis of the trends in financial support.

That official development assistance has been in decline is not in doubt. Since the mid-1990s, 16 of the 21 donor countries in Europe, North America and Asia have reduced their levels of development commitment to developing nations as a proportion of their gross domestic products. Between 1996 and 1997, Sweden reduced its foreign aid by 5.9%, Germany by 11%, the United States by 35%, and Italy by 45%. Not far behind is the OECD which reduced its assistance by 23% between 1998 and 2001 (Heyneman 2005:112). The reasons advanced for the decline are multifaceted, ranging from waning political support for aid in the donor nations, political as opposed to economic rationale for aid, and lack of absorptive capacity in aid recipient nations. Central to my thesis, however, is that this decline in official development assistance is part state retreat in development assistance, a distinguishing phenomenon of globalization and marketization of development. No longer is the state considered central in stimulating national development. Rather, the market is considered as being more efficient in determining developmental needs through the forces of demand and supply. State role is limited to regulation of the various developmental actors in a competitive market environment.

A decomposition of the United States' official development assistance data as administered by USAID in 2003 is presented in Figure 1. Ideological and strategic needs, it appears, override developmental challenges in decisions about funding. The centrality of Asia in United States ideological and strategic interests provides a reasonable justification for devoting 45% of aid to that region alone. Another geopolitical region of significance is the Middle East. Four countries in this region—Egypt, Israel, Jordan, and the West Bank and Gaza—benefited from 35% of all the official development assistance in that year, more than Africa and Latin America combined. Such a skewed aid disbursement neither promotes long-term development nor equity in development partnership.

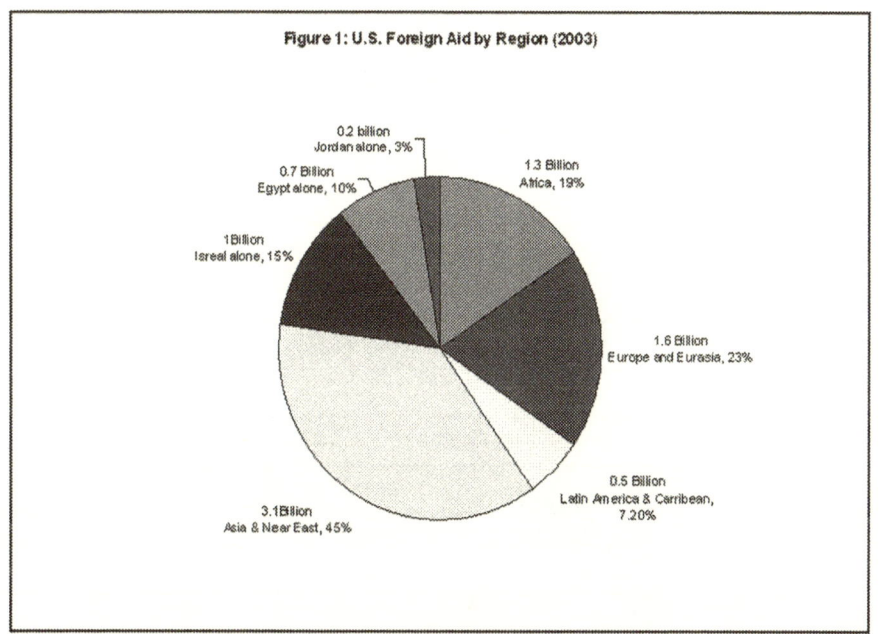

Figure 1: U.S. Foreign Aid by Region (2003)

Source: USAID 2003

The regional focus of major donors, those with five or more large projects in African higher education for the years 2001-2004 is presented in Table 1. Both private and government agencies are included. There is a tendency for agencies to focus their attention on specific regions. For United States, there is a clear preference for the government agency, USAID, to concentrate major project funding in East Africa. This contrasts sharply to the Canadian and Netherland government agencies, CIDA and NUFU, respectively, which have had their funding spread out relatively uniformly in the four major regions of the continent. The United States' case demonstrates the significance it attaches to its regional strategic interests in determining assistance to Africa's higher education.

Table 1: Regional Funding Focus by Major Organizations by Region, 2001-2004

Region	Main Funding Organization	No. of Projects
East Africa	NUFU	12
	CIDA	7
	USAID	6
	World Bank	5
	Ford	5
	JICA	5
Horn	NUFU	9
Southern Africa	Ford	27
	NUFU	14
	Carnegie	9
	NFP (Netherlands Program for HE & Training	8
	CIDA	8
	European Union	6
	Rockefeller	5
West Africa	World Bank	14
	CIDA	12
	MacArthur	7
	NUFU	6
	CoL	5

Table 1: Regional Funding Focus by Major Organizations by Region, 2001-2004 (Continued)

Francophone	AUF (Agence Universitaire de la Francophonie	5
All Africa	AAU (Association of African Universities)	6
All Sub-Saharan	UNESCO	5

Source: Kubler 2005:17

The Education for Democracy and Development Initiative (EDDI) in Africa, 1998-2003

The EDDI project provides another important lens through which to examine the important aspects of United States' support for African higher education. Funded by the American government's USAID through the Association Liaison Office (ALO) for University Cooperation in Development, the aim of the project was to "strengthen African educational systems and promote Africa's integration into the world community of *free-market democracies*" (ALO 2003, emphasis added by me). ALO, founded in 1992 by six of America's higher education associations, promotes strategic engagement between the higher education community and the USAID. With representation from the United States Departments of Agriculture, Education, Defense Labor, State and the National Security Council, the EDDI had these long-term objectives among others: (a) increasing knowledge about and access to technology, (b) establishing on going linkages between African institutions and American partners, (c) strengthening African democracies, and (d) preparing countries to be integrated into the world communities.

In Table 2, funding under this project is disclosed. Projects related to science and technology, workforce development, as well as teaching and learning innovation, received the bulk of the funding. Lowest funding was in programs related to Islamic Studies, which entailed sponsoring two academic staff exchanges in terms of visiting professorships. It bears observing that a common denominator for the top three funded areas was computing technology, the linchpin in the move towards globalization, and how it could be integrated in the realm of university education, secondary and elementary education, as well as in worker education programs. Due to this technological bent, the bulk of the collaborating United States' institutions were community colleges in contrast to African partner institutions which were the lead institutions in the home countries. Significantly, most funding went to countries in Central, Eastern, Western and Southern Africa, with South Africa being the most favored recipient nation. Missing is the Arab-speaking Northern Africa.

Table 2: The Education for Democracy & Development Initiative (EDDI) in Africa Funding, 1998-2003

Category	Amount of Funding	Country
AIDS/HIV/Health	$1,829,701.00	South Africa (3 projects) Senegal Uganda
Science-Tech	$3,424,644.00	South Africa (7 projects) Kenya Ethiopia (2 projects) Malawi Nigeria Senegal Ghana
Workforce Dev.	$2,842,139.00	South Africa Uganda Namibia (2 projects) Eritrea Zambia Tanzania
Teaching-Learning	$2,713,226.00	South Africa Ghana Angola Malawi Kenya
Islamic Studies	$202,062.00	Nigeria

Source: Adapted from ALO 2003

To sum up, the key point to note here is that nearly all funding went to programs that sought to link universities directly to the market and to American institutions. Technology is the key to this integration into the global political economy. In this category, I should also add HIV/AIDS which has become a globalized disease due to the global interconnectedness of nations. This is in addition to the global market that exists for any innovation that targets this disease.

Regional disparities in funding distribution are also apparent with South Africa being the most favored aid recipient.

Higher Education Partnerships for Global Development: Knowledge, Cooperation and Results, 2000-2004

Like EDDI, this project was sponsored by USAID and implemented by ALO on behalf of the development agency. The goal of the project was to harness and integrate knowledge to address developmental challenges in Third World countries. Through the emergent collaborative partnerships, knowledge networks pertinent to development would be established in all participating countries including the United States. The key institutions in the generation and transmission of knowledge networks for development would be higher education institutions in both the United States and in the developing world. The networks, notes ALO (2004:111), facilitate joint programming among partner institutions and sharing of resources, alongside facilitation to pursue large funding resources that would not otherwise be available to institutions.

In Table 3, the names of African countries, regions, number of institutions funded along with the total funding received are presented. While no particular reason is provided in the document for this funding distribution, it is clear that, once again, South Africa as a country was the single most favored destination of funding. In terms of region, the leading regions in terms of number of funded countries include South, West and Central Africa, while North Africa had the least number of countries funded. The programs funded included the following: agriculture and agribusiness, community development, democracy and governance, economic growth and trade, environment and natural resources management, AIDS/HIV, population and nutrition, and Internet and communications technology and distance education. The significance of these projects rests on the fact that they are the cardinal areas key to globalization, since they entail applied knowledge networks that seek to connect nations to the global free market economy.

Table 3: Partnership for Global Development Funding, 2000-2004

Country	Region	Institutions Funded	Total Funding
Algeria	North	1	$329,018
Angola	South	1	$ 2,053,066
Benin	West	1	$157,692

Table 3: Partnership for Global Development Funding, 2000-2004 (Continued)

Country	Region	Institutions Funded	Total Funding
Botswana	South	1	$ 747,740
Dem. Rep. of Congo	Central	1	$100,000
Egypt	North	3	$1,571,194
Eritrea	East	1	$562,120
Ethiopia	East	7	$1,680,713
Ghana	West	2	$1,251,618
Kenya	East	3	$2, 471, 827
Lesotho	South	1	$201, 457
Malawi	Central	4	$4,393,885
Mali	West	2	$890,156
Morocco	North	1	$343,086
Mozambique	South	1	$371, 843
Namibia	South	2	$900,330
Nigeria	West	3	$808,430
Rwanda	East	1	$5,234,851
Senegal	West	2	$314,106
South Africa	South	22	$7,240,290
Tanzania	East	4	$877,432
Tunisia	North	2	$200764
Uganda	East	1	$523,141
Zambia	Central	1	$630,168

Source: Adapted from ALO 2004

This is further underscored by the project's perception of higher education, which derives its inspiration from the community college model of the United States. In articulating this vision, the project statement on workforce development affirmed:

In this era of globalization, these institutions [community colleges] bring the same *demand-driven* approach to their partnerships abroad and, in the process, they influence the way *international educators think* about higher education ... An increasing number of developing countries seek to adapt the U.S. community college model to their own higher education contexts to increase access to postsecondary education and produce the educated and well-trained workforce that is needed for sustainable development.... The process of *higher education reform* can be very complicated and can involve a number of legal, institutional, and even political obstacles. Despite these challenges, supporters are optimistic that the strengths of the community college system will become evident and that similar models will emerge around the world (ALO 2004:49, emphasis added by me).

Funding goals have an agenda that supersedes the mere training of workers. It seeks to transform African universities from institutions of critical consciousness into training colleges offering market-oriented programs, the marketization dimension of higher education globalization. Little wonder that junior colleges, the United States' community colleges, have been paired with senior national universities in Africa in this endeavor. Underlying this agenda is the belief that African universities have been a failure, a perception first fronted by the World Bank.

Salient Features of United States Aid to African Higher Education: Implications for Equitable Partnerships

The preceding overview of the trends in American aid to African higher education provides an opportunity to delineate the salient features of this assistance. I have already noted some in the discussion of the trends, while others will be addressed in this section. The overriding goal of this section is to demonstrate that the assistance cannot just be considered as a friendly gesture on the part of the United States. Rather, it is inextricably interwoven with the country's ideological considerations, including globalization and the attendant marketization principles, the new kids on the block higher education transformation, and international relations as well. As I proceed with the analysis, I will speculate on the broader macro level consequences of the current trend in United States' assistance and the micro level impact at the institutional and individual faculty level. The essential features of this analysis are presented graphically in Figure 2.

Globalization Interactive

We have noted that at the macro level the United States has systematically decreased the level of development assistance to education and other sectors since the mid-1990s. Apparently, this is also the same period that tenets of globalization and marketization became vogue after the collapse of Communist Europe. The state has been regarded as an inadequate actor in national development and inferior to the market. The market, it is reasoned, is more efficient in stimulating development by enhancing competition within and across sectors. The state's role should be that of redressing market imperfections such as monopolistic or near monopolistic tendencies. The failure of donor-driven aid to radically transform Africa from abject poverty to wealth and development in the mould of United States' Marshall Plan in Europe after the Second World War has added impetus to this state retreat from international development assistance.

References have been made about how the current assistance reinforces globalization in higher education. Here, I wish to underscore the pressure for a uniform economic system, essentially capitalistic and market-centered as practiced in the Western, industrial nations epitomized by the United States and facilitated by information technology that represents the benchmark of this globalization (Edgell 2003:5). Prime institutional movers in the globalization agenda are the World Bank, the IMF, and now the World Trade Organization (WTO), all with a substantial American influence. The emphasis on information technology in current USAID higher education support has also been noted and highlights the globalization bent of the developmental assistance.

Also, higher education has an additional link to globalization which the development assistance bolsters. As economic competition increased in the western industrial nations in the 1980s, so did the corporate sector pressure governments in the United States, the United Kingdom, and Australia to steer financing of higher education in directions aimed at securing inventions, innovations and product developments in order to make the nations globally competitive. The result has been legislation and policy edicts that emphasize university-industry partnerships, biotechnology and information technology research, and training and contractual relations between public universities and national governments on institutional funding. This may explain the significant emphases on HIV/AIDS, computer technology and workforce development, science and mathematics in most sector-wide funding evident in America's support for African higher education. They mirror the key funding interests pursued by the United States federal government in its contractual relationship with American universities.

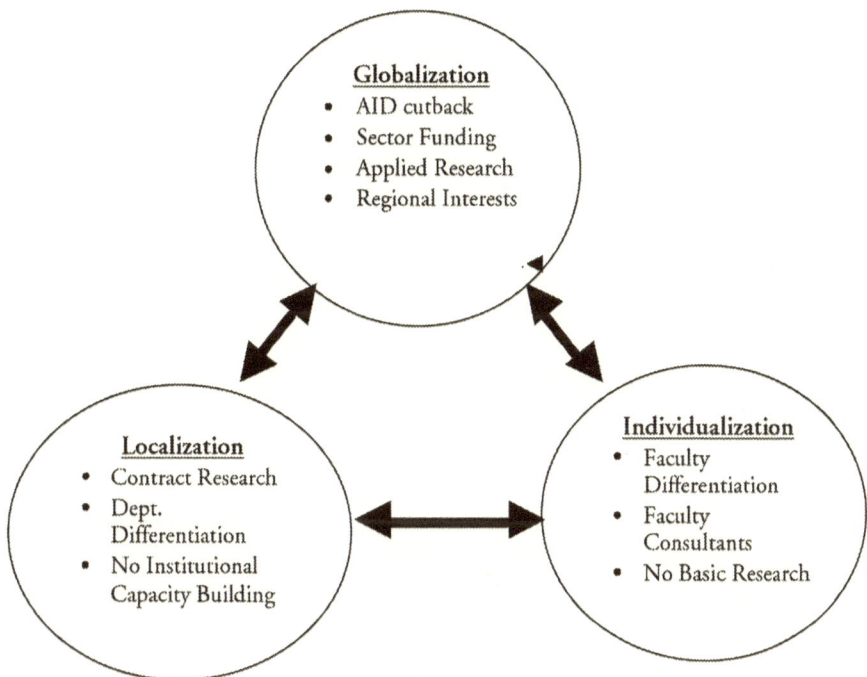

Figure 2: Globalization Interactive

Needless to say that state action is not only analyzed by what it does but also by what it does not do. As evident from the data provided, only minuscule funding is directed towards programs in the humanities and the social sciences. The overemphasis on funding projects with a seemingly immediate market value sends a clear signal that the humanities and the social sciences are not highly regarded. This likely undermines the larger social goals of higher education, such as the promotion of social justice, public criticism, humanistic development, and democratic citizenship, all of which are inculcated through teaching in the humanities and the social sciences.

These developments are in tandem with the criticism of the excessive instrumentality in knowledge production that characterizes the contemporary market university. According to Gibbons et al. (1994), the increasing globalization and marketization of universities has led to the decline in Mode 1 knowledge production—the basic sciences, arts and humanities—which lacks an immediate market value. Mode 2 knowledge—applied, short-term, demand-driven knowledge—has, on the other hand, continued to register tremendous growth, thanks to donor funding and government support. Programs in public health (HIV/AIDS), information technology, computer science, and business are some of the applied disciplines that have been a favorite for United States' support for higher education in Africa. The end result is a potential for undermining long-term, sustained research capacities of universities in all disciplines.

Not only does the sector-based assistance to African higher education by the United States threaten long-term research capacity in non-applied disciplines, but it also leads to disciplinary based faculty differentiation in prestige. As Slaughter and Leslie (1997) have accurately observed, contract monies are crucial for universities not only because they are raised competitively, but also because universities are prestige maximizers. Most faculty teach, most perform community service, but very few win competitive research and contract grants especially the kind that the USAID doles out. These grants are a mark of prestige to the faculty and the departments that win them. At the University of Nairobi in Kenya and Makerere University in Uganda, faculty differentiation based on donor funding to particular departments has been particularly apparent leading to the inability to articulate a common voice about faculty issues. Furthermore, this is likely to buttress the view that some departments are more important than others, thereby creating undesirable distinctions within the universities besides steering them off their crucial mission of teaching and engaging in basic research. A cursory look at the mission statements of departmental Web sites as well as faculty Curriculum Vitae at the University of Nairobi shows that most have the term "consultant" incorporated in their work, reflecting a desire to capture contract donor funding.

The data so far presented have suggested that the United States has some favored destination for assistance in higher education. I have noted the favored status of South Africa, Egypt and the East African region. The rationale for this favored status is beyond the ambit of this chapter. It suffices to state that nations have every right to make funding decisions based on perceived ideological and strategic interests. Indeed, with increasing globalization of the economy and the attendant demands for accountability, wealthy nations have been forced to scale back the amount of development assistance as well as demonstrate that it has practical results. It comes in handy if there are nations in which donor assistance could be linked to strategic and practical problems. South Africa, the youngest independent African nation, has been undergoing rapid transformation from an apartheid state to a democratic one. Egypt, on the other hand, has been the strongest America ally in Arabic-speaking Africa. The downside to this country-specific assistance is that it discourages interregional collaboration between neighboring countries on developmental challenges of mutual concern such as HIV/AIDS.

Underlying the modalities of the assistance, nonetheless, are the questions of priority. What is the priority? Who sets the priority agenda and the implementation modalities? These are important questions that are germane to our understanding of the current practice. In appreciating the extent to which the United States sets the agenda, it is appropriate to quote Pugh and Spear who capture the rationale for control of the agenda and the consequences for equity in partnership in higher education:

> The accountability push on development aid agencies has forced them to seek more control of projects to secure desired measurable results. The more an agency takes control, the less critical thinking and creativity is required by developing country, further diminishing that country's ability to help itself, and undercutting its ownership of the project. There is a shift in helping developing country develop skills by which it can help itself to producing results such as "number of trained teachers" for annual reports to the donor agencies' governments. Or as Ellerman states 'instead of helping people to learn how to fish for themselves, the task managers need to show that they have 'given out a certain number of fish' or even better they have helped set up a 'fish distribution system' (2005:46).

The main point worth noting here is the insistence on market-oriented accountability measures to evaluate results of assistance. Immediate short-term accountability measures are in tandem with goals of the global political economy for higher education systems. Significant also is omission of long-term institutional capacity building in terms of staff development which may not exhibit immediate measurable results, albeit crucial for university functioning. It is not easy to ascertain whether the local African institutions that received project funding were the actual initiators of the programs, since this is not explicitly stated. What is indisputable, however, is that the programs fall within the funding priority of the United States.

The problem of agenda setting is also seen in the United States government's Millennium Challenge Account (MCA), a commitment by the American government to raise its grant aid by a factor of 50% over the next three years and will lead to a $5 billion annual increase over current foreign aid levels. MCA is America's contribution to the Millennium Development Goals (MDG) which has become the architecture for international development assistance. Common to both MDG and MCA is their vision of how aid should work in developing countries, as well as the priorities that should form the core of funding. Informing the philosophy guiding MCA is the belief that international aid works well in an environment characterized by "fiscal balance, low inflation, openness to international markets, intelligent property rights, and strong institutions with a history of low corruption" (Heyneman 2005:113). That openness to international market is a condition for accessing MCA funding underscores the globalization intent of the assistance program. King (2004) rightly posits that MDG is owned by northern industrial states that also set the target goals to be achieved in the millennium. The MDG is minimalist in its approach to development, argues King, with target goals in education being universal basic education and gender equity in basic in education as opposed to a comprehensive strategy of educational growth and development.

The Road Less Traveled: Proposals for Equitable Partnership in Higher Education

How can partnership between African higher education and an American policy be equitable? Subsumed in this question is a problematic proposition, since the American financial clout necessarily means an unequal power relationship between the two actors. Granted that he who pays the piper necessarily calls the tune, it may be difficult to envisage a situation in which African governments and institutions will enjoy great leeway in determining how resources from United States will be utilized for higher education. Even as accountability demands escalate in donor home countries, including the United States and as tenets of globalization and attendant marketization wiggle their way through higher education, there exist possibilities for soft landing that would provide opportunities for equal partnership between the United States and African higher education. The following are some suggestions.

Embryonic Projects Strategy

Setting the funding agenda at the macro level is, as I have argued, a task overwhelmingly at the hands of the donor countries. This leaves little voice for the receiving countries. One way of ensuring local participation in determining the funding agenda besides project ownership is through what is known as embryonic project funding. The process involves determining what the institutions are doing and what they need. This is followed by a consideration of how funding will contribute to the productive efforts.

This may look rather simple; but when examined critically, it discourages the donor agency from initiating projects. Donors look for changes taking place at the institutions and provide development incentives. Such projects address a felt need that universities are trying to address and are locally owned. Ellerman (2004) has referred to this type of assistance as "just-in-time aid." Both the donor and the aid recipient institution benefit from the mutuality of objectives—aid is dispensed, but rooted in goals originating at the institutional level.

This approach could be beneficial in the sector-wide funding approach that USAID has adopted for university support. As already indicated, the sectors being funded are those that have been deemed strategic by Washington and not necessarily by African institutions. Indeed, it begs the question whether it is realistic to identify a narrow set of focus areas as being the most vital to direct donor assistance in a continent as diverse as Africa with a multiplicity of developmental challenges. Embryonic funding would open additional sectors which local academics have judged to be critical and worthy of funding as a way to combat poverty. There is no doubt that embryonic project funding approach entails considerable outlay in manpower and man hours by the donor, but it is a minimal price to pay for ensuring equity in partnership. This strategy shifts funding from globalization to glocalization; global funds are used as a catalyst for development prioritized by local African institutions.

Continental and Regional Research Organizations (CARRO) Support Strategy

Supporting Continental and Regional Research Organizations (CARRO) which have active links with African higher educational institutions provides a good strategy for the United States to engage the continent's universities on the basis of a relatively equal partnership. Through these efforts, the United States can play a critical role in institutional revitalization, maintenance of local research and developing research capacity. In addition, these African-founded and African-based organizations provide a suitable buffer that mediates the effects of globalization tendencies in African universities. An examination of the most prominent of these bodies is important in demonstrating the role of these organizations in strengthening African universities and the opportunities that abound for collaboration with the United States.

The Council for the Development of Social Science Research in Africa (CODESRIA) has been the leading organization in the development of social science research in Africa. As a continent-wide body, its programs and activities permeate the breadth and width of Africa's universities. With donor support from public and private agencies in the Nordic countries, Europe and Canada, CODESRIA has developed the following programs: Multinational Working Groups (NWG), National Working Groups (NWG), Small Grants Programs for writing Theses and Dissertations, and Training Institutes. These diverse activities have enabled universities build not only their research capacities but also develop staff and pioneer appropriate research methodologies that are germane to the African context. United States collaboration with CODESRIA could go a long way in strengthening research in the social sciences and the humanities which received only a modicum of financial support in the current dispensation.

The Association of African Universities (AAU) is another continent-wide body that has played a key role in the development and management of African universities. AAU has also been instrumental in supporting research in the higher education crisis in the continent. Founded in 1967 following the UNESCO-sponsored conference on higher education in Africa in 1962 held in Antananarivo, Madagascar, its membership today comprises of African universities, both public and private. With an initial membership of 34 institutions, its membership today consists of around 199 institutions, cutting across language and other divisions.

AAU supports institutional capacity building in two important areas. First, with Dutch and Swedish financial support, it has established the Study Program on Higher Education Management in Africa. The aim of this program is to develop the capacity to undertake indigenous research on issues confronting higher education management in Africa and seek local solutions to the problems, thereby enhancing African higher education policymaking. Through this scheme, research grants have been awarded in areas as diverse as information and data gathering, resource mobilization, higher education and work, higher education cost and financing, higher education access, graduate and employer survey, and privatization of higher education. Second, AAU also supports the development of general research that seeks to strengthen the linkages between higher education institutions and the society. These include Regional Cooperation in Graduate Training and Database of African Theses and Dissertations (DATAD); African Universities Responding to HIV/AIDS, Coordination of Internet Communications Technology Initiatives, and Developing Quality Assurance Systems.

American support for AAU would go a long way in enhancing institutional capacity building as it relates to institutional governance and management. This is critical, since African universities are undergoing radical transformations as state funding declines, demand increases and private universities begin to define the continent's higher education landscape. African-based training and reflection on policies with American support provides a better option for strengthening institutional capacity building than overseas training. Institutional governance and management blend well with United States' commitment to democratic governance in Africa. Indeed, there is no better place to embark upon training in democratic principles than in African institutions of higher learning.

Two regional organizations are also worth mentioning as possible partners with which the United States' government could collaborate. The Organization of Social Science Research in Eastern and Southern Africa (OSSREA) is a membership-based organization dedicated to the development of social science research in Eastern and Southern Africa. With donor support from Ford Foundation, Swedish International Development Agency (SIDA), Norwegian Agency for Development Cooperation (NORAD), the Netherlands Ministry of Foreign Affairs and Canada's International Development Research Center (IDRC), OSSREA has mounted activities in publishing, training workshops, conferences, competitive research grants and sabbatical programs for senior scholars in universities. Additional resources from the United States would strengthen the capacity of OSSREA to provide post-doctoral training and sabbatical opportunities within African universities. This would contribute immensely to local institutional capacity building.

The African Regional Postgraduate Program in Insect Science (ARPPIS) is a 31-university membership organization dedicated to training insect scientists at masters and doctoral levels. Funded by European government agencies and the United Nations Food and Agriculture Organization (FAO) among others, the program has three sub-regional centers, Eastern, Southern and Western Africa. ARPPIS remains one of the most successful African-initiated scientific research programs. American support could go a long way in providing additional scholarships for doctoral studies for those who will take academic leadership positions in African universities.

To sum up, I have argued that continental and regional organizations provide a buffer through which the United States' agenda could be meshed with that of African universities to come up with an accommodative position that would allow for equity in higher educational partnership. In addition, it would put the goals of research development and institutional capacity building within African educational leaders. Finally, it would enhance academic activities in the humanities and the social sciences through additional resources from the United States which have been on the decline.

Counter-penetration Strategy

In view of the diminished Fulbright opportunities for African scholars to travel to the United States on academic exchange, a case can be made for the United States to consider supporting what Mazrui (1992) has christened as "the therapy of counter-penetration." While financially supporting African-based initiatives as discussed above is a welcomed development, there is a need to ensure that African scholars are not excessively isolated and disengaged from the rest of the global academic community. A two-pronged approach is envisaged in this counter-penetration strategy which would seek to engage African academics and their American counterparts through academic exchanges.

The first would be for the United States to leverage American dollars from the public-funded Africa-America Institute to support academic visits by African scholars who could take part in teaching and joint collaborative work with their American counterparts. Using African-based academics to team-teach courses on African culture, geography, economics and political systems among other African disciplines would add a refreshing perspective than when it is taught by a non-African. In addition, it would be a powerful weapon to fight prejudices against Africa that have materialized overtime due to negative media coverage.

Besides supporting African scholars to visit the United States, America could support initiatives that seek to strengthen bonds between Africans and African Americans. Both groups have a common heritage, but nurturing this brotherhood and sisterhood bond has always been a victim of poverty. Africa in general and its higher education institutions in particular have been in financial dire straits just as the historically black colleges and universities in the United States. Opportunities exist for student and staff exchanges between these institutions. African Americans could attend college in African universities and vice versa. By providing financial and programming resources that could strengthen academic bonds between these institutions, the United States will make a strong statement about its commitment to equity in partnership in higher education.

Finally, support for staff exchanges needs to go beyond African Americans and also support other Americans who would seek to undertake teaching and research assignments in collaboration with their African counterparts. Although some of this is in progress, thanks to the Fulbright program, the number remains miniscule, and there is potential for increasing the level of cooperation as well as the areas of academic focus.

9

Transnational Scams

James T. Gire

Introduction

Globalization, aided and sustained by advances in technology, especially information technology, has been welcomed as a very positive phenomenon that is presumed to be responsible for the unparalleled pace and level of economic development for most of the world. Unfortunately, globalization has also been credited with the expanded scope and magnitude of transnational crime, both by organized criminal groups and opportunistic, freelance criminals. The combined profits from transnational criminal activities are estimated to be more than one trillion dollars annually (Center for Strategic and International Studies 2004). Tragically, the benefits of globalization seem to have eluded Africa even as it is increasingly identified with the criminal side of transnational crime, which has expanded dramatically in Africa, especially West Africa (Williams 2004), particularly with regard to drug trafficking, people-trafficking and fraud. The focus of this chapter, however, is limited to fraud, especially the advance-fee fraud. The main aim of this chapter is to briefly describe the problem of transnational scams and how this is damaging to both the West, especially the United States, and Africa. The chapter examines how the problem has been conceptualized and addressed from the Western viewpoint that essentially has ignored both the origins of the problem and how it is viewed from the African perspective. The chapter concludes by proposing an integrationist solution that, if adopted by the main stakeholders, is more likely to reduce the problem.

According to the United Nations Office on Drugs and Crime (UNODC) (2005), authorities in the United States estimated that in the mid-1990s, Nigerians were responsible for at least 58 per cent of fraudulent insurance claims and, that overall, Nigerian fraudsters accounted for US $20-26 billion worth of fraud a year in the United States alone. Specifically, the same report suggests that the

Nigerian advance-fee fraud named "419" corresponding to Section 419 of the Nigerian Criminal Code scams victims of several hundred million dollars a year. The advance-fee fraud typically involves "attempts to obtain pre-payment for goods or services that do not actually exist or which the proposer does not actually intend to deliver" (UNDOC 2005:24).

I need to state at the outset that many people in different countries outside Africa engage in advance-fee fraud. In the same vein, citizens of other African countries beside Nigeria also participate in this type of fraud. A disproportionate number of cases that have been brought to the fore, however, have involved Nigerian citizens operating either within Nigeria or in other countries. In fact, some have suggested that even the cases of advance-fee fraud reported in other African nations such as Ghana, Sierra Leone, and South Africa are either engaged in by Nigerians directly or by Nigerians in consort with local collaborators.

As early as 1996, Jonathan Winer, the then Assistant Secretary for International Narcotics and Law Enforcement Affairs, indicated the following in a statement before the Subcommittee on Africa of the House International Relations Committee:

> Our law enforcement agencies attest that Nigerian criminal enterprises are organized and active in at least 60 countries around the world. They are adaptable, polycrime organizations. They launder money in Hong Kong, buy cocaine in the Andes, run prostitution and gambling rings in Spain and Italy, and corrupt legitimate business in Great Britain with their financial crimes. Nigerian drug trafficking rings are notorious. The presence today of hundreds of convicted Nigerian traffickers in Indian, Pakistani, Thai, Turkish, and other international prisons is indicative of the international reach of the Nigerian crime rings. Nigerian trafficking organizations have continued to evolve. Where once they limited themselves top to bottom to members of ethnic-based clans, they have come to recognize that international law enforcement targets Nigerian nationals. Accordingly, Nigerian trafficking organizations today favor surrogate couriers, especially young women. In the area of white collar crime, the U.S. Secret Service conservatively estimates that Nigerian advance free fraud letter scams cost Americans $250 million a year" (1996:2).

In a similar vein, Alemika (2004) indicated that 122 out of 138 countries represented at an Interpol meeting in 2003 complained about Nigerian involvement in financial fraud in their countries. Consequently, Nigeria will be used more or less as a case study in this chapter.

The picture painted above illustrates that the problem of transnational scams is indeed serious and has a lot of implications for Africa, especially as it relates to its desires for attracting investment from the international community, especially in the Western world. In fact, Waziri (2005) a retired Assistant Inspector General of Police (AIG) of the Nigerian Police Force and the first head of Nigeria's Special Fraud Unit (SFU) that was created specifically to tackle this problem, considers the problem of transnational scams as a national security problem, since it has negative effects on Nigeria's economy and international image. This view is shared by Howard Jeter, the former United States Ambassador to Nigeria who suggested that the "419" fraud not only hurts Nigeria's image, but it also hinders potential foreign investment and trade. Because of these fraudsters, legitimate Nigerian businessmen attempting to establish trade links with the United States and the European Union countries or who strive to solicit foreign investments are greeted too often with negative reactions based on suspicions of the "419" fraud schemes (Crossroads 2001).

The Typical Response to Advance Fee Fraud from the U.S. and the West

Before delving into the typical response from the West, it is imperative to examine an example of this scam to determine whether these responses are deemed the most appropriate, given the context of the scam. Here is an example of one such scam, probably millions of which have been sent across different locations in the world. In fact, I have personally received many of these (and did get one just on October 31, 2006), as I am sure many among the readers also have. This is unedited:

STRICTLY CONFIDENTIAL

Engr. Amos Okoti   Tel 234-1-4923287
ATTN: THE PRESIDENT   Fax: 234-1-4922341
Lagos—Nigeria
Sir,

REQUEST FOR URGENT BUSINESS RELATIONSHIP

My colleague and I, have after some due deliberations finally decided to send forth to you this proposal.

We succeeded in procuring safely, the sum of thirty four million five hundred thousand U.S. Dollars (US$34.5) which has been laying a suspense account with Central Bank of Nigeria. This amount of money resulted from an already executed contract for and on behalf of my Ministry which we over-invoiced to the tune of US$34.5.00 this was done deliberately, it was a deal between me and my colleagues.

As you may rightly want to know my colleagues and I are top officials of the Nigerian national Petroleum Corporation (NNPC) and in cooperation with our colleagues who are also officials of the Federal Ministry of Finance (FMF) and Central Bank of Nigeria (CBN) will use our position to influence and authenticate the payment, as we have craftily manipulated and secured the approval of this payment.

At this juncture it has become imperative that we present an international business outfit to represent the contractors and as such can now apply and subsequently claim the amount in question. In this regards, contract with you has become almost indispensable. You will however, be required to furnish us these documented informations:

1.   A copy of your company's letter headed papers stamoed and signed underneath.

2.   A copy of your company's proforma Invoice, stamped and signed underneath.

3.   Your banker's address. Telephone, Fax and Telex numbers.

Your private phone number and fax numbers for confidentiality and easy communication the documents/information should be sent to me through fax immediately. These will enable us apply for payment of the fund from concerned government agencies.

SHARES

For providing the account into which the money shall be remitted, you will be entitled to 30% of the money 60% will be for me and my partners while 10% has been mapped out of the total sum as reimbursable fund to cover expenses that may be incurred in the course of transacting this business.

For further inquiries, you can reach me by this Tel/Fax numbers above needless to remind you that this is not exactly an open business contact. Therefore discussion on this issue are highly limited, please adhere strictly to this as we are still in service of government.

NB: Alternatively you can call my attention, so that I will Fax to you the text which you will type in your invoice and letter head papers and should stamped and sign then you send them to me by fax, for approvals and payment of this sum.

Thanks for your cooperation.

Yours sincerely,

ENGR. AMOS OKOTI

The preceding scam letter is representative of the schemes proposed in a majority of these "419" letters. There is a common saying that it is very difficult to cheat an honest man. There is no question that the intent in this letter involves a solicitation to defraud: in this case, government agencies of a foreign government. The person's ("victim's") assistance is solicited to defraud another government. Coomassie, the former Inspector General of Police, the overall head of the Nigerian Police Force, stated that advance-fee fraud usually involves "a conspiracy between some dubious Nigerians and gullible foreigners to transfer illegally, abroad, non-exiting funds" (1994:1). Similarly, responding as to whether foreigners so affected are victims or collaborators, the former Director of Foreign Operations of the CBN, Alhaji Rasheed, indicated that they were clearly would-be co-conspirators when he stated the following: "So far, there has been no case of an innocent victim who participated in the scam. The various 'business proposals' *ab initio* manifest fraudulent intentions, which should ordinarily put any respectable corporation or individual on enquiry" (1997:8).

The predominant response from the United States and other Western nations, however, is to regard the would-be co-conspirators as victims. Drastic measures are taken or contemplated, but none of them are aimed at addressing the fundamental reasons for why these crimes are committed, nor the United States or other Western component in the fraud. The following statement by Winer in the report to the Subcommittee on Africa captures much of the overall approach and refers to a plan that has:

> … its basic objectives reflect long-held U.S. law enforcement goals in Nigeria. These include identifying those Nigerian organized crime activities that threaten U.S. national security, and those of its citizens; strengthening U.S. law enforcement capabilities and activities against Nigerian organized crime; fostering change in Nigerian political and legal institutions in order to decrease the threat posed by Nigerian organized crime and to protect Americans who do business with or visit Nigeria; dismantling Nigerian-controlled drug trafficking and criminal networks around the world; increasing public awareness of the threat posed by Nigerian organized crime; and creating regional capabilities to combat Nigerian organized crime in affected areas of the world.

In addition to going after Nigerian heroin and cocaine trafficking, we are targeting Nigerian financial crimes like 419 frauds, insurance frauds, credit card frauds, and money laundering; Nigerian counterfeiting and false documents; trafficking in persons, including alien smuggling and prostitution, and contraband; and Nigerian corruption. Efforts against these crimes will require not only cooperation among many different parts of the U.S. Government, but with other governments, with the private sector, and ultimately, with the Nigerian Government and people" (1996:3-4).

Other measures center on working to improve Nigerian law enforcement efforts, upgrade Nigerian crime and extradition legislation, especially as it applies to financial crimes, and public information programs to educate American citizens and companies on how to recognize and avoid Nigerian scam operations. It is instructive that none of these measures aims at discouraging or prosecuting their citizens who are intent on colluding to defraud other nations. Rather, the tendency is to give a lukewarm acknowledgement of some of the efforts undertaken by the Nigerian government by way of new legislation and arrest of the fraud perpetrators at the Nigerian side of the fence and to indicate that such efforts are not enough. Owing perhaps to this unidimensional focus, and the fact that it fails to attack the root causes of the proliferation of these scams, the issue has been perceived differently by some citizens in Nigeria and non-Western settings.

An Alternative and More Comprehensive View of Transnational Scams

I need to state at the outset that you will find few persons who view transnational scams in a positive light. Most Nigerians and other Africans detest the practice and are aware of how the proliferation of scams has dented the image of their countries and the developmental consequences associated with these financial crimes. They are frustrated, however, at the seeming lack of acknowledgement by the United States and the European Union countries in recognizing the culpabilities of their citizens in these crimes and for not taking stern measures on their citizens that they require of Nigeria and other African nations. This seeming impotence is viewed as blatant examples of double standards, or at best sour grapes. The contention among many honest citizens in Africa is that these financial crimes are magnified only because, for a change, the Western would-be fraudsters have been outsmarted by their Nigerian or African partners in crime. I had been interested in this dimension before, but what got me thinking in terms of writing about it was a song that I heard by accident. I was visiting a colleague at a university in Nigeria, when, as a way of entertainment, he played a musical VCD that contained a song entitled "I go Chop your Dollar" by Nkem Owoh. This song represents a strong example of the point made here, so I have duplicated it below with an attempt at interpretation in parenthesis since the song is in Pidgin English.

I Go Chop Your Dollar

> *I don suffer no be small (I have suffered a lot)*
> *Upon say I get sense (Since I have sense/intelligence)*
> *Poverty no good at all (Poverty is not good)*
> *Na im make I join this business (that's why I joined this business)*
> *419 no be thief (419 is not theft)*
> *It's just a game everybody dey play am (it's a game that everybody plays)*
> *If anybody fall mugu, ah my brother I chop am (if anyone is that foolish, my brother I will "eat it")*
>
> *CHORUS*
>
> *National Airport na me get am (I own the national airport)*
> *National Stadium na me build am (I built the national stadium)*
> *President na my sister brother (The president is my sister's brother)*
> *You be the mugu, I be the master (You are the fool, I am the master)*
> *Onyinbo man I go chop your dollar (White man I will "eat" your dollar)*
> *I go take your money disappear (I will take your money and disappear)*
> *419 is just a game; you are the loser I am the winner (this is self-explanatory)*
>
> *The refinery na me get am (I own the refinery)*
> *The contract na you I go give (I will give you the contract)*
> *But you go pay me small money make I give you (You have to give me a little money so that I can give you)*
> *You be the mugu, I be the master (You are the fool, I am the master)*
> *When Oyinbo man play wayo (When a white man plays tricks)*
> *E go say na new style (He will say it's a new style)*
> *When country man do im own (But when countryman does his own)*
> *Dem greedy (they are greedy)*

I say dem greedy (I say they are greedy)
I don see dem tire (I am tired of seeing them)
That's why dem enter my trap (that's why they get into my trap)
I dey show dem fire (I will show them fire (hell?)).

The clear message from this song is that the 419 scams were the result of extreme hardship. The notion here is that these crimes were not common place when things were relatively good for a majority of Nigerians. It was the discomfort of extreme hardship that made some of these people to get these plans. Moreover, the scams look clearly fraudulent even for the most casual observer. It is the consumption with greed that makes people get lured by most of these obviously flaky scenarios. Thus, the reference to "victims" as fools. Another factor, and one I already alluded to earlier, is the point that complaints coming out of the United States and other Western nations about these scams are sour grapes arising from the realization that, for a change, the "White man" is at the losing end. Thus, the song suggests that when a White person does this kind of scheme, it is viewed as a new plan. However, when a Black person succeeds, the Black person is frowned upon. Above all, it captures the notion that a majority of people who have succumbed to these frauds are victims of greed.

It is important to subject these main assertions to greater scrutiny to determine if there is any basis to these claims. Let me first begin with the notion of changing economic fortunes as contributors to the proliferation of transnational scams in Nigeria. In tracing the historical determinants of "419"-type scams, Waziri (2005) indicated that even though fraud had long existed in Nigeria, it was after the oil boom that was followed by a crash due to falling oil prices throughout much of the 1980s and 1990s that fraudulent crime emerged as a major problem. In order to obtain loans from international agencies such as the International Monetary Fund (IMF) and the World Bank, Nigeria had to implement crushing structural adjustment programs (SAP). Notable among these were mass retrenchments of civil servants and people working in government corporations, loss of access to health care, housing and other amenities hitherto enjoyed by these people, and alienation. In addition, the suddenly dire condition by people who had experienced an acceptable quality of life, coupled with the absence of jobs for young people graduating from tertiary institutions affected the youth who no longer had an assurance that a university degree would guarantee them a decent job. Consequently, a good number of these people resorted to illegal activities, notably advance-fee fraud.

The other issue relates to why people easily succumbed to these scams that ought to look very obviously fake to a prospective "victim." The answer lies in previous successes of foreign citizens who had successfully connived with some Nigerians in government to defraud the Nigerian government and people of large sums of money. As Alemika indicated:

> "The common element in these was that through collusion between government officials and foreign businesses, imported goods were over-invoiced, resulting in the transfer of huge resources from the country without the supply of goods and services. The West became used to money being stolen into foreign countries with the collusion of foreigners. This was the precursor to the current financial scam and the reasons why western conspirators actually believed the financial scam perpetrators ... The process of liberalization also reduced the foreign exchange controls and led to the deregulation of financial and banking services, which may have contributed to the crime" (2004:7).

The interesting point made by this quote is that the current vulnerability to financial scams stems from earlier successes by mainly citizens of the United States and European Union countries in colluding with a few corrupt officials to defraud the Nigerian government of billions of dollars. At the time, however, there was no concern, let alone the vigor to arrest and prosecute citizens of these Western nations who had participated in these scams. It was as if the problem did not even exist. It is only now when the co-conspirators who have lost out in these scams are from the West that financial scams have been assigned the top priority billing that they currently enjoy. A common question that is asked by many Americans is the following: "Why do they hate us?" The answer appears to be double standards. In a discussion over the menace of "419" scams recently with a colleague from Africa, he indicated that while he was against the criminal element in the scams, he was irritated with the label of victim tagged on the co-conspirators in these scams. He illustrated his point with the following example: If an African were to be approached by a United States citizen about some terrorists that were desperately looking for weapons of mass destruction and that he had (the United States citizen) access to it but needed some money to move it in order to obtain the premium price that the terrorists were willing to pay, would he do so? Suppose further that there really were no weapons and that the said terrorists did not actually exist, but instead the whole plot was used to scam money from the African, a scenario very much along the lines of the scams currently under discussion, what would be the consequence? Suppose then that the African paid this money upfront only to realize that he had been scammed by the American and, thus, took his case to United States authorities, what would happen? How did I think the United States authorities would view the African "victim?" Even as I was considering the scenario, he went forth to give me the answer. In his view, he believed that the African would be arrested, probably as an enemy combatant, or at best charged with a conspiracy to commit a terrorist act. He suggested that he would not view such an action as unreasonable, and then asked: "Why can't the United States do the same with these would-be fraudsters who lose out in what they believed to have been a criminal act?"

The perception of double standards is reflected in another area where the West is viewed as a haven for Africa's stolen wealth. Just recently, in a speech at the opening ceremony of the Extractive Industries Transparency Initiative (EITI) in Oslo, Norway, on October 16, 2006, the President of the World Bank, Paul Wolfowitz, declared that Nigeria had lost about $300 billion of oil wealth to corruption over the past four decades. Almost all this money has been siphoned and hidden in Western financial institutions. Many Africans are of the view that various government agencies in the West know the identities of the people who have stolen the monies in question and where the money has been stashed. They are, however, unwilling to share these data with the nations from where this wealth has been stolen with the view to returning the stolen wealth to the affected countries. Nor have any actions been taken against the financial institutions that are the custodians of the stolen money, even when the transactions in question ought to have aroused the suspicions of even the most naïve person as to legitimacy of the money. The situation has not changed even in the current modifications in the documentation and reporting of finances brought about by the recent United States declaration of the global war on terror in which stringent laws calling for a close monitoring of financial transactions have been enacted. Intentionally or not, the disparity in determining the financial transactions that would be subjected to scrutiny and those to which to give a blind eye have accentuated the feeling of resentment by many Africans. It has also led to the current indifference or benign support among non-Westerners to the plight of Westerners who, for a change, are at the receiving end of transnational scams.

An Integrationist Approach to Tackling the Problem of Transnational Scams

As indicated in the preceding discussion, transnational scams have become a global problem involving billions of dollars a year and have as victims individuals and governments. There is, thus, an urgent need to find solutions to this growing problem. Thus far, only the law enforcement approach has been used; and, even then, it does not appear to be evenly applied. Sticking to an exclusively law enforcement strategy, however, is tantamount to treating the symptoms of a disease without regard to the underlying causes. One major strategy that is very popular involves public enlightenment. This approach has been used widely by American agencies and those of other nations almost to the point of declaring every Nigerian a potential fraudster. Public awareness, however, can only go so far. In fact, as Waziri (2005) has indicated, the Central Bank of Nigeria has placed numerous advertisements in newspapers and other outlets in different languages and in different countries warning foreigners about the scam letters fraudsters. Unfortunately, many foreigners continue to fall prey to the fraudsters and report to authorities mostly only after they have already been scammed.

From the law enforcement perspective, the Nigerian government has enacted and expanded on laws dealing with various facets of transnational scams. There also have been increases in the enforcement as evident from the growing number of those arrested and prosecuted. Nonetheless, the problem persists, as I indicated that I received another of such letters only a few days ago. Waziri (2005) has also suggested an amendment to the current Nigerian law on advance-fee fraud to include the prosecution of foreigners currently deemed victims on charges of conspiracy to defraud or engage in an illegal activity. This is an interesting suggestion and may be more effective than the current drive to provide warnings about the scams. It may also have the effect of removing the current argument against double standards and potentially attract more cooperation from the general public.

Another approach involves attacking some of the root causes of the scams by way of improving opportunities for educated people who would have alternatives for upward mobility. Even though those who engage in these scams have varying backgrounds, an emerging profile is instructive. Because these people now use E-mail and other aspects of information technology, it is obvious that they are well educated enough to perform these electronic transactions in a manner that would not be easily traceable. It also demonstrates that they have enough knowledge of international government and business practices to present credible enough scenarios to attract the greedy and gullible. They are also known to work with lawyers, accountants and sometimes security agencies that they pay for their services. With these skill levels, these individuals can, when provided an enabling economic environment, legitimately make a good living. In addition to providing resources to security and law enforcement agencies in Nigeria and elsewhere in Africa to tackle transnational scams, as the United States and European Union countries currently do, they should also provide financial and technological inducements to increase the opportunities for citizens of these countries. The

additional variables proposed would probably not curb international scams completely, but they would hopefully result in a meaningful reduction of the problem
and should certainly be more effective than the prevailing strategies.

There appears to be a similar policy along these lines with respect to the
attempt to control the cultivation of opium by Afghan farmers. Afghanistan is by
far the largest producer of opium in the world, accounting for 92% of the world's
supply in 2006 (MacKenzie, Amani & Ibrahimi 2006). Not surprisingly, opium
accounts for 52% of Afghanistan's gross domestic product (GDP) (UNODC
2005). Thus, attempts to eradicate opium production without a substitute source
of income threaten to place a heavy burden on an already economically impover-
ished population. A popular option among several that are in various stages of
implementation, and one preferred by some scholars, non-governmental organizations, as well as the international community is the so-called "smart" counter-
narcotics strategy. This approach encompasses both law enforcement action
against opium trade and the substitution of other cash crops for opium poppies
and the creation of new economic activities (Drug War Chronicle 2007). A mod-
ification of this strategy should be applied in the area of transnational scams,
whereby law enforcement approaches will be combined with alternative legal economic options by way of job training programs and small loans to computer literate and enterprising young people in Africa. This alternative approach will be
slow and its results will become evident only in the long-term, but it certainly is
worth a try.

10

Natural Resource Conservation

Abdul Karim Bangura [1]

Introduction

In his chapter titled "A Natural Resource Conservation Initiative for Africa" (in Kansteiner III and Morrison 2004), Nicholas Lapham identifies three areas for enhanced United States engagement and leadership in natural resource conservation in Africa and offers six recommendations for tackling the issues. The three areas are: (1) trans-boundary natural resource conservation, (2) governance of natural resources, and (3) unsustainable commercial wildlife exploitation. The six recommendations include the United States (1) scaling up and sustaining diplomatic, technical and financial assistance aimed at conserving major trans-boundary ecosystems; (2) prioritizing improved natural resource management as a major component in promoting good governance; (3) expanding and better coordination of government activities to deal with the African bush-meat situation; (4) developing stronger programs and incentives to more effectively engage the American diplomatic corps in Africa on natural resource conservation issues; (5) restoring and expanding technical assistance programs that build the capacity of African practitioners and political leaders in natural resource conservation; and (6) increasing American investment in African parks and protected areas. While Lapham's diagnosis of the problem and suggested medicine for curing it are quite sound, the shortcoming is not one of commission, but one of omission.

First, Lapham does not address a significant question: i.e. in light of the current United States' record on environmental matters, does it command the moral

---

1. The author draws greatly from his notes taken during courses dealing with environmental issues while a student at Stockholms Universitet in Sweden and the works of Anders Forsse, Hans Blix, Calestous Juma, Sven Bergström, Varis Bokalders, Anders Rapp, Lasse Berg, Rolf Edberg, Lars Sundgren, and Marianne Enge through the Swedish International Development Authority.

authority to get African governments to adhere to good environmental practices? Second, a corollary to the first omission, Lapham focuses solely on the actions of Africans for their environmental problems and ignores those by the United States and other industrialized countries. For example, Lapham points out the corruption of African leaders, but he does not mention the fact that most of the stolen money ends up in Western banks, thereby perpetuating the corruption. Third, Lapham pays greater attention to those areas that are geared more towards United States' interests. This chapter deals with these omissions and discusses other issues that will provide ideas for an equitable partnership between Africa and the United States in the area of natural resource conservation.

America's Moral Credibility as Champion of Conservation

The assertion by Lapham that the "United States has a distinct comparative advantage—above and beyond Europe, Japan, and other industrialized countries—in helping Africa address conservation concerns" (2004:88) is hardly a matter of dispute. Whether the United States has the moral credibility to get African governments to adhere to good environmental practices is another matter. This is in light of the assault by the Republican-controlled Congress and White House on environmentally protected areas in the United States, the current George W. Bush administration's continued refusal to even entertain the idea that global warming is possible, and the United States being one of only two countries in the world (the other country being Australia) that have failed to ratify the Kyoto Protocol. (The Kyoto Protocol is an agreement made under the United Nations Framework Convention on Climatic Change—UNFCCC. Countries that ratify this protocol commit to reduce their emissions of carbon dioxide and five other greenhouse gases, or engage in emissions trading if they maintain or increase emissions of these gases.)

The United States in recent years has been reneging on its historical role as a leader in environmental regulation. At the same time, the European Union, motivated by political integration, has enacted many, new environmental legislation and taken a leadership role in promoting global environmental sustainability. While European and American policies may seem somewhat similar in terms of domestic regulation, they are clearly diverging in the current environmental concerns, which include such global problems as climate change, international trade, and sustainable development (Vig and Faure 2004).

The Law of Change

Humans, like all other animals, and all plants, influence their environment, and they are in turn influenced by it. Mutual influence is part of life itself, a fundamental force behind development, through millions of years, of the many living things on our planet. We can envision this force as a law of nature: i.e. the law of change.

The concept *ecological balance* is often employed to simplify matters. The term implies a situation where the law of change works in various directions in a system of animals and plants, and that the various forces countervail in order to stabilize the system as a whole. But in a broader perspective, and in the long run, it makes no sense to speak about equilibrium, as the law of change is omnipresent. It works sometimes incrementally, with course corrections, sometimes by leaps and bounds, as ancient species and ways of life give way to the new.

A very long time ago, Africans, like other humans, were hunters, gatherers and fishermen. They needed large tracts of land. If the population density became too high, starvation or ethnic war, or both, were the inexorable result. Had these hunters, gatherers and fishermen achieved equilibrium with their environment? At any rate, they appear to have been unable to bring about great or rapid change. Arms and tools were slowly improved upon, and Early Human and Early Dog found it to be to their mutual advantage to extend their cooperation to each other's clans. But this did not represent the law of change in more than its snail's pace version.

Then, a few thousand years ago, there was the great leap forward ushered in Africa in that the art of systematic growing of useful plants was developed instead of just collecting seeds and fruits in their natural habitats. In one stroke, Homo sapiens developed much improved means of guiding their destinies. The mechanism of collaboration could be utilized more efficiently, the physiological capacity of the brain could be used for planning, storing, foresight and prediction in a manner vastly different from what had been possible when all one could do was to run after wild quadrupeds in the wild forest. Humans were coming seriously to the fore, beginning to influence their environment in a way that was very different than ever before—it began very slowly at first, but then more rapidly, to fill the earth.

The influence of agricultural human on nature was and is by no means destructive as a rule. Indeed, the classical farming land constitutes a better and more pleasant environment than the preceding virgin forest, not only to humans, but also to many other living things. Large parts of Africa have achieved their present vegetational appearance as a result of ancient agricultural practices and animal husbandry that have been going on for thousands of years, due to the great grass fires which Africans in many places start every year to improve grazing conditions. This practice has also benefited many wild herbivores. Much of what we call nature is largely the creation of humans, and it is dependent upon humans for its continued existence and, therefore, unstable in the sense that we choose to apply when we wish to pretend that humans are not part of nature. It is evident, however, that instability becomes manifest when Nature's son/daughter modifies his/her way of life for one reason or another.

Industrialization, so far incomparably the greatest intervention by the law of change in our existence and environment, is due to accumulated cleverness, inventiveness and organizational talent. But we now see the limits of what the new concoction can provide: pollution of air and water, din, acidity of lake water, maltreatment of nature, the health hazards of many products and production processes, mega-crowds, the breakdown of traditional groups and values. All these are consequences of industrialization or, at least, of a too rapid and, in part, obviously unpremeditated process of industrial growth. These consequences are the price we have paid for our un-paralleled supply of goods and services per capita and our un-paralleled growth in numbers. Most of us became genuinely aware of these consequences very late in the game.

One corrective seems to be coming along all by itself: i.e. the tendency towards decreasing child-births and, consequently, decelerating population increase. It is comforting to reflect that, at least in one respect, humans seem to conduct themselves differently from bacteria in a nutritious concoction. While many learned arguments have been made to explain this development, it is commonly agreed that it has something to do with high or improving material standards, with the attendant general education and emancipation of women. Improved contraceptive methods are a help, but they are not decisive for demographic developments. Modern contraception was hardly in the picture when the population in France stagnated in the late 19th Century, at the same time as living standards rose. Nor is it evident that contraception has constituted any significant brake on population increase in African and other Third World nations. That contraception should form an essential part of modern health care is quite a different matter.

It is imperative to keep in mind the link between material well-being and interest in environmental improvement when we consider the problems which African countries face with regard to soil, vegetation and water. The existence and increasingly critical nature of these problems are generally recognized and

eloquently described. That the United States, as well as other donors of development assistance, should try to help towards their mitigation is undisputable. The
least aid donors can do is to avoid causing further damage through the support of
poorly planned development projects, such as gravely polluting industry, or water
for cattle in such geographical concentration as is liable to cause overgrazing and
trampling of the vegetation. In addition, they can provide expertise, equipment
and money to stimulate and support such attempts at preservation or restoration
of the natural environment as are proposed or initiated in African countries.

Indeed, it is not industrialization which constitutes the main environmental
dilemma for African countries. Industrialization has not gotten very far in Africa;
the law of change has not yet had the same impact there as in the United States
and other industrialized countries. Agriculture and animal husbandry, generally
on the subsistent level, constitute the dominant pattern of the African economy.
Formal Western-style education, especially of women, has not reached a level
which would lead us to expect rapid demographic change. In their pursuit of survival, peasants exploit ever more marginal soil, ever poorer grazing grounds.

The problem of Africa, when it comes to the natural environment, as well as
in most other respects, is not an over-hasty development, but a too sluggish one,
or none at all. The exposed land would be best preserved by being left alone, and
this would be possible if people could do something else than trying to cultivate
it—for instance, pursue industrial development. But this is precisely what African
countries are short of the means—management capacity, know-how, trained
manpower, and capital—to do.

Direct measures of assistance to soil conservation and other forms of preservation of the environment are vital, and they are already part of America's battery.
But what will be decisive, in the long run, for the prospects of African nations to
remedy soil and water problems as well as other environmental problems is their
success in improving the low productivity of their people and the prospects of
economic progress. What is needed is the stimulation of productivity to enlarge
the scope for economic activity. That would be pushing the law of change forward, and that is what Africa needs.

Environmental Crises in Africa and the United States: A Brief Comparison

The environmental crises in Africa and the United States are Janus-faced: i.e.
whereas the environmental crisis in Africa is one of under-consumption and inadequate technology, the environmental crisis in the United States is one of mass
consumption and advanced technology. That patterns of production and con-

sumption in the United States have had a severe impact on the nation's environment is now becoming fatefully apparent to every American.

Today, about 20 percent of Americans refuse to drink water from their taps, at least partly because they doubt its safety, the dangers of floods (increased by the clearing of forests for farms and timber), the leaching of garbage buried in landfills, and pesticide runoff in irrigation waters from agriculture. Many Americans are worried about the ways the society generates energy and the resulting global warming, air pollution (as much of the 2,500 gallons of air inhaled in the United States each day contains exhaust fumes, lead, and asbestos), and ozone depletion and its relationship to skin cancer (Blatt 2004).

The relationship between poverty and environmental abuse is not so widely understood. Even so, on closer examination, it, too, seems inevitable. This relationship is painfully apparent in Africa. Affluent societies' appetites for exotic hardwoods do, of course, contribute to the rampant devastation. American, European and Japanese corporations, constrained by severe restrictions at home, have been able to operate quite uninhibited in Africa. The royalties the developed countries have paid for laying waste African lands have been welcomed by African governments as much-needed nest-eggs for their countries' "development." Now, albeit late in the game, a few African leaders are beginning to slam on the brakes.

Nonetheless, native slash-and-burn farmers are also contributing to the problem, as they cover ever wider territory to eke out food for the day from temporary croplands. In addition to the farmers, there are hosts of landless peasants who wage a desperate struggle to ward off hunger and malnutrition. Yet still, millions are in desperate need of firewood, especially for cooking. The scarcity of firewood is the real energy crisis for a majority of Africa's people. Anything and everything that could be burn is being torn out of the soil; naked circles around villages are widening. Gathering food for cooking is beginning to take all day for many.

Where the forest is gone, wells dry up, rivers alternate between flooding and running dry, topsoil is leached and washed away, and dams clog with silt. In this way, the poorest of our fellow humans are literally destroying their own future, as the very basis for future generations' existence goes up in smoke.

Marine environments are also being subjected to ruthless destruction. Mangrove forests and coral reefs, havens for young fish and a buffer against the land-eating onslaught of the tides, are being exploited and ravished at a scary pace. Substandard technology further leads to serious pollution, of water in particular. Waters in which two-thirds of the world's fish mature from egg to adulthood are now in jeopardy. Supplies of drinking water are in many places impaired or endangered.

Thus, no form of assistance from the United States can be more important than assistance with the aim of saving the prerequisites of life of coming generations. No economic assistance can be more economically sound than assistance to emergency efforts to protect threatened biotypes. The scale of America's advanced technology and overall approaches to problems is frequently ill suited to such efforts. Assistance efforts encounter a crucial difficulty in the very fact that all assistance presumes a form of knowledge transfer. Another prime difficulty resides in the fact that many African governments are often quite removed from those most in need of assistance. Consequently, United States officials must reach out to the people in the villages, listen to their views, their accumulated wisdom, get them involved, and get them to realize that it is a question of their day-to-day existence. In essence, it is in small communities of individuals around the world that the great work to save our global environment must be carried out.

Poverty and Hunger

Are the problems of pollution and environmental degradation really the sole headache of the industrialized countries? Problems of conservation are mounting in African and other developing countries as well, but they are generally of a different kind compared to those in the industrialized countries: desertification (i.e. the process whereby vegetation and soil are debased to the extent that more or less permanent areas of desert-like barrenness materialize in arid tracts outside actual deserts), the wholesale razing of tropical rain forests, the pollution of highly productive coastal waters, etc. As such, the United States and other aid donors must consider the environmental impact of projects beforehand, so that they and the recipients need not spend future time and effort repairing the damage the "aid" has done.

In the last three decades, increasing attention has been paid to environmental questions in the debate on foreign aid and development. The reason is obvious. In many African and other developing countries, there is now taking place a ruthless exploitation of scarce natural resources and a dramatic degradation of the environment which is threatening the basis of human existence. Thus, the customary view that environmental degradation is only a problem for the industrialized countries, and that environmental protection is a luxury which the developing countries cannot afford, appears increasingly obsolete. There should be no conflict between environmental protection and development in African nations. In many places, environmental degradation constitutes a direct threat to development. This is especially true of the efforts to improve the living conditions of the numerous poor in the rural areas. Active environmental protection is in many cases a prerequisite for development.

Environmental degradation in African countries is principally a result of over-exploitation of natural resources. This is, for instance, true of arable land, pasture, groundwater and forests. Even though there is profit-motivated devastation, especially in the case of the felling of forests, over-exploitation is mainly due to poverty. To subsist, people are forced to use natural resources in a way that drastically reduces the capacity of those resources to provide yield in the long term. The energy and food crises have created a vicious circle of poverty which has led to an ecological disaster in many areas.

To reverse the present trend, steps must be taken to combat poverty, from which the environmental problems of African countries actually emerge. To begin with, the general economic and social conditions in the rural areas must be improved. Steps must be taken to find new ways of earning a subsistent living. Alternative kinds of energy and a technology that is better adapted to African countries must be introduced. Furthermore, a better integration of environmental aspects in development work is imperative. Development must be adapted to the conditions laid down by nature. The limits set by the natural environment and natural resources must not be exceeded. At all times, attention must be paid to the close connection between natural resources, the environment and development.

The decisive importance of environmental aspects has been better documented at the international level, and it has also been recognized more widely in recent years. For many years, Sweden has been working diligently in bringing that about. A United Nations symposium convened in Stockholm in 1979, financed by Sweden, drew attention to the necessity of recognizing the connection between population growth, natural resources, the environment and development. Sweden believes that only through the integration of the aspects of natural resources and the environment into the development process can a development which is ecologically tenable be guaranteed. Since then, a Swedish initiative has been taken to establish a United Nations program—the United Nations Environmental Program (UNEP)—aimed at ensuring that greater attention is paid to these fundamental links.

A World Conservation Strategy was initiated in 1980 by a number of international organizations both within and outside the United Nations system. This strategy emphasizes the connection between social and economic development and the natural environment, and suggests alternative approaches to development that take this connection into consideration. For the United Nations Environmental Program (UNEP), environmental development is a major component of its work. The aim is to achieve an integration of the environmental and resource aspects in all of the United Nations' development efforts and to work out methods of integrating them into the development work of the individual countries.

All development and development assistance cooperation must hinge upon the wishes of the recipient countries. Consequently, the frequently discussed question of choosing a suitable technology for a development project should be, first of all, a matter for the recipient country. The task for development assistance should be to help the recipient country to develop its own capacity to assess, receive and adapt the technology that is exported.

African countries and the United States must markedly increase their commitments in the sphere of land management, principally in village forestry, and the combating of desertification. The problems of soil erosion and desertification seem especially acute in the Sahel area, where the advance of the desert constitutes an ecological disaster of enormous proportions. The very basis of human existence is being rapidly eroded over large areas by the desperate search by the poor for shrinking grazing land for their livestock, for fuel, for water, etc. Bilateral projects which must be brought to the fore should include planting of trees and village forestry, providing more efficient stoves which use less wood, restoring of areas around water-holes, etc. which have been over-grazed in countries like Burkina Faso.

A corollary to poverty, inevitably, is hunger. The reasons for hunger in Africa are many; environmental degradation is one. Another is that African countries today produce raw materials for the industrialized countries that pay very little for them. In order to feed their own peoples, African countries are then forced to increase their production of the raw materials at the expense of the environment.

There already exist signs of stress on the world's bio-productive resources. If the production of major commodities of biological origin is viewed in per capita terms, it is evident that many of them have already exceeded their peaks. And as population and per capita consumption continue to increase, it is likely that more commodities will reach their peaks in the near future.

Some studies have shown that the earth's physical resources and expanding technology can sustain an average growth rate in food production of about five percent. Even a humble population growth of 2.1 percent per year, however, would lead to increased pressure on resources, higher real costs and environmental deterioration—factors which would further undermine the global food prospects. Humankind has entered an era of scarcity as far as arable land is concerned. The declining availability of arable land suggests that expanding food production will depend on a wide range of resource-augmenting inputs like fertilizers, pesticides and high-yielding varieties.

But this leads to another problem. Not only is the production of fertilizers and pesticides energy-intensive, it is also expensive and dependent on the global petroleum prospects. Producing one ton of nitrogen requires about 1.8 tons of oil-equivalent. Much of the fertilizer applied to farms is not utilized by crops and leaches into water systems where it poses environmental health risks through nitrate contamination. The presence of nitrates in drinking water may induce a disease called methaemoglobinaemia, through which the capacity of the blood to carry oxygen from the lungs to the rest of the body is reduced. Infants are most vulnerable to this disease. Moreover, the leaching of nitrogen fertilizer may lead to the problem of eutrophication. It has been estimated that more than 70 percent of the nitrogen entering surface water comes from agricultural activities. If eutrophication is modest, it may be a source of food for numerous herbivorous animals, which in turn are fed upon by fish. But if the bloom becomes excessive, it may choke waterways and hinder navigation. And when the bloom decomposes, it depletes oxygen and may affect the fish population.

Most of the pesticides used in Africa and other Third World countries include persistent organochlorines like DDT, aldrin, dieldrin, and heptachlor—all of which have already been banned or are heavily restricted in developed countries. Pesticides poison at least one person every five minutes in the Third World, making a total of 250,000 people a year, of who about 10 percent die. This estimate, however, does not include the thousands who suffer from cancer, have miscarriages and still-births, bear deformed children or suffer from the effects of pesticide contamination. The world produces about 1.8 tons of pesticides each year, an equivalent of 14 ounces per person on earth. Approximately 360,000 tons are exported to the developing countries. Despite this massive production of pesticides, the problem of pests is far from being solved; the bugs are fighting back by developing resistance against pesticides.

Future growth in agricultural resources will depend on the provision of more water and better water management in the arid and semi-arid areas. It will also depend on the drainage and management of surplus water in the humid and wet areas which account for well over 50 percent of the world's remaining reserves of arable or potentially arable land. Water will continue to be a major limiting factor to food production. Producing one kilogram of dry wheat grains needs at least 0.75 tons of water, and irrigating a hectare or rice requires up to 787,400 cubic inches of water in a season.

Food production faces the challenges of soil deterioration, despite the fact that some of the previously unutilized land is being brought under the plough. Soil deterioration is mainly a result of desertification, waterlogging, salinization, alkanization, deforestation, loss of farmland to other uses and general soil erosion. The problem is compounded by the lack of effective technology for reclaiming salinized and waterlogged farmland. And bringing more land under irrigation may reduce the availability of pastureland and intensify pressure on the remaining pastures.

Forests and Trees

The threat to tropical forests is a threat to hundreds of people's chances to survive on agriculture. The devastation of tropical forests in Africa has created an energy crisis that is of concern to most people. The slaughter of rainforests is radically changing our climate and life condition, in spite of the denial by some policy makers and observers. The threat comes from transnational forest companies pursuing maximum profit and slash-and-burn farmers struggling to eke a living, but signs of resistance are beginning to emerge.

The rainforest is a 60-million-year-old ecological system that is unique in its stability. It rains constantly in the rainforest, often at the same time every day. It is permanently warm and no wind penetrates into it. Eternal dusk prevails under leaves that form an impenetrable valve 110-140 feet up towards the sun.

Over millions of years, each species in the rainforest has developed a continuously higher degree of specialization. Birds exist that would die if touched by sunlight, and the richness of various species among insects, animals, plants and birds is tremendous. According to some estimates, half of the world's 10 million living species are in the rainforests, even though these forests cover only one-seventeenth of the earth's mainland.

Some generations ago, there were 840,000 square miles of rainforests in the world. About half of them have already been devastated and transformed into poor agricultural plots, ashes, infertile plains or toilet paper and luxury furniture. About a quarter of a million square kilometers of rainforest disappear each year. At this rate, this would mean that within a span of a generation, there would be no such forests left on this earth. What happens when a rainforest disappears? One outcome is certain: the rainforest will never reappear. It is even questionable whether an ordinary forest will ever grow out of this devastation.

The rainforest is a perfectly functioning biological entity. The sunshine and rains keep in motion a system that is almost totally closed. Dead plant matter is reborn at a staggering speed into new growing plants. The nutrients from smoldering leaves and branches are sucked up in new growing plants. The rest is immediately carried away by the permanently streaming rainwater. Under this thick skin of life, the ground is sterile. This is why it is difficult to create a new rainforest there, or fertile agricultural fields or grazing land without the help of extensive fertilizing. A new rainforest will never grow up again. Erosion will be thousand-fold. The result is that the rainforests disappear. With them millions of people's environmental conditions are destroyed. With them, we renounce our heritage, as aesthetical and biological resources that took nature tens of millions of years to create vanish. And with them also disappear the genetic materials from millions of living species which could have enriched our knowledge of medical plants or given us better grains, new fruit trees, root plants resistant to disease.

In addition, modern climatic research points out that clear-cutting of rainforests can heavily add to the increase of carbon dioxide content in the atmosphere created by the burning of fossil fuels. Stockholms Universitet in Sweden undertakes research in this field, and it has received international attention. Meteorologist Anders Björkström, a leading scientist on carbon dioxide content and greenhouse effects on climatic conditions, has found that the content has increased by approximately 15 percent. Simple prognoses indicate that there will be a twofold increase of carbon dioxide between the years 2025 and 2050, which is hastened by the clear-cutting of rainforests. Estimates as to how much this contributes to climatic changes vary: from negligible amounts to amount comparable to, or even larger than, what derives from oil or coal burning. A doubling of carbon dioxide content in the atmosphere would mean a rise in the average temperature by roughly three degrees Centigrade. But such a rise in temperature will be unevenly distributed on the earth. At lower latitudes, it would only become one or two degrees warmer; at higher altitudes, it would get considerably warmer—up to 7-9 degrees. This is rather worrisome. One can imagine a certain melting of ice caps. This rise in temperature can lead to a general transformation of the climatic pattern on earth so that, for example, extremely dry areas would move north in the northern hemisphere and parts of presently existing agricultural areas would lose their ability to maintain a population.

Who is to blame for all this? The forest companies—Weyerhaeuser, International Pacific, Sunitomo, Honshu Paper, Volkswagen, Unilever, etc.—say not them. They argue that they only undertake a smaller part of the clear-cutting. For them, it is the fault of the slash-and-burn farmers. But it is the transnational forest companies that carried the biggest trees to their sawmills. In its original shape, the rainforest is much too dense and big for the local people to clear for their own agricultural needs. When the foresters go in and take away the biggest trees, the people move in as a result. They cut the smaller trees and burn the remaining vegetation and plant vegetables in the ashes. This particular area has never been cultivated before. As soon as the bigger trees have been removed, the slash-and-burn farming means a total change in the structure of the forest. Grass goes in and the forest is completely destroyed. The sun can burn the soil into a hard crust. In essence, the slash-and-burn farmers simply conclude the transnational forest companies' work: i.e. kill the forest for good.

Indeed, the future of Africa is intimately bound up with the future of its trees. Wood and charcoal are African households' most important fuels. Furthermore, trees provide shade and protect crops from the scorching sun. They help retain moisture in the soil, thereby combating erosion. But more trees are felled than are being planted. Turning the tide to avert catastrophe requires planting millions of trees each year. Fuel, too, must be used more efficiently. With an average population growth of about 3.2 percent per year, Africa's problem is acute, requiring mass mobilization and a firm political will to solve the deforestation problem.

Despite the abundant oil reserves in Africa, most of which has not even been tapped, the continent is facing two energy crises at once: an oil crisis in the modern sector and a wood fuel crisis in the traditional sector. The crisis in the modern sector is one of rising oil prices. Oil is mainly used in transport and industry. Increases in oil prices have meant that an ever smaller share of the economy is available for development. The crisis in the traditional sector has to do with the fact that more trees are felled than are planted, as noted earlier. Moreover, waste (plant mortality) is substantial: roughly three out of every five seedling trees are destroyed, with only two surviving 10 years after planting. In addition, the potential energy in the wood is used inefficiently. In rural areas, food is prepared over open hearth consisting of three stones. Such hearths have a fuel efficiency of roughly four percent: i.e. only four percent of the energy in the wood is utilized in cooking. In the towns, meals are prepared on simple charcoal stoves without chimneys, with a fuel efficiency of just about 10 percent. The charcoal, in turn, is manufactured in primitive coal pits which, too, have an efficiency of about 10 percent. Some coal is further lost in the distribution process, as charcoal is transported in jute sacks. In sum, town-dwellers utilize less than one percent of the gross energy content of the wood they consume.

Planting trees is one of the most important tasks facing Africans today, and it will require considerable efforts. A continental-wide reforestation program would cost billions of dollars, but no other course of action offers the same advantages at that price. The value of trees cannot be overestimated: as mentioned earlier, trees shade the soil and crops against the scorching heat of the sun; they help retain moisture in the soil and mitigate the effects of seasonal drought; they inhibit erosion, a severe problem in Africa; they pump up nutrients from deeper layers of soil; they provide fodder for livestock and food, fuel and timber for people.

In order to stimulate such a reforestation program, more money should be channeled directly to the planting groups, so that more people can be activated in the projects. The problem is so serious that governments alone cannot solve it without mobilizing the people. Bottlenecks in reforestation projects usually involve the supply of seeds and seedlings, shortages of automobiles for transport and implements and watering cans for use in planting. Seed collection and founding nurseries must get under way promptly.

The International Center for Research in Agroforestry (ICRAF) is an organization that studies the co-cultivation of trees and crops to see what systems are best suited to different types of soil. It has found that over the years, Western agricultural practices, with large-scale monocultures that leave the earth bare from time to time, are poorly suited to African soils and climatic conditions. Combining agriculture and silviculture produces better yields, while combating erosion. This leads to better harvests and more trees, which is important inasmuch as food production is vital and cannot be made to compete with energy sources.

One out of every two Africans is under the age of 15, and it should therefore be a vital strategy to engage these young people and the schools in reforestation efforts. First, they have more reason to think ahead; second, the tree plantations would serve a major learning purpose in increasing young people's understanding of ecological relationships.

Energy must be used effectively in every phase, and there is a lot of room for improvement. Simple wood stoves, built of local materials, might increase the efficiency of wood use. It is vital, however, that the stoves be inexpensive, so that many people can afford them. An expenditure of any magnitude will not attract many users, even though households in many areas spend as much on wood as they do on food each year. A conceivable solution might be to introduce portable, effective kilns of the type developed by the Food and Agricultural Organization (FAO), the Cusab kiln. The kiln could be transported, making local purchases of wood. This model can also make charcoal of brush and wigs. The manufacture of briquettes might reduce wastage in transport by binding the coal dust. Coffee bean hulls, coconut shells, grass and other agricultural refuse can also be mixed into the briquettes. More efficient charcoal burners would also help increase fuel efficiency. Such braziers are already in the market, but they are more expensive than ordinary charcoal stoves without chimneys. It may be necessary to subsidize them in order to increase their sale and usage.

In the long run, alternative energy sources such as solar, wind and water will contribute to Africa's energy supply. But for the present, most people on the continent rely on wood. Hydro-power can be further exploited to provide more electricity for the modern sector. One problem with this energy source is that dams and reservoirs tend to clog with sift as a consequence of soil erosion. Therefore, hydroelectric power, too, is dependent on the success of reforestation and soil conservation efforts.

Geothermal energy has begun to be exploited in some areas of Africa. For example, in Olkaria, some 62 miles north of Nairobi, Kenya, a hole was drilled 353 feet into the earth. Steam is produced and harnessed to drive the turbines of a generator to produce electricity. Drilling was done at several other sites, so that geothermal electricity can contribute approximately 11 percent of Kenya's electricity.

Bio-gas (methane), derived from the manure of livestock, can be produced and utilized on large farms, albeit it is unlikely to contribute on a large scale, as cattle are grazed sparsely scattered over vast areas. Ethanol, or ethyl alcohol, can be produced from molasses, a by-product of sugar refining. Ten percent ethanol can be mixed with gasoline to reduce Africa's need of imported gasoline. But efforts to increase ethanol production further will be at the expense of foodstuffs. Producing methanol (methyl or wood alcohol) offers greater promise.

Solar cells are used for telecommunications, to drive pumps in isolated places, and to electrify fences to keep animals out of cultivated fields. They are too expensive, however, to have a major impact on the total energy strategy. Solar radiation is used to heat water and to dry various crops. The prospects for expanding this type of energy are vast. The sun can heat water for schools, hospitals, institutions of various kinds, hotels and homes. It can also be used to dry coffee and tobacco. The drying of tobacco leaves today consumes vast quantities of wood—approximately 30 trees per hectare of tobacco. Thus, in the short term, only mass mobilization to plant trees, coupled with more efficient use of wood fuels, can solve the energy crisis in the traditional sector.

Desertification

In 1973, two words became prominent in newspapers and television news around the world: Sahel and desertification. Sahel is an Arabic word denoting the belt of steppe and arid savannah south of the Sahara—from Senegal on the Atlantic Ocean to the west to the Sudan and Ethiopia on the Red Sea to the east. This roughly 310-496 mile-wide belt normally receives 2.5-15 inches of precipitation per year, but several years between 1968 and 1973 brought far below normal amounts of rain. Grass and other fodder disappeared, and millions of head of livestock perished. Deaths due to starvation among the nomadic herdsmen and small farmers of the Sahel were estimated at 200,000. The disastrous cycle of crop failure, famine, devastated pasturelands and cultivated fields has gone down in history as "The Sahel Catastrophe." It also resulted in considerable degree of desertification—defined earlier in this essay as the process whereby vegetation and soil are debased to the extent that more or less permanent areas of desert-like barrenness materialize in arid tracts outside actual deserts.

Several types of land abuse can result in desertification. Two cases of the devastation of arable land in the arid regions of Africa are considered here: (1) Tunisia, an example of the situation on the northern fringes of the Sahara; and (2) the Sudan, an example of sub-Saharan Sahel conditions.

The Mediterranean climate is characterized by long, dry summers and intensive periods of rain during the winter—a pattern that can lead to significant soil erosion if natural ground cover is weakened through farming, over-grazing, or the felling of bushes and trees. The same practices denuded the mountains bordering the Mediterranean to the north and east some 2,000 years ago. Greece, Italy, Lebanon, Spain, Turkey, among other countries, offer numerous examples. As the population of Tunisia has grown rapidly (about eightfold) over the past 100 years, the pressure on land, water and wood resources in that country has intensified. Consequently, the following six ecological effects have been noted:

1. Over-grazing occurs because too many animals are allowed to graze freely on steppe land for long. Grazing and the trampling of hooves of goats, sheep and, to some extent, camels weaken the natural ground cover. As a result, topsoil is pulverized and is easily blown away by the wind or rinsed away by heavy rains.

2. Over-cultivation of marginal lands that are extremely sensitive to erosion by water and/or wind results in permanent impairment of the fertility of topsoil and its ability to retain moisture after only a few seasons of farming. Disc-plowing by tractors, introduced over the past several decades, has caused particularly severe problems in Tunisia. It is a case of a highly inappropriate technology in a sensitive milieu, and many of the new flecks of desert that have come into existence in the steppe zone are directly attributable to this over-cultivation. The larger of these

flecks, several miles in length, are clearly visible in satellite and aerial photos.

3. Wood derived from the cutting of trees and brush for household fuel, fencing or building material bares the soil, paving the way for ensuing erosion. Each family of farmers cut approximately one hectare of marquis each year to meet fuel needs. The areas are cleared and then planted, making them extremely vulnerable to erosion.

4. Salinization of irrigated land results because the bedrock of southern Tunisia contains salt that in many places contaminates groundwater as well as soil water. Deposits of gypsum have caused the formation of alkaline crusts in the soil and salinization with gypsum in irrigated fields. Salinization due to insufficient drainage is believed to have ruined vast irrigated tracts in ancient Babylon, contributing to the fall of the empire more than 2,000 years ago.

5. Water erosion and siltation in reservoirs are the outcome of the many fluvial reservoirs that have been built in Tunisia. Most of them lie in the mountainous and less arid northern reaches of the country. Dams have been constructed to supply the cities with drinking water, to irrigate various agricultural districts, and to control flooding. All of the reservoirs, however, are filling rather quickly with sediment.

6. Wind erosion is symptomatic of the effects of the tremendous dust storms that carry soil particles from North Africa across the Mediterranean to southern Europe. Soil leaves Tunisia in other directions as well—e.g., eastward and southward. Clouds of red dust from Africa have descended from time to time on the Alpine glaciers—where the snow is colored red—and on European coasts and cities. The precipitation occurs in the form of dry dust or as clumps of mud in rainstorm. Each of these storms represents the loss of millions of tons of African soil. The loss of wind-borne sand and soil particles from the Sahara and the Sahel over the Atlantic is even greater.

The Sudan, the largest country in Africa, with an area of 967,247 square miles, contains a variety of climatic zones, ranging from Saharan desert along its northern borders to mountainous rain forests along the Uganda-Congo frontier to the south. The Sudan probably has more territory affected by desertification than any other country in Africa.

A 1944 report by a Sudanese government commission on soil conservation revealed that the problem was known even at that time. The commission's conclusion was that soil degradation and erosion were more a consequence of human beings and their domesticated animals than of a change in climate. Its recommendation mainly concerned regions surrounding towns, where it advised planting green windbreaks of trees and bushes around some centers. As we know today, the commission was only partly correct about both its diagnosis and suggested medicine.

Between 1968 and 1973, the arid and semi-arid reaches of the Sudan suffered as severe a drought as hit the countries of the West African Sahel, from Senegal to Chad. Three factors helped to lesson the impact on the Sudan, compared to its neighbors, Chad to the west and Ethiopia to the east: (1) Sudanese herdsmen and their animals moved south, (2) domestic relief supplies were available from the surplus of Nile Valley agriculture, and (3) there was a certain degree of awareness and preparedness among policy makers of the necessity of combating desertification.

A detailed and well-thought out plan for the effort was drawn up under the sponsorship of the Sudanese Research Council and presented to the United Nations Conference on Desertification (UNCOD) convened in Nairobi, Kenya from August 29 to September 9, 1977. The plan entailed (a) an inventory of the forms and extent of soil degradation and erosion, and (b) a pilot program for soil conservation and desert control. Unfortunately, the Sudanese efforts to engage the industrialized countries and oil-rich neighbors in a common cause against desertification fell on deaf ears. Even the conference planned to be held in the Sudan in 1978 had to be cancelled due to lack of interest among the invited countries. Nevertheless, the Sudan started, with its own funds and probably support from United Nations organs and bilateral assistance, several successful pilot projects that have shown that soil conservation is possible even in areas of extreme aridity. These projects include windbreak plantations along the western fringes of the Nile Valley bordering on the Sahara. Sweden also supported plantations near the town of Atbara.

In essence, it is not an overstatement that the need to conserve basic resources like water, productive soil and vegetation in Africa is greater now than ever. Soil erosion is one of the most serious threats to the health and welfare of Africans today, especially marginalized groups, which are forced to live on the fringes of arable land. Traditional forms of land use can no longer support them. There is no place left for them to move should their present land be debased or destroyed. Soil conservation for long-term productivity must become a more central concern in the United States' development assistance programs than has been the case to date.

Water

Long, tiring treks for a bucket of water have been the plight of most women in Africa; and for many of them, it still is. Indeed, a growing number of villages have been furnished with piped water and taps within easy walking distance. An immediate and feasible goal of any African society's water program, to which the United States could contribute, should be for every villager to walk less than 300 yards to clean water.

Fetching water has always been an endless drudgery for most women in Africa. They have had to walk several miles for a pail of water. Whole families have had to make two or three buckets of water last several days. There were times when mothers had to even deny their children a drink when they are thirsty to make the water last. Policy makers recognize the importance of adequate water supplies for industry, for mines, for herding and for a country's overall development, but they seem not to be equally impassioned about life in the village, even though many of them are descendants of villages.

It is obvious that when women no longer have to make the long, tiring treks just for a pail of water, they will have more time and energy to take better care of their homes and families and to do more creative work. They can, for example, begin their own small businesses and earn money. They can raise more vegetables, thereby giving their families more nutritious diets. A clean house, clean children and clean food are all important for improving people's standard of health.

Most women avoid fetching water in the heat of the midday sun, so demand on the water system peaks twice a day: between 8:30 and 11:00 a.m. and 5:00 and 6:30 p.m. The water pressure falls so that it sometimes takes twice as long to fill a bucket as it does other times of day. But the women seem not to mind waiting, as it gives them a chance to chat with their friends. When the buckets are full, the women lift them carefully up onto their heads and walk home. There they empty the buckets into large clay jugs, which keep the water cool. The jugs have no lids; and when the women sweep the ground outside their doors in the morning, clouds of dust swirl up and settle down over the jugs, forming thin films on the water.

Sometimes, too, hens drink right out of the jugs, or toddlers fetch drinking water in mugs that have been left on the ground and licked by dogs. Water is generally clean when it leaves the faucet, but it becomes polluted due to dirty buckets and poor storage facilities. Many village households still use the traditional clay jugs without lids. Households that store their water in big plastic tanks with caps are considered "modern."

When school is out in the afternoon, one often sees children in their school uniforms with water buckets on their way to a tap. Teachers say that there is a significant correlation between a well-functioning water supply and less absenteeism from school. Among school-aged children, girls fetch water more than boys. Only when the household fetches its water in a large tank that has to be hauled with a donkey-cart do the men help out, as men are traditionally responsible for handling draft animals.

According to the World Health Organization (WHO), a person should use at least eight gallons of water a day in order to keep him/herself clean and healthy. Many African families manage on far less, perhaps a little less than three gallons per person. Nonetheless, they all look clean and neat. The young children are bathed in a little water in a basin every evening; dishes and kitchen utensils are always clean, even though they are washed in the least amount of water imaginable. The average family uses about 53 gallons of water per week for cooking. Approximately 45 gallons go to personal hygiene. Adults bathe every day, using between one and two buckets of water each time. School children generally wash their faces, hands and legs each morning before going to school. Young women tend to bathe more frequently than older women and men because they want to be "attractive."

Laundry is washed twice or thrice a week, each washing requiring four to five buckets of water. This means an average of 30 gallons of water per week for laundry. Household laundry done once a month requires even more water. Households located near community taps wash their clothes when they need washing rather than letting them accumulate. Some women take their laundries to the wells to wash there, but this practice is not encouraged. Instead, authorities have sought to interest villagers in building small laundry stations near their taps, but these remain to be built.

Water use in villages peaks in July and August after the harvest, when people return to their villages after spending the planting season in huts near their fields or cattle posts. As a result, there are more people in the villages than at other times. Also, this is the time of year when people tend to repair their houses. Most village homes are built of stone plastered with a mixture of clay, cow dung and water. The plastering of a family's walls, floors and low compound walls requires between 100 and 800 gallons of water. In addition, local beer is brewed after the harvest. Each batch requires approximately 40 gallons of water. Brewing, with the attendant beer consumption, has been found to increase sharply as access to water improves through drilled wells and piped water in the villages.

Water supply development has progressed faster and even more effective in some African countries. Advanced technology has made it possible to drill many wells in a short time, but one disadvantage has been the almost complete reliance on foreign expertise. Training of African personnel has not kept pace with the extension of modern water facilities. Maintenance of pumps and piping has been a major problem in many countries. Generally, foreign assistance has not covered maintenance, and most countries have used the money on investments, installations, and neglected maintenance.

A major figure in the functioning of the system is the pump-man. Often, he is elected at village meetings and sent to a training course to learn how to take care of the pump, pipes and taps. The pump-man maintains the pump, cleans and lubricates it, but does not undertake any repairs on either the pump or the pipelines. In case of trouble, maintenance personnel from the district water board are sent. When a tap does not work, people do not get angry; they simply go to another one.

Much of the water obtained through drilling is contaminated with a variety of substances, which, of course, is a major problem. Salt is one common contaminant, as are nitrates and the presence of bacteria. Efforts must be redoubled to see that people get pure water. In many villages, the water well is in the middle of town. As villages grow in size and as more latrines, installed over holes in the ground, are built, some serious cases of pollution have developed. The risk of contamination must be a prime concern in the planning and drilling of new wells. Meanwhile, existing wells must be fenced-in so that livestock cannot pollute the water supply. Chlorine is added to disinfect the water in some villages, but villagers complain of the taste. Another factor underlying their dislike of chlorine may be that chlorinated water is not good for brewing beer.

In some African countries, Family Welfare Educators (FWEs) stationed in villages play a significant role in teaching people how to handle their water. Chosen by villages, FWEs are trained and then work together with the personnel of local health clinics. They make house-calls and lecture mothers on health, hygiene and the importance of vaccinations when they visit the clinics with their children. First, people were weary of the FWEs and did not want them to make house-calls. Nowadays, the people understand the importance of the visits made by the FWEs. It is a difficult task to change people's attitudes. It is one thing to give people medicine and vaccine; it is quite another to get them to change their way of thinking, their diets, how they raise their children. On home-calls, FWEs can see for themselves how well cared-for the children and household are. They can point out, for instance, that the water jugs should be covered or that water should be boiled if a child has diarrhea. If the children look undernourished, they can refer mothers and children to a nutrition clinic in the village.

Global Warming

In June of 2006, the government of Niger requested that its citizens pray and fast so that it would rain. The country has had three consecutive years of drought and the situation was getting desperate. Could anyone in the United States imagine three years without a drop of rain? This is commonplace in parts of East and Southern Africa.

The major reason for this and other deleterious effects that have resulted from the global climate change, according to Dr. Sama Banya, Honorary President of the Conservation Society of Sierra Leone, is the reckless manner in which some developed countries are misusing the earth's natural resources and polluting the atmosphere with greenhouse gases. He suggests that while Africans have no control over the way the industrialized countries are causing climate change leading to global warming, Africans can minimize the effects of those changes by the way they treat their local environment.

That the effects of global warming are being felt on the continent of Africa is hardly disputable. As Godwin Obasi (in Ramsay and Edge 2004:241) points out, global meteorological observational records show that Africa is now warmer than it was 100 years ago. Warming through the 20th Century was at the rate of about 0.05 degrees Centigrade per decade, with slightly greater warming from June to August and from September to November than at other times. The five warmest years in Africa have all occurred since 1988, with 1988 and 1995 being the two warmest years. Africa's rate of warming has mimicked those of the rest of the world. Obasi adds that a comprehensive characterization of regional climate change projection for Africa for the 21st Century is that future annual warming will be from 0.2 to more than 0.5 degrees Centigrade per decade—i.e. ten times the rate during the 20th Century. The warming is expected to be greatest over the interior semi-arid margins of the Sahara and Central and Southern Africa.

According to the Sciencebase Section News, in May of 2005, researchers from the University College of London found that the fabled equatorial icecaps in the Rwenzori Mountains will disappear within two decades because of global warming. The Rwenzori Mountians, also known as the "Mountains of the Moon," are at the border between the Democratic Republic of Congo and Uganda. The mountains are home to one of the four remaining tropical icecaps outside of the

Andes and are well known for their spectacular and rare Afroalpine flora and fauna. The legendary status of these mountains can be traced back to the 2nd Century when Greek geographer Ptolemy proclaimed that the River Nile was supplied by snow-capped mountains at the equator of Africa. In his words, they were "The Mountains of the Moon whose snows feed the lakes, sources of the Nile" (Sciencebase Section News, May 15, 2006).

The glaciers were first surveyed a century ago, and the glacial cover over the entire range was estimated at the time to be 4.3 square miles. Recent field surveys and satellite mapping of the glaciers conducted by the University College of London, Makerere University and the Ugandan Water Resources Management Department reveal that some glaciers are receding tens of yards each year and that the area covered by glaciers halved between 1987 and 2003. The researchers also found that since the 1960s, there have been clear trends toward increased air temperature around the Rwenzori Mountains without significant changes in precipitation. If present trends continue, the less than one square mile of the remaining glaciers will disappear within the next 20 years. It is not clear, however, how the projected loss of the glaciers will affect tourism and the traditional belief systems of the BaKonzo linguistic group. Nzururu, the BaKonzo word for snow and ice, is the father of the spirits who are responsible for human life, its continuity, and its welfare. The irony of global warming as it pertains to Africa is best stated by Dr. Richard Taylor, the lead researcher from the University College of London, as follows: "Considering the continent's negligible contribution to global greenhouse-gas emissions, it is a terrible irony that Africa, according to current predictions, will be most affected by climate change. Furthermore, the rise in air temperature is consistent with other regional studies that show how dramatic increase in malaria in the East African Highlands may rise, in part, from warmer temperatures as mosquitoes are able to colonise previously inhospitable highland areas" (Sciencebase Section News, May 15, 2006).

The Youth

Work, having a purpose, is what gives us our identity. In African countries, children and young people often have to work too hard; but they serve a vital function in the families' lives and in society at large. These children are quite sure that they are needed. In the United States, this is seldom the case; consequently, young people are forced to seek their identity by other means. A number of toys and gadgets tend to play a significant role in their lives. Meanwhile, society and the schools ask them to be active, responsible citizens, to get involved in important issues concerning the environment, waste of resources, the plights of their less fortunate counterparts at home, in Africa and in other parts of the world. How does all this add up? How can this course be changed?

Leading our children to the playing field and teaching them how to dribble a soccer ball has a powerful learning effect. Such an effect cannot be matched by any classroom discussion on the fine art of soccer. This is because the rewards the schools offer are usually quite inferior to those offered in life outside the classroom, even in the case of soccer. Teachers' scolding weighs less compared to convenience or the glint of admiration in a child's parents' eyes. Still, remarkably enough, children are usually those who hesitate the most before following the flock in a soccer game. Now this section is not about soccer; it is about how we learn certain important attitudes and values, among other things, about our environment and threats to it.

Is it at all realistic to try to correct bad habits on the soccer field and other aspects of life by means of information that appeals to reason and tries to influence people's attitudes? Educators and psychologists have long noted that it is almost impossible to change a person's behavior by advocating a different attitude—i.e. "preaching" (e.g., in teaching). Marketing executives are particularly aware of this and sell whole lifestyles in which gadgets and toys become necessary attributes. It seems that people develop habits, often as a result of pressure from their environment, due to prevailing circumstances or some other—unconscious—reason. With habit established, people then formulate or adopt a value or attitude, a rationale, that legitimizes the habit in question. If we consider what our institutions of education try to teach with regard to the environment, natural resources and economic distribution, we can make a number of interesting, albeit perhaps mainly depressing, observations.

Some years ago when alarming numbers of American teenagers were using illegal drugs, members of the United States Congress were asking about what schools have done about the problem. Some educators responded that they do not make or sell the illegal drugs, a response that reflects a profound understanding of the phenomenon known as the "hidden curriculum." Thus, it may be fitting to take a new tack on the question and ask what the schools have done to take account of that insight—i.e. taking as one's point of departure the fact that attitudes on such questions are often formed by already established patterns of behavior.

How do American schools provide for learning respect and awareness of the environment? Unfortunately, it is more the rule than the exception that students are asked to learn "respect for conservation" while the school milieu in effect systematically trains them to the contrary. When many American school children and children attending day-care centers feel thirsty, they normally have no other option than to go to a dispenser, pull out a plastic cup, fill it with water, drink up and toss the cup into a trash can. Thirsty again an hour later, they repeat the same procedure. School lunches can be a continuation of the same indoctrination—plastic cups, plastic spoons, plastic forks, plastic knives, half cartons of milk, foil wrappers around the butter, leftovers, etc. thrown into the trash cans. If you ask the students in American "plastic-wrap schools" from where the plastic comes, you will get some quite informative answers: "From oil, which entails this and that environmental risk in extraction, transport and refining, not to mention that it is scarce, expensive and most of it imported. Plastic in our refuse, when burned, produces so-and-so pollution, etc."

Therefore, in a traditional sense, the teaching has been effective to a point. Students know all they need to know, but seldom if ever does their knowledge affect, nor is it permitted to affect, their behavior. On the contrary, they are systematically trained to behave in ways which, during certain segments of their school day, they have learned are wrong. The examples of such contradictions are just too numerous to discuss here.

The big problem, of course, is that the whole society outside the school—indeed, children's overall situation in industrialized societies—constitutes an effective training ground in behavior that in both the short- and the long-term is devastating to the environment and finite resources. From a global perspective, the situation is morbid. In the classroom, young people learn that oil, paper and numerous other commodities are in scarce supply and, above all, that they are extremely inequitably distributed and consumed. Out of class, they see plenty evidence to the contrary. The major tragedy is that this contradiction is even apparent in the schools themselves.

The schools are part and parcel of the predominant lifestyle in the wealthy countries. Naturally, they reflect the mainstream pattern of behavior. Indeed, they help reinforce it, with a few cosmetic amendments here and there in the form of slick slogans. "The population explosion in Third World countries" is still singled out as the most serious threat to natural resources and the environment, with no mention whatsoever of the far more invidious consumption explosion taking place in the industrialized societies, which hardly brightens the picture. The schools even carefully avoid making any links between abundant wealth and rampant waste in the industrialized countries on the one hand and the exploitation of developing countries during and since colonialism on the other. Being kept in the dark, today's American students are not equipped to understand the environmental problems of developing countries.

Put differently, the schools make no serious effort to counteract or rebut the economic rationale behind the squandering of natural resources and the pillage of the environment. Neither could they hope to bring about any fundamental change acting alone. The few teachers who attempt to do so are hounded and threatened with losing their jobs by right-wing neoconservatives who call them "unpatriotic liberals." But the schools in general could do more than they are doing if they are united in the pursuit of truth that will benefit the society at large. The schools are also pitted against a number of other factors that have made the youth in the United States, among other industrialized countries, particularly inclined toward the various attributes of the lifestyle of overdevelopment and over-consumption. They have been trained in the ideology of consumerism, a world of disposables, the latest gadget, of built-in obsolescence, in which possessions form a very central part of existence. A society that has given them everything: from iPods to satin satchels in which to keep their dogs' pajamas.

It may be difficult to fully grasp what growing up in such an environment means and the nature of the underlying mechanisms. A few comparisons with certain features of most African children's lives may be useful. Practically anywhere in Africa, one will see most of the children coming home from school, hanging up their book bags and, entirely on their own volition, going to take care of the family's most prized possession: a farm, a garden, cattle, or a kiosk, etc. Once home, they continue with household chores. These children have a purpose: filling a natural function within the family circle and in village life. How, then, do their American counterparts spend their afternoons and evenings? They may have two wheels with a ten-speed transmission or the latest GameBoy. Others spend the entire afternoon and evening on the basketball court or some other athletic arena. Still others walk around committing crimes or harassing their peers and elders.

African children with their gardens, farms, or cattle, etc. have a role in the family. Sometimes, the chores are too many and too heavy—which is not good, let alone idyllic—but that is up for debate. Feeling that we are needed, that we count, is a basic human need, common to all, regardless of age. Our work, the role we play, is what gives us identity. Lacking such a role, the individual must seek to establish his/her identity by other means: for instance, by being first on the block to own an iPod, the latest designer jeans, etc. Those who cannot be the first will have to "borrow" their identity, emulating those who were. They will have to creep into the protective shell of the latest fashion, acquire the right kind of high-tech gadget and mannerisms, to do the "cool" things. This creates a virtual insatiable market for all sorts of gadgets and fads. This market is bountiful.

Fads come and go at astonishing pace: witness the recent cycles of cellular phones.

Is it a hopeless venture to try to change the status quo? The answer depends on one's perspective. For the long run, we must recognize that comprehensive changes in American society will be necessary for classroom input to have a significant impact. But since the youth and children spend so much of their time in school and nursery schools or day-care centers, it should be possible to exert some influence that, in turn, might at least lead to perhaps hastened social change. The acceptance of this premise calls for a recognition that the schools must become more consistent, more consonant with their stated objectives. Plastic cups and the like must be banished if the schools are to have any credibility as advocates of non-consumerism and conservation. Meanwhile, child-care institutions must also make far greater use of the opportunities that do exist to let children feel capable, useful, needed: i.e. to develop a positive identity of self-image.

How can children be taught about respect for Nature when they no longer know that Nature provides things that are vital to our day-to-day existence? The answer hinges upon throwing out all kinds of so-called pedagogical toys—plastic beads mounted on Masonite, styrofoam Easter chicks and Santa Clause. Bring in reality, instead! What happened to pine cones, acorns and interestingly-shaped pebbles? Or take, for example, a meal of fresh red snapper. A mess of fish is all full of lessons. One can count them. How many red snappers to the pound? One can compare them in length and width. There is the icky-sticky-gooey fun of cleaning them. One might stop to consider what they eat (by looking in their stomachs) and what eats them. One can look for milt and roe, etc. This is a natural part of the conversation over the common activity of preparing the meal, which is exactly the way children used to learn in their homes: doing useful work together with adults.

Classes can cultivate useful plants. Many American day-care centers and schoolyards are surrounded by thorny hedges. Why not plant berries, instead? The berries can be harvested, prepared and eaten. Meanwhile, the children will have a natural opportunity to learn all sorts of things about how nature works; they can work with their hands and minds. Is mental dexterity not better developed by dicing onions for meatballs that one can serve his/her classmates for lunch than mounting plastic beads on Masonite? Besides being able to assume a greater responsibility for their environment, older children might run a flea market exchange for second-hand items such as roller-skates, sports equipment, toys, games, clothes, shoes, books, CDs, etc. This should function as an antidote to the latest gadget craze. Where such activities yield a profit, the money might be donated to a worthy cause in an African country. The main thing is that the youth have the initiative. They certainly want to be trusted with the responsibility. Schools might also become centers for repairs and recycling projects of various sorts. Classes might also undertake fact-finding studies for local government agencies.

Any study on crime prevention that queries numerous schools on what measures had proved most effective in discouraging absenteeism and vandalism would yield answers concerning measures involving a greater measure of self-determination on the part of students themselves. There are actually many interesting examples of successful efforts to change teaching routines and the whole school experience to allow the schools to exert the kind of influence discussed here. Far more important would be to give each school greater freedom in drawing up local study plans designed to achieve curricular goals with respect to environmental issues and the conservation of resources. Furthermore, teaching with the aim of promoting resource conservation and environmental awareness can be economical. (This is not to suggest that the efforts should be promoted as money-savers, as that would put a serious constraint on such a program before it even gets started.) Such efforts have proven to be most effective when students and teachers together have been given whatever money their innovations have saved.

Anyone who suspects that young folk might just run to the store and buy candy with the profits from their initiatives will take comfort from the example of students in Kiruna in arctic Sweden who run the school café. These students have introduced a utilitarian pricing scheme, whereby mark-ups (surcharges) on such items as Danish pastry are used to subsidize more healthy foods like fruits and salads. It appears that adults are less utilitarian-minded than the youth.

Another major goal is to develop active, socially aware, responsible citizens. There is a strong connection between individuals' propensity to take action and the extent to which they are able to exert influence on their own surroundings. Generally speaking, those who are unable to influence their immediate environment and day-to-day situations tend to have the least interest in environmental issues, people in other parts of the world, etc. Indeed, if African and American policy makers want not only to give the youth an awareness of environmental problems but to also move them to do something about those problems, then the elements of a program relating to school democracy, student participation, self-determination, etc. must be among the most vital policy repertoires.

Conclusion

Dealings between Africa and the United States that relate to natural resource con-servation are part and parcel of American development assistance to the conti-nent. And since neither Africa nor the United States has shown any signs (as of this writing) for terminating this relationship, it can best be characterized in terms of the type of "interdependent," albeit unequal, relationship between devel-oped and developing nations: i.e. on the one hand, United States development assistance to Africa appears more as a means to strengthen American economic and geopolitical interests in Africa; on the other hand, Africa benefits by having a peaceful relationship with the United States and employing American aid to pro-mote government programs. More basically, then, the issue can be raised as to whether or not the present American mode of pursuing its interests in Africa crip-ples the ability of the continent to control its own destiny. For implicit in United States development assistance is an ethnocentric view that prevents it from seeing what is good in "underdeveloped" Africa and to feel justified in treating Africa as standing in need of American "know-how."

This ethnocentric view hampers innovation and change and results in social isolation. This explains why some African leaders often reject American solutions to their development problems, and see no need to change what they feel is already a good thing from their perspective. At worst, it leads to stagnation; at best, it results in retarded growth and development. The fragmentation of United States development programs in Africa is the additional negative consequence of this ethnocentric view.

Since the United States government possesses most of the needed technologi-cal and financial resources for development, or enjoys access to them, the United States understandably "aids" the development efforts of Africa only to the degree that such activity enhances American objectives. And since the United States is technologically and economically more powerful, transfers of resources, informa-tion, and personnel consolidate the dominant American position and further accentuate the dependency of an economically weak Africa.

When development techniques are transferred from the United States to Africa, only a fraction of the entire process of technical change is bound to emerge within Africa when the technique is implemented. It is those parts of the process that are taking part outside the United States that dictate the basic prop-erties of the technique. These characteristics are shaped by the social organization and the factor endowment of the United States where the inventions and innova-tions are made. And for those techniques that are generated within American transnational corporations, it is obvious that they will be geared toward those corporations' maximum profitability in their international corporations, and not necessarily adapted to the conditions in Africa. Most frequently, Africa is able to choose only among techniques generated in American transnational corporations. This limitation gives rise to a structural technical dependency by Africa in terms of American projects in the continent.

This being the case, a more coherent American foreign assistance program for Africa calls for terminating project aid and converting it to outright security assistance. This will allow Africa to spend its aid dollars on programs that it perceives important to its development needs (a relationship that will parallel that between the United States and Israel), putting Africa fully in charge of its own economic destiny.

The major consequence of such a foreign aid policy, however, will hinge upon the American public's attitude towards its government. This attitude, which must be conditioned by trust, calls for clarity and honesty with which American leaders explain the African situation and argue for actions they believe are necessary to meet the critical challenge in that part of the world.

Such a foreign aid policy cannot be expected to lead the United States to a foreign policy consensus, but it can play a role in generating domestic support for African initiatives if it is explained honestly in terms of what it is and what it will do. It should neither be explained as a humanitarian program nor as a development program, since security assistance programs are not primarily designed to spark self-sustaining economic growth (Israel is a good example).

A United States foreign aid program for Africa that is comprised of security assistance entirely would increase Africa's maneuverability; and what it will do with this ability will depend on its priorities and capabilities. This will also allow the African governments to increase their odds of survival—no government can pursue effective development policies if its future is in doubt.

This is why the application of security assistance compels different rules. The unpredictable nature of African politics and the uncertainties inherent in intra-African relationships, in particular, suggest that such a security assistance program for Africa will carry with it the potential for excesses. This could lead to charges of waste and inefficiency by its critics. While such outcomes are inevitable, they can nevertheless be kept in check through careful management.

In essence, United States development assistance to Africa should be used to reinforce both actors' political, economic and moral objectives. If these purposes are sound, then United States aid will become an effective form of foreign policy for strengthening America's interests in Africa. The continent, on the other hand, will be able to buy breathing space in maintaining stability as it works to meet its development needs.

In conclusion, the modern system of communication has overcome the geographical barriers between Africans and Americans and expanded their horizons. Africans, especially, have become more acutely aware of the state of affairs in the United States than ever before. They are hauntingly reminded of America's affluent style of living. Many in the United States have also been frequently moved to help Africans work towards eradicating poverty and causes of disease and unrest. Many in Africa grow restive to achieve a higher standard of living, to emulate the American way of living. Both Africa and the United States stand to benefit from increased prosperity in Africa and from mutual trade.

11

Micro-franchise in Economic Development

Ciyata Dinah Coleman

Introduction

This chapter explores a phenomenon that could prove quite useful for promoting an equitable partnership between Africa and the United States: i.e. micro-franchise (MF) as an alternative form of economic cooperation in Africa's development. Micro-franchises are replicable small businesses that follow proven marketing and operational practices that are facilitated by a network of small entrepreneurs offering the same market products or services.

This chapter draws upon the works of development economists and social scientists who have emphasized the potential of entrepreneurship to transform development through the enabling environment of micro-franchises. Especially noted is Kirk Magleby (2006), who promotes research on the role of micro-franchise in the elimination of poverty. The exploration of the role of MF in economic development contributes to the ongoing discussion on the relevance of entrepreneurial growth in Africa's development.

Development economists continue to assess how various forms of entrepreneurial development models might contribute to job creation, expansion of the tax base, and promotion of democracy and sustainable economic development in Africa. MF has become an important topic of academic research, allowing for the increased understanding of new business models that promote positive economic, cultural, and environmental outcomes for the poor (Brigham Young University Center for Economic Self-Reliance 2005).

The chapter proceeds as follows. First, it discusses a list of characteristics associated with entrepreneurship in Africa intended to provide an understanding of why the micro-franchise model might be beneficial in Africa's entrepreneurial development. Second, it provides two examples of MF in Africa. Finally, it concludes with a general discussion of the micro-franchise and related forms of entrepreneurial models in development.

Entrepreneurship and Micro-franchise in Africa

Entrepreneurial growth in Africa has been associated with a multiplicity of factors tied to the individual entrepreneur and to social, political and legal environments. Kiggundu (2002) discusses entrepreneurship in Africa in terms of three broad categories: (1) characteristics unique to the entrepreneur, (2) characteristics more specific to the African entrepreneur firm, and (3) characteristics more linked to the external environment in which the entrepreneur operates.

Examples of these characteristics complemented by other identifying traits of the African entrepreneur are listed below and suggested in this chapter as relevant in assessing the potential for the success of the *micro-franchise model* in Africa's development:

1. Small entrepreneurs face the constraints of limited equity capital, inadequate managerial skills and undue social influences of the family and community.

2. There exist many small family entrepreneurs dependent upon a strong authoritarian father and a closely knit family structure (Benedict 1979).

3. Female entrepreneurs tend to faced more operational and strategic impediments than male entrepreneurs (Rutashobya 2001:31-37). Keyser, de Kruif and Frese, however, found that among Zambian entrepreneurs, age or gender made no significant differences in determining entrepreneurs' success (Frese 2000).

4. Small-scale trading (commerce) dominate the micro-enterprise sector.

5. African entrepreneurs have difficulties establishing and maintaining business networks and clusters.

6. Entrepreneur activity in Africa is generally linked to self-employment, given the lack of appropriate public and private employment opportunities. Many potential entrepreneurs have the drive and vision to pursue self-employment and become economically self-reliant, but they often lack basic business managerial skills.

The MF model of entrepreneurial development is considered potentially relevant in eliminating the financial and managerial constraints small African entrepreneurs face in development. The following are some of the benefits MF might offer existing and potential entrepreneurs in Africa (Magleby 2006):

- MF offer low-income potential entrepreneurs a proven business opportunity that comes with considerable institutional support: that is, the opportunity to follow well-established business policies and procedures.

- The symbiotic and supportive relationship embodied in MF insulates the individual entrepreneur from many of the shocks of the open market and provides the small entrepreneur an institutional infrastructure, a degree of stability, security and predictability. MF is built upon a mutually profitable contractual relationship of shared ownership, and it promotes and supports a mutually beneficial product or service brand.

- MF allows for the sharing of the costs, risks, financing and profits between an enabling franchisor and an implementing franchisee or local business partner. MF promotes a self-governing peer-to-peer network of entrepreneurs. The small or local entrepreneur provides local knowledge, contacts and contributes to start-up capital.

Two examples from sub-Saharan Africa illustrate the impact MF is having on the lives and income of the entrepreneurs and the local communities:

1. The HealthStore Foundation in Kenya operates micro-franchise pharmacies, which provide a living wage to their owners while also contributing to the health of the local community through the distribution of medications for the treatment of malaria, worms, and respiratory infections (Kramer and Katz 2006).

2. The Vodacom Community Services program in South Africa uses a franchise model to promote local entrepreneurship and reduce startup capital requirements. It is a shared service model for providing telecommunication services to poor communities in South Africa. Much of Vodacom business with lower income customers comes from prepaid phone cards which are serviced from retail storefronts. Vodacom maintains a network of "phone centers" throughout the country. Vodacom owns the structures and some fixed equipment. Local franchisees own their equipment, inventory and customer relationships. The benefits of Vodafone entrepreneurs to the local community are manifold: allow

families to keep in touch with one another (especially migrant workers), manage family affairs, and help people to keep in touch with business partners (www.omidyar.net).

The preceding examples are limited to two sectors of the economy: namely, the health and telecommunication retail sectors. Nonetheless, MF is having developmental impacts in other economic sectors, such as agriculture, agro-business, energy, financial and other professional service sectors (UNDP 2001).

Studies have shown that MF allows small entrepreneurs to find income generating opportunities and have access to technology. MF allows the prospective entrepreneur to seize an opportunity and to be innovative. Social scientists emphasize that MF engages people at the base of the income pyramid as business partners and customers, building sustainable enterprises by introducing appropriate disruptive technologies and innovative business models.

The MF model allows for the creation and replication of successful private and social enterprises in developing economies. MF enables locally-owned small businesses in developing countries to create diversified and sustainable employment and income generating opportunities. MF has been identified as a catalyst for the creation of unique private market institutions to address the challenges of poverty alleviation and long-term economic development.

MF is promoted in development because of its "empowering solutions," as opposed to "imposed or donated solutions." For example, over time, social scientists have recognized that the traditional short-term relief aid and dependency approaches to economic development have not altered the underlying institutional basis of poverty. MF is viewed as a liberating business network model that given a favorable legal environment can enable the owners to increase their productivity as successful entrepreneurs and, thus, function as a catalyst in poverty elimination (Prahalad and Hart 2004).

MF models in development can take on characteristics of different organizational forms. For example, the *Bottom of the Pyramid (BOP) Protocol* promotes entrepreneurial development in less developed countries through partnership with multi-national and non-profit organizations (Cornel University n.d.). The success of this model of entrepreneurial development is linked to the adherence to the triple bottom line principles of economic profitability, environmental sensitivity, and social responsibility. Another example is the cooperation of micro-franchise with non-profit organizations (NGOs) and the private sector in development. For example, a multi-national corperation (MNC) operating in the developing world could adopt a form of the micro-franchise business model in partnership with NGOs to penetrate low-income markets. An example is the Shell Foundation work in global pro-poor energy initiatives with Micro-Franchises in developing areas Magleby 2006).

An interesting aspect of research on MF is determining the impact on the lives and income of the owners and poor communities in development. By understanding the profiles of the owners and the businesses of MF, one can more effectively approach a measure of the impact of MF in development.

Examples of other forms of economic cooperation can also provide lessons on how seemingly related entrepreneurial models have been implemented at different levels of economic development and the resulting impact on the income of the owners. A classic example of entrepreneurial development from the Federal Republic of Germany has been of special interest, given the success of entrepreneurial cooperatives such as the *Raiffesen and Volksbanken* in generating incomes for the members and creating employment opportunities in the local communities. The characteristics of the basic micro-franchise model can be viewed as complementary of the economic development model of the German cooperatives (*Raiffeisen and Volksbanken* organizations). Success of small-and medium-sized German cooperatives, in which members cope with resource constraints through the provision of professional advisory services, operational resources, and training by the secondary and tertiary level of the organizational structure, are well documented and recommended in development (Guinnane 1995). Such models have also been suggested and implemented (with qualifications for the local conditions) in Africa's entrepreneurial development. Many of such cooperatives in Africa, however, have been formed as state owned enterprises benefiting from government subsidies and considerable public funds.

Conclusion

MF has the potential for achieving greater success in overcoming the managerial and financial resource constraints in development. Both public and private institutions have begun to direct resources and the political willingness to promote private sector initiatives, as exemplified in the MF model, to ensure sustainable development (Government of South Africa 2001).

The successful application of the entrepreneurial model in Africa's development will ultimately depend on an enabling legal and business environment that rewards innovation and deter corrupt practices (e.g. illicit, and improper legal business conduct) (Klapper 2006). Success will also depend on how the MF model adapts to changing social, market and technological conditions.

Note: I am continuing my study of micro-franchise and other forms of entrepreneurial development in Africa to facilitate a comparative investigation of how replicable the MF entrepreneurial model is across geographical regions.

Bibliography

Abrahamsen, Rita. 2000. *Disciplining Democracy: Development Discourse and Good Governance in Africa.* London & New York: Zed Books.

Achebe, Chinua. 1991. "An Image of Africa," *Research Literature.* 9, 1978, cited in Jean and John Comaroff. *Of Revelation and Revolution, Colonialism and Consciousness in South Africa Vol. I.* Chicago: University of Chicago Press.

Aderinokun, Kunle. December 12, 2004. "Shell, JV Partners Commit $8.5 BN to NLNG," *This Day News.*

Aderinwale, Ayodele (ed.). 1995. *Corruption, Democracy and Human Rights in Southern Africa,* organized jointly by the Africa Leadership Forum and the Transparency International in Pretoria, South Africa, 31 July-2 August.

Africa Leadership Forum. November 17-18, 1990. *Origins of the Conference on Stability, Security, Development and Cooperation in Africa*, Addis Ababa, Ethiopia. http://www.africaleadership.org/CSSDCA.htm

Ake, Claude. 2000. *The Feasibility of Democracy in Africa.* Dakar: CODESRIA.

Ake, Claude. 1996. *Democracy and Development in Africa.* Washington, DC: The Brookings Institution.

Alemika, E.O. April 2, 2004. *Organized crime: Nigeria.* Paper presented at UNODC Seminar, Dakar, Senegal.

Alemika, E.O. April 2, 2004. *United Nations Transnational Organized Crime Assessment Form: Nigeria.*, Paper presented at UNDOC Seminar, Dakar, Senegal.

Allen, John. December 6, 2006. "Kabila Inaugurated Amid Tight Security," posted on *allAfrica.com.*

ALO. 2004. *Higher Education Partnerships for Global Development: Knowledge, Cooperation and Results.* Vol. IV 2004. New York: The Association Liaison Office for University Cooperation in Development.

ALO. 2003. *Report on the Collaboration Between The Education for Democracy and Development Initiative (EDDI) in Africa & The Association Liaison Office for University Cooperation in Development (ALO) 1998-2003.* New York: The Association Liaison Office for University Cooperation in Development.

Amanpour, C. (Producer) September 23, 2006. "Where have all the parents gone?" *CNN.*

Amoako, K.Y. 2005. *Forward, in Striving for Good Governance in Africa.* Synopsis of the African Governance Report by the United Nations Economic Commission for Africa.

Aronowitz, Stanley and Heather Gautney eds. 2003. *Implicating Empire: Globalization & Resistance in the 21st Century World Order.* New York: Basic Books, chapter one.

Atumba, Honoré N'Gbanda Nzambo Ko. 1998. *Ainsi Sonne Le Glas! Les Derniers Jours du MaréchalMobutu.* Paris: Éditions Gideppe.

AVERT. 2006. *Providing drug treatment for millions.* Retrieved on October 28, 2006 from http://avert.org/drugtreatment.htm

Ayad, Christophe. August 1, 2006. "RDC: boycott raté pour Thisekedi." *Libération.*

Bage, L. Sept-Nov, 2004. "HIV/AIDS in Africa: shifting the horizons of development" *UN Chronicle.* United Nations Publications.

Bajpae, Chietigj. October 7, 2005. "Sino-US Energy Competition in Africa," Power and Interest Report in Global Policy Forum.

Banya, Sama. July 6, 2006. "Apart from Climate Change What Else?" *Concord Times* (Freetown, Sierra Leone).

Barrow, John. 1801-1804. *An Account of Travels into the Interior of Southern Africa in the Years 1797 and 1798.* 2 volumes, London: Cadell & Davies.

Benedict, Anderson. 1996. *Imagined Communities*. London: Verso.

Benedict, B. 1979. "Family firms and firm families: a comparison of Indian, Chinese and Creole firms in Seychelles." In S.M. Greenfield, A. Stricken & Aubey, R.T. (Eds.), *Entrepreneurs in cultural context*. University of New Mexico Press.

Bergsten, C. Fred. March/April, 2004. "Foreign Policy for the Next President," *Foreign Affairs*."

Benot, Yves. 1991. *La démence coloniale sous Napoléon*. Paris, France: La Découverte.

Biddle, Jr., A. J. Drexel. "Memorandum: A Digest of Opinion of Norwegian Informed Observers Bearing on European Outlook and War Tendencies." In President Franklin D. Roosevelt's Office Files, 1933-1945, Part 2: Diplomatic Correspondence File. Washington: Library of Congress. Hereinafter FDR's Office Files, followed by the year and Part number. Biddle served as United States Ambassador to Norway from 1935-1937.

Blatt, Harvey. 2004. *America's Environmental Card*. Boston, MA: The MIT Press.

Bond, Patrick. 2004. *Talk Left Walk Right: South Africa's Frustrated Global Reforms* (Scottsville, South Africa: University of KwaZulu Natal Press, p. 193, 202-4.

Boston Globe, August 4, 2002 cited in Patrick Bond's *Talk Left Walk Right South Africa's Frustrated Global Reforms*.

Bottom of the Pyramid Protocol. n.d. BOP, Cornell University, http://www.johnson.cornell.edu/sge/BoP%20Protocol.pdf,

Braeckman, Collette. 2003. *Les Nouveaux Prédateurs: Politique des puissances en Afrique centrale*. Paris: Fayard.

Braeckman, Collette. 2002. *Lumumba, un Crime d'État*. Bruxelles: Les Éditions Aden, The full text of Lumumba's independence speech is reproduced in this book.

Braeckman, Collete. 1999. *L'Enjeu Congolais: L'Afrique centrale après Mobutu.* Paris: Fayard.

Brigham Young University. n.d. Center for Economic Self-Reliance, Annual Report 2005.

Brown, Drew. November 27, 2006. "U.S. stepping up anti-terrorism efforts in Africa," *Star & Stripes.*

Cartothers, Thomas. 1999. *Aiding Democracy Abroad.* Washington D.C: Carnegie Endowment for International Peace.

"Catholic Bishops Say Electoral Process Flawed," posted on *allAfrica.com* on 21 July 2006.

Center for Voting and Democracy. n.d. *What is Proportional Representation?* www.fairvote.org

Center for Strategic and International Studies. 2004. Transnational threats update. http://www.csis.org/media/csis/pubs/ttu_0412.pdf.

Chambers, Robert. 2006. Poverty Underperceived: Traps, Biases and Agenda. Institute of Development Studies at the University of Sussex, Brighton.

China Daily. August 1, 2006. "Energy Partnership with Africa based on equality."

Clinton, Bill. October 18, 2006. Africa: Speech of William Jefferson Clinton Accepting the 2006 Africare Humanitarian Award.

Clough, Michael. 1992. *Free At Last? U.S. Foreign Policy Toward Africa and the End of the Cold War.* New York: Council on Foreign Relations Press.

"Combined Joint Task Force-Horn of Africa," *Source Watch*, November 27, 2006.

Committee on International Relations. United States House of Representatives. 2005. "U.S. Response to Global AIDS Crisis: A Two-Year Review." Government Document 1617-6-01.

Coomassie, I. September 28-October 4, 1994. *Advance fee fraud.* Position paper presented at the 63rd Interpol General Assembly, Rome, Italy.

"Congo may face toughest test after vote," posted on *cnn.com*, 31 July 2006.

Conrad, Joseph. 1995. *Heart of Darkness*, edited by Robert Hampson. London & New York: Penguin Books.

Conrad, Joseph. 1983. *Heart of Darkness*. New York: New American Library, pp.147, 153.

Coquery-Vidrovitch, Catherinne. 2001. *Le Congo au temps des grandes companies concessionaires, 1898-1930.* Paris: Editions de l'EHESS.

"Country's Rich Promise," July 27, 2006, posted on *allAfrica.com*.

Creating a Development Dynamic-Final report of the digital opportunity initiative, 2001 Accenture, Markle Foundation, United Nations Development Programme, http://www.optinit.org/framework/pages/contents.html

Crocker, Chester. December 10, 1985. Statement by the Assistant Secretary of State for African Affairs, Before the United States' Senate Sub-Committee on African Affairs.

Crossroads. August-October, 2001. *Exploits of the "419" Scam.* Vol. 8, No. 8. U.S. Embassy, Nigeria. http://Abuja.usembassy.gov/wwwhxrdaug13.html.

Dao, James. September 19, 2002. "In Quietly Courting Africa, U.S. Likes the Dowry: Oil," *New York Times*.

Davidson, Basil. September 8, 1951. "Africa: Emergent Colossus." *The Nation*.

Deen, Thalif. July 27, 2006. "UN Readies for Biggest Ever Poll," posted on *allAfrica.com*.

De Witte, Ludo. 2001. *L'assassinat de Lumumba.* Paris: Karthala, 2000; translated in English by Ann Wright & Renée Fenby as *The Assassination of Lumumba.* London & New York: Verso, pp. xiii-xiv, xxii. A Belgian Parliamentary commission of enquiry into the assassination of Lumumba acknowledged Belgian responsibility in this affair and prompted the Belgian minister of foreign affairs, Louis Michel, to offer official apologies to the Congolese people, together with symbolic monetary compensation to Lumumba's descendants.

Dokubo, Charles. 2000. "'An army for Rent', Private Military Corporations and civil Conflicts in Africa: The case of Sierra Leone." *Civil Wars*, Vol. 3, No. 2, pp51-64.

Drug War Chronicle. January 5, 2007. Afghan opium dilemma sparks new calls for alternative development, "normalizing" the poppy crop. Issue #467. http://stopthedrugwar.org/chronicle/467/
afghan_opium_dilemma_sparks_calls_alternative_development_normalize
_poppy_crop

Dumbuya, Peter A. 1995. *Tanganyika Under International Mandate, 1919-1945.* Lanham: University Press Of America.

Dunn, Kevin C. 2003. *Imagining the Congo: The International Relations of Identity.* New York: Palgrave-Macmillan.

Edgell, Alvin. 2003. Globalization and cultural encounters. *International Third World Studies Journal*, XIV:1-9.

Eisemon, Tom and M. Kourouma. 1994. Foreign assistance for university development in Sub-Saharan Africa. In Jamil Salmi and Adrian Verspoor, eds. *Revitalizing Higher Education*. Washington, DC: World Bank.

Elkins, Caroline. 2005. *Imperial Recokoning: The Untold Story of Britain's Gulag in Kenya.* New York: Henry Holt and Company.

Ellerman, David. 2004. Autonomy in education and development. *Journal of International Cooperation in Education*, 7, (1):3-14.

Ellerman, D. I. 2004. *Helping People Help Themselves: From the World Bank to an Alternative Philosophy of Development.* Ann Arbor, Michigan: University of Michigan Press.

Elliot, George Fielding. April, 1955. "Africa, Key to Western Security." *American Mercury*.

Energy Information Administration. March, 2003. "West African Gas Pipeline (WAGP) Project."

Energy Information Administration. December, 2000. "Annual Energy Outlook 2001."

Fallah, Bob. 2006. "Bad Governance Is Africa's Major Problem." In *The Perspective*, Atlanta, May 12.

Flipo, Blandine. July 25, 2006. "Au Congo, les soldats européens contre les mauvais perdants." *Libération.*

Freedom House. 2006. Freedoms in the World. www.freedomhouse.org/uploads/Chart18Files.pdf. Accessed on October 28, 2006.

Freedom House. 2003. Freedoms in the World. New Jersey: Piscatemy Transaction Publisher.

French, Howard W. 2004. *A Continent for the Taking: The Tragedy and Hope of Africa.* New York: Alfred A. Knopf.

Frese, M. 2000. *Success and Failure of Micro Business Owners in Africa: A Psychological Approach*, Westport, CT: Quorum Books.

Ganado, Leburah. October, 2006. "Ogoni: Why Shell is Unpardonable." *Nigeriaworld.*

Gellman, B. 2000. Western media attention to AIDS in Africa. Avert.org. Retrieved September 9, 2006 from http://www.globalissues.org/Geopolitics/Africa/AIDS.asp

Gettleman, Jeffrey. October 30, 2006. "Despite Tensions, Millions Vote in Congo," *The New York Times.*

Gibbons, M. *et. al.* 1994. *The New Production of Knowledge: Science and Research in Contemporary Societies.* London: Sage Publications.

Glaser, Antoine and Stephen Smith. 1994. *L'Afrique san Africains: Le Reve Blanc du Continent Nois.* Paris: Editions Stock.

Gleijeses, Piero. 2002. *Conflicting Missions: Havana, Washington, and Africa, 1959-1976.* Chapel Hill: University of North Carolina Press.

Global AIDS Alliance. 2002. Former South African President and Nobel Laureate Nelson Mandela, February 17, 2002. Retrieved from http://www.globalaidsalliance.org/quotes.cfm (10/19/2006).

Goldschmidt, Walter. 1958. *The United States and Africa.* New York: Columbia University Press.

Goldwyn, David L. and Robert E. Ebel. 2004. "Crafting a U.S. Energy Policy for Africa." In Walter H. Kansteiner III, and J. Stephen Morrison, eds. *Rising U.S. Stakes in Africa: Seven Proposals to Strengthen U.S.-Africa Policy.* Washington, D.C.: The Center for Strategic and International Studies Press.

Gondola, Ch. Didier. 2002. *The History of the Congo.* Westport, CT: Greenwood Press.

Gouahinga, François. November 15, 2006. "Joseph Kabila re-elected," posted on *allAfrica.com.*

Government of South Africa. July, 2001. "A New African Initiative: Merging the Millennium Partnership for the African Recovery Program (MAP) and the Omega Plan."

Guinnane, T. W. September, 1997. "Regional Organizations in the German Cooperative Banking System in the Late 19th Century." *Research in Economics*, Volume 51, Number 3, pp. 251-274(24), Publisher: Academic Press, ttp://www.earthinstitute.columbia.edu/cgsd/documents/guinnane.pdf

Hall, Luella J. 1971. *The United States and Morocco, 1776-1956.* Metuchen: Scarecrow Press.

Harris, Joseph. 1987. *Africans and their History.* New York: Penguin, p. 23.

Hart, Stuart. 2005. "Capitalism at the Crossroads: The Unlimited Business Opportunities in Solving The World's Most Difficult Problems."

Hartley, Aidan. July 28, 2006. "Congo's Election, the UN's Massacre," *The New York Times.*

Heyneman, Stephen. 2005. "Foreign Aid to Education: Recent U.S. Initiatives—Background, Risks, and Prospects." *Peabody Journal of Education*, 80, (1):107-119.

Hilferdig, Rudolf. 1988. 1877-1941 in *Finance Capital*. New York: Routledge.

Hobson, J.A. 1904. *Imperialism: A Study*. Hobson distinguished late 19th Century imperialism from previous ones in two ways: competition of several empires against each other predominance of finance capital over mercantile capital. He rejected the idea that capitalism would help improve poor peoples' conditions.

Hochschild, Adam. 1998. *King Leopold's Ghost: A Story of Greed, Terror, and Heroism in Colonial Africa*. Boston: Houghton Mifflin Company.

Homely delivered by Archbishop Emmanuel Kataliko, Roman Catholic Archbishop of Bukavu (DRC) on Christmas Day 1999, in Letter from the World Council of Churches' General Secretary to WCC member churches in the DRC, Geneva (24 July 2006); available at http://www. oikoumene.org/index.php?id=2354.

Hope, Kempe Ronald, Sr. 2005. "Child Survival, Poverty, and Labour in Africa." *Journal of Children and Poverty*, Vol. 11, No. 1.

Howe, Russell Warren. 1975. *Along the Afric Shore: An Historic Review of Two Centuries of U.S.-African Relations*. New York: Barnes and Noble.

Human Development. August, 2001. *Challenging the Challenger: Understanding the response of Universities in Africa to HIV/AIDS*. p.144-48.

Human Rights Watch. 2003. http://www.hrw.org/reports/2004

Human Rights Watch. 2005. World Report. New York: Human Rights Watch.

Human Rights Watch. 2004. World Report. New York: Human Rights Watch.

Human Rights Watch. 2003. World Report. New York: Human Rights Watch.

Human Rights Watch. 2002. World Report. New York: Human Rights Watch.

Human Rights Watch. 2001. World Report. New York: Human Rights Watch.

Human Rights Watch. 2000.World Report. New York: Human Rights Watch.

Human Rights Watch.1999. World Report. New York: Human Rights Watch.

Human Rights Watch. 1998. World Report. New York: Human Rights Watch.

Human Rights Watch. 1997. World Report. New York: Human Rights Watch.

Human Rights Watch. 1996. World Report. New York Human Rights Watch.

Human Rights Watch. 1995. World Report. New York: Human Rights Watch.

Human Rights Watch.1994. World Report. New York: Human Rights Watch.

Human Rights Watch. 1993. World Report. New York: Human Rights Watch.

Human Rights Watch. 1992. World Report. New York: Human Rights Watch.

Human Rights Watch.1991. World Report. New York: Human Rights Watch.

Human Rights Watch. 1990. World Report. New York: Human Rights Watch.

Huntington, Samuel P. Summer, 1993. "The Clash of Civilizations?" *Foreign Affairs* 72, No.1. pp. 22-49.

Ifedi, Afam and J. Anyu Ndumbe. September-December, 2005. "West African Gas Pipeline (WAGP) Project and It's Impact on the Region's Development," *Journal of Development Alternatives and Area Studies* (formerly *Scandinavian Journal of Development Alternatives and Area Studies*), Volume 24, Nos. 3 and 4.

Inter Press Service. August 2, 2002.

Inter Press Service. July 31, 2006. "A Three-Week Countdown," posted on *allAfrica.com*.

International Crisis Group (ICG). July 20, 2006. "Escaping the Conflict Trap: Promoting Good Governance in the Congo." *Africa Report* No. 114.

ICG. July 20, 2006. "Escaping the Conflict Trap: Promoting Good Governance in the Congo." *Africa Report* No. 114, i.

ICG. January 9, 2006. "Katanga: The Congo's Forgotten Crisis." *Africa Report* No. 103 [http://www.crisisgroup.org/home/index.cfm?1=1&id=3861].

ICG. October 19, 2005. "A Congo Action Plan," *Africa Briefing* No. 34). www.crisisgroup.org/home/index.cfm?1=1&id=3758.

Jackson, Henry. 1982. *From The Congo to Soweto: U.S. Foreign Policy Toward Africa Since 1960*. New York: William Morrow and Co.

Joskow, Paul L. n.d. "U.S. Energy Policy during the 1990s." Analysis of United States' policy effort relies substantially on this National Bureau of Economic Research (NBER) working paper, 8484.

Kagan, Robert. March/April, 2004. "American Crisis of Legitimacy," *Foreign Affairs*, Vol.83, No. 2.

Kalb, Madeleine G. 1982. *The Congo Cables: The Cold War in Africa, from Eisenhower to Kennedy*. New York: Macmillan Publishing Co., pp. 194, 196.

Kamitatu, Cléophas. 1971. *La grande mystification du Congo-Kinshasa: les crimes de Mobutu*. Paris: François Maspéro, 2ème edition, pp. 97-99.

Kansteiner III and Morrison, eds. 2004. *Stakes in Africa-United States Relations: Proposals for Equitable Partnership*. Washington, DC: The Center for Strategic and International Studies Press.

Kankwenda, Mbaya J. 2005. *L'économie politique de la prédation au Congo Kinshasa: Des origines à nos jours, 1885-2003*. Kinshasa, Montréal & Washington: Éditions de l' ICREDES.

Kanza, Thomas. 1972. *Conflict in the Congo: The Rise and Fall of Lumumba*. Baltimore: Penguin Books.

Karlstrom, Mikael. 2003. *On The Aesthetics and Dialogics of Power in the Postcolony*, Africa 73 (1).

Kieh, George Klay. 1988. "The Reagan Administration's Policy Toward Liberia: A Critical Analysis." *ACAS Bulletin*. No. 25:8-11.

Kiggundu, Moses N. October, 2002. "Entrepreneurs and Entrepreneurship in Africa: What is Known and What Needs to Be Done." *Journal of Developmental Entrepreneurship*.

King, Kenneth. 2004. "The External Agenda of Educational Reform: A Challenge to Educational Self-Reliance and Dependency in Sub-Saharan Africa." *Journal of International Cooperation in Education,* 7 (1):85-96.

Klapper, Leora. November, 2006. "Entrepreneurship—How Much Does the Business Environment Matter?" *Viewpoint.* Note Nr.3 http://rru.worldbank.org/PublicpolicyJournal

Kramer, William and Robert Katz. January, 2006. "Health-Store: Health Care at the Bottom of the Pyramid." World Resources Institute.

Kraxberger, Brennan M. Fall 2005. "The United States and Africa: Shifting Geopolitics in an 'Age of terror,'" Africa Today, Volume 52, Number 1.

Kubler, Jay. 2005. "African Higher Education Activities in Development: The AHEAD Database." London: Short Paper Series on African Higher Education Development, Policy Research Unit, Association of Commonwealth Universities.

Lancaster, Carol. 1993. *United States and Africa: Into the Twenty-First Century.* Washington D.C.: Overseas Development Council.

Lapham, Nicholas P. 2004. "A Natural Resource Conservation Initiative for Africa." In Walter H. Kansteiner III and J. Stephen Morrison, eds. *Rising U.S. Stakes in Africa: Seven Proposals to Strengthen U.S.-Africa Policy.* Washington, DC: The Center for Strategic and International Studies Press.

Lenin, Vladimir. n.d. *Imperialism: the Highest stage of Capitalism.* New York: International Publishers. He argued during this period imperialism was characterized by dominance of monopolies & Finance capital.

Letter from the World Council of Churches Secretary General to WCC member churches in the DRC, Geneva, 24 July 2006; posted on http://www.oikoumene.org/index.php?id=2354.

Liberia Research and Information Project. 1988. Liberia Alert. Chicago: LRIP.

Lindqvist, Sven. 1996. *"Exterminate All the Brutes" One Man's Odyssey into the Heart of Darkness and the Origins of European Genocide*, referring to a speech by Lord Salisbury, prime minister of England. New York: W.W. Norton & Company.

Llon, Lynn. 2003 "Foreign Aid Financing of Higher Education in Africa" In P. Altbach and D.Teferra, eds. *African Higher Education: An International Reference Handbook*. Bloomington & Indianapolis: Indiana University Press, 2003:6-71.

Lumumba, Patrice Émery. July 15, 1960. "Address to Parliament," in Yves Bénot, *La mort de Lumumba*, pp. 132-3.

Luxemburg, Rosa. 1951. *The Accumulation of* Capital. New York: Monthly Review Press.

Machiavelli, Niccoli. 1994. *The Prince*. New York: Penguin Books.

MacKenzie, J., Amani, W., & Ibrahimi, S.Y. December 7, 2006. "Afghan Opium: A Failed Jihad?" *Environment News Service* (International Daily Neswire) http://www.ens-newswire.com/ens/dec2006/2006-12-07-02.asp

Macmillan, Graham. n.d. "Corporate/MFI Partnerships that Are Profitable for the Corporation, the MFI, and the Clients." Scojo Foundation, United States, from http://www.microcreditsummit.org/papers/Workshops/9_Macmillan.pdf

Madsen, Wayne. 1999. *Genocide and Covert Operations in Africa, 1993-1999*. Lewiston, NY: The Edwin Mellen Press.

Magleby, Kirk. 2006. "Micro-Franchises as a Solution to Global Poverty." MicroFranchises.org http://ascendalliance.org/fckeditor/editor/filemanager/upload/php/file.php?id=338

Magubane, Bernard. 1996. *The Making of a Racist State: British Imperialism and the Union of South Africa 1873-1910*. Trenton, NJ: Africa World Press.

Majumder, Sanjoy. September 8, 2006. *Indian Women to keep Liberia Peace*. BBC News in Video and Audio, (Printable version). Http://News.bbc.co.uk/2/hi/south_asia/5323140.stm

Mann, J., Grunskin, S., Grodin, M., and Annas, G. J. 1999. (Edited). *Health and Human Rights: A Reader.* Routkedge, New York, NY.

Martin, Guy. 2002. *Africa in World Politics: A Pan-African Perspective.* Trenton, NJ: Africa World Press.

Martin, Guy. Winter 1998. "Reflections on Democracy and Development in Africa: The Intellectual Legacy of Claude Ake," *Ufahamu* 26. pp. 102-109.

Martens, Ludo. 2002. *Kabila et la révolution congolaise: Panafricanisme ou néocolonialisme?* Tome 1 (Anvers: Éditions EPO.

Masango, David. July 27, 2006. "DRC Confident of Successful Elections." posted on *allAfrica.com.*

Matos, Narciso. October 5-9, 1998. Speech of Professor Narciso Matos, Secretary-General of the Association of African Universities. In *Plenary: World Conference on Higher Education*, UNESCO, Paris. Vol. V. Document No. ED-99/HEP/WCHE/Vol.V-NGO-2. Paris, UNESCO.

Mayamba, Serge. July 25, 2006. "Police Disperse Anti-Poll Demonstrators." posted on *allAfrica.com.* Mayumba is in charge of Youth Affairs in the UDPS.

Mazrui, Ali. 1992. "Towards Diagnosing and Treating Cultural Dependency: The Case of the African University." *International Journal of Educational Development*, 2 (2):95-111.

McGhee, George C. July 16, 1951. "Africa's Role in the Free World Today." *The Department of State Bulletin.* Vol. XXV, No. 629.

McKay, Vernon. 1963. *Africa in World Politics.* New York: Harper and Row.

Memmi, Albert. 2002. *Portrait du colonisé, précédé de Portrait du colonisateur.* Paris: Folio-Actuel/Gallimard.

Mendell, G. September, 2005. "Living with AIDS" *National Geographic*, pp. 66-73.

Menkiti, Ifeanyi A. 1999. "Normative Instability and political Disorder in Africa." In *New Political Science*, Volume 21, Number 1.

Meredith, Martin. 2005. Merlier, Michael. 1962. *Le Congo, de la colonization belge à l'indépendence*. Paris, France: François Maspéro.

Merivale, Herman. 1996. 1838 Oxford Lectures on "Colonization and Colonies." In Sven Lindqvist. *"Exterminate All the Brutes" One Man's Odyssey into the Heart of Darkness and the Origins of European Genocide*. New York: W.W. Norton & Company.

Morse, Edward L. and A. M. Jaffe. n.d. "Strategic Energy Policy: Challenges from the 21st Century," Report of an Independent task Force, James A. Baker III Institute for Public Policy of Rice University and the Council on Foreign Relations.

Mueni wa Muiu. 2002. "Fundi wa Africa: Toward a New Paradigm of the African State" *Journal of Third World Studies* (volume xix, no.2):23-42.

Myers C. N. & A. E. Henn. In Robert I. Rotberg, ed. 1988. *Africa In The 1990s And Beyond: U.S. Policy Opportunities And Choices*. Algonac, MI: Reference Publications.

Nabudere, Dani. 2004. "Africa's First War, Mineral Wealth, Conflicts and War in the Great Lakes." Occasional Paper No. 8. African Association of Political Science.

New York Times. October 29, 2006. "Africa's World of Forced Labour, in a 6-year Old's Eyes," vol. civi, no. 53,747.

New York Times. October 4, 2006. "An African Dumping Ground."

Ngawi, Joseph. July 28, 2006a. "The Economy a Major Factor in Elections." posted on *allafrica.com*.

Ngawi, Joseph. July 25, 2006b. "Elections Capture the Attention of Africa." posted on *allAfrica.com*

Nicholas, H.G. 1975. *The United States and Britain*. Chicago: University of Chicago Press.

Ntuli, Zibonele. July 19, 2006. "Successful Elections to Open up Unprecedented Prospects," posted On *allAfrica.com*.

Nzongola-Ntalaja, Georges. 2002. *The Congo from Leopold to Kabila: A People's History*. London & New York: Zed Books.

Nkrumah, Kwame. 1970. *Class Struggle in Africa*. New York: International Publishers.

N.S.C. 5818. August 26, 1958. "U.S. Policy Toward Africa South of the Sahara Prior to Calendar Year 1960." White House Office of the Special Assistant for National Security Affairs. *The Declassified Documents Quarterly Catalog*. Vol. VII, No. 3. Washington: Carrollton Press, 1981.

Noble, R. 2006. "Providing Drug Treatment for Millions." Avert.org. Retrieved, October 28, 2006 from http://avert.org/drugtreaqtment.htm.

Nzouankeu, Jacques Mariel. 1998. "Major Problems and Emerging Trends with Respect to Governance in Africa." United Nations: Group of experts on the United Nations Programme on Public Administration and Finance, 14th Session, May 4-12.

Obasi, Godwin O. P. 2004. "Embracing Sustainability Science: The Challenge for Africa." In F. J. Ramsay and W. Edge, eds. *Africa* (Global Studies, 10th ed.). Guilford, CT: McGraw-Hill/Dushkin Company.

O'Brien, Conor Criuse. 1996. *To Katanga and Back: A U.N. Case History*. New York: The Universal Library/Grosset & Dunlap, pp. 238-40

Okomo, Mojubaolu Olufunke. 2005. "The Nature of the State, Gender Politics and the Empowerment of Women in the Twenty-First Century." In E. Ike Udogu (ed). *Nigeria in the Twenty-First Century*. Trenton, NJ: Africa World Press, pp. 91-112.

Olsen, Gorm Rye. July, 2004. "Challenges to the Traditional Policy Options, Opportunities for New Choices: The Africa Policy of the E.U." *The Round Table*, Vol. 93, No. 375, 425-436.

Ottaway, Marina. June 8, 1999. *Statement Before the U.S. Senate Subcommittee on Africa*. Ottaway is a Senior Associate with the Carnegie Endowment for International Peace.

Outstanding Example of SME Development via the Franchise Business Model. n.d. http://www.omidyar.net/group/poverty/file/0.98.11067702980/get/Vodafone%20Phone%20Shops.doc

Owoh, N. n.d. I go chop your dollar. Lyrics to a VCD song.

Paiewonsky, D.and García, 2006. M. *Gender, Remittances and Development.* United Nations International Research and Training Institute for the Advancement of Women (INSTRAW).

"Pan-Sahel Initiative" *Source Watch*, November 27, 2006.

Penfield, James K. June 8, 1959. "The Role of the United States in Africa: Our Interests and Operations." *The Department of State Bulletin* (Vol. XL, No. 1041).

Piot, P., Feachem, R. G., Jong-wook, L., and. Wolfensohn, J. June 25, 2004. "A Global Response to AIDS: Lessons Learned, Next Steps" *Science Magazine.* Vol. 304, No. 5679, pp. 1909-10. Available at http://www.sciencemag.org/cgi/content/summary/304/5679/1909

Plank, David. 1993. "Aid, Debt and the End of Sovereignty: Mozambique and Its Donors." *Journal of Modern African Studies* 31, 3. Quoted in John S. Saul, *The Next Liberation Struggle: Capitalism, Socialism and Democracy in Southern Africa.* Toronto & New York: Between The Lines/Monthly Review Press, 2005.

"Records of Maji Maji Rebellion 1905-1907 cited in Robert O. Collins, ed. 2001. *Documents From the African* Past. Princeton: Wiener Publishers, p. 306.

Prahalad, C. K. 2004. *The Fortune at the Bottom of the Pyramid: Eradicating Poverty through Profits.* Upper Saddle River, NJ: Wharton School Publishing.

Pugh, Marilyn and Mary Spear. 2005. "Can Higher Education Partnerships Teach a Person to Fish?" *Journal of International Cooperation in Education,* 8 (1):45-59.

Rasheed, R. A.. August 6, 1997. "Advance Fee Fraud (419): A Scam that Feeds on Itself." Paper presented at the joint conference of the Central Bank of Nigeria and the Nigeria Police, Special fraud Unit, Lagos, Nigeria.

Robinson, Mark. 2006. *The political Economy of Governance in Uganda.* Institute of Development Studies at the University of Sussex, Brighton.

Roosevelt, Franklin D. 1933-1945, Part 2. *President Franklin D. Roosevelt's Office Files, 1933-1945, Parts 1 and 2: Diplomatic Correspondence File.* Washington: Library of Congress.

Rutashobya, L. 2001. "Female Entrepreneurship in Tanzania: Constraints and Strategic "Considerations." Proceedings of the International Academy of African Business and development, Washington, D.C., pp. 31-37.

Schatzberg, Michael G. 1991. *Mobutu or Chaos? The United States and Zaire, 1960-1990.* Lanham: University Press of America.

Schraeder, Peter J. 2004. *African Politics and Society: A Mosaic in Transformation.* Belmont, CA: Wadsworth/Thomson Learning.

Schraeder, Peter J. 1994. *United States Foreign Policy Toward Africa: Incrementalism, Crisis and Change.* Cambridge: Cambridge University Press.

Sciencebase Section News. May 15, 2006. "Disappearing Equatorial Icecaps." Posted by Africans_Without_Borders@yahoogroups.com on May 15, 2006.

Sengupta, Somini. March 29, 2004. "Attack in Congo Capital Mars Peace Transition," *New York Times.*

Shannon, Ulric. 2000. "Human Security and the rise of Private Armies." *New Political Science,* Volume 22, Number 1.

Simons, Paul E. August 1, 2006. "U.S. Seeks Energy Security through International Partnership." *Energy News.*

Skinner, Elliot P. 1992. *African Americans and U.S. Policy Toward Africa 1850-1924: In Defense of Black Nationality.* Washington: Howard University Press.

Slaughter, Sheila. and Larry Lesile. 1997. *Academic Capitalism: Politics, Policies and the Entrepreneurial University.* Baltimore: The Johns Hopkins University Press.

Southern African News Features. July 27, 2006. "Candidates Contest for 189 Constituencies." Posted on *allAfrica.com*

Stiglitz, Joseph. 2002. *Globalization and Its Discontents*. London: Penguin.

Stolberg, S. and R. Stevenson. January 30, 2003. "The President's Proposals: AIDS Policy; Bush AIDS Surprises Many, but Advisers Call It Long Planned." *New York Times*, retrieved August 30, 2006 from http:// query.nytimes.com

Swedish International Development Authority. 1981/82. *Report, Theme: The Environment*. Stockholm, Sweden: SIDA Information Division.

Tang, Sello and Silindiwe Dube. July 21, 2006. "Nine Days to DRC Elections and the Country Says It's Ready." posted on *allAfrica.com*.

Task Force on Higher Education and Society. 2000. "Higher Education in Developing Countries: Peril and Promise." Washington, DC: World Bank. Retrieved July 20, 2006 from www.tfhe.net/about/about.htm

Taulbee, James Larry. Summer 2002. "The Privatization of Security: Modern Conflict, Globalization and weak States." *Civil Wars*, Vol.5, No.2, pp.1- 24.

The history of cooperatives, Deutsche Genossenschafts-und Raiffeisenverband e.V. n.d. http://www.dgrv.de/en/cooperatives/historyofcooperatives.html.

"The Minerals of the Democratic Republic of Congo" [http:// euromin.w3sites.net/Nouveau_site/gisements/congo/GISCONe.htm]

The Punch. November 1, 2006. "Nigeria, China sign $8.3bn rail contract."

The World Development Movement. 1999.

ThisDay Online. October 17, 2006. "Wolfowitz: Nigeria Has Lost $300 Billion to Corruption." http://www.thisdayonline.com/nview.php?id=60860

Thomas-Slayter, Barbara and Sodikoff, Genese. 2001. "Sustainable Investments: Women's Contributions to Natural Resource Management Projects in Africa." *Development in Practice*, Vol. 11, Number 1.

Udogu, E. Ike. 2005. "General Introduction." In E. Ike Udogu *Nigeria in the Twenty-First Century*. Trenton, NJ: Africa World Press.

UNESCO. *General History of* Africa, Vols. II 1980; III 1988; IV 1984. Heine-mann, California, Paris: NESCO.

UNODC. 2005. Summary findings of opium trends in Afghanistan. http:// www.undoc.org/pdf/afghanistan_2005/annex_opium-afghanistan-2005-09-09.pdf.

UNODC. 2005. *Transnational Organized Crime in the West African Region*. New York: Author.

UNODC. 2005. *Why Fighting Crime Can Assist Development in Africa*. New York: Author.

United Nations Chronicles Online System Watch. 2005.

United Nations Economic Commission for Africa. 2005. "Striving for Good Governance in Africa, Synopsis of the 2005 African Governance Report." Prepared for the African Development Forum IV.

United Nations Integrated Regional Information Networks (UN-IRIN). April 12, 2004. "DRC: 25 People Hacked to Death Discovered in North Kivu, UN Mission Says." posted on http://allafrica.com.

UN-IRIN. July 27, 2006. "Thousands Displaced in Katanga Return Home." posted on *allAfrica.com*.

United Nations News Service. April 12, 2004. "UN Mission in DR of Congo Finds Bodies After Report of Gunmen Killing Villagers." posted on *allafrica.com*.

United States Agency for International Development. 2003. *Budget 2003*. Retrieved June 14 2006 from www.usaid.gov

Vansina, Jan. 2004. *How Societies are Born: Governance in West Central Africa Before 1600*. Charlottesville, Virginia: University of Virginia Press, pp. 206-272

Varg, Paul A. 1978. "Missionaries." In Alexander DeConde, ed. *Encyclopedia of American Foreign Policy* (Vol. II). New York: Charles Scribner's Sons.

Vig, Norman J. and Michael G. Faure. 2004. *Green Giants? Environmental Policies of the United States and the European Union.* Boston, MA: The MIT Press.

Villard, Henry Serrano. 1965. *Affairs at State.* New York: Thomas Y. Crowell Company.

Volman, Daniel. 2006. "U.S. Military Programs in Sub-Saharan Africa, 2005-2007." Working Paper. Association of Concerned Africanist Scholars.

Volman, Daniel. 1993. "Africa and the New World Order." *Journal of Modern African Studies*, Vol. 31, No.1.

Wallerstein, Immanuel. 1975. "Africa, the United States and the Third World Economy: The Historic Bases of American Policy." In Frederick S. Arkhurst, ed. *United States Policy Toward Africa.* New York: Praeger Publishers.

Walton, P. June 22, 2006. *U.S.-Africa partnership aims to help "poorest of the poor."* Federal Information and News dispatch, Inc. Retrieved on August 30, 2006 from http://wf2la2.webfeat.org/GrVIG1122url=http://web.lexis-nexis.com/universe/

Wangila R., & Akukwe, C. 2006. "HIV and AIDS in Africa: Ten Lessons from the Field." Retrieved August 9, 2006 from http://www.worldpress.orf/Africa/2445.cfm 9/9/2006

Waziri, F.M. 2005. *Advance Fee Fraud, National Security and the Law.* Ibadan, Nigeria: Book Builders Editions Africa.

Warren, N. P. N. June, 2000. "AIDS and the Worldbank: global blackmail?" *A&U Magazine.* Retrieved September 9, 2006 from http://www.globalissues.org/Geopolitics/Africa/AIDS.asp

White, Carol. 1980. *The New Dark Ages of Conspiracy.* New York: New Benjamin Franklin House.

White, E. H. 2004. "AIDS in Africa: A Security threat?" Master's Thesis, the Fletcher School, Tufts University. Retrieved October 14, 2006 from http://fletcher.tufts.edu/research/2004/White-Elizabeth.pdf

Wikipedia, Free Encyclopedia. 2006. AIDS Epidemic. Retrieved September 23, 2006 from http://en.wikipedia.org/wiki/AIDS_pandemic.

Willame, Jean-Claude. 1999. *L'Odyssée Kabila: Trajectoire pour un Congo nouveau?* Paris: Karthala.

Williams, P. May, 2004. "The Global Implications of West African Organized Crime." *Input paper: West Africa Assessment Project.*

Wilson, Woodrow. January 8, 1918. "Address of the President of the United States Delivered at Joint Session of the Two Houses of Congress, January 8, 1918." Akron: Woodrow Wilson Papers, Bierce Library, University of Akron.

Winer, J. September 11, 1996. *Nigerian Crime.* Statement before the Subcommittee on Africa of the House International Relations Committee, Washington, DC. http://www.fas.org/irp/congress/1996_hr/h960911w.htm

Wolfowitz, P. October 16, 2006. Paul Wolfowitz speech at the third plenary conference of the extractive industries transparency initiative, Oslo, Norway.

World Bank, Small and Medium Enterprises http://rru.worldbank.org/Themes/SmallMediumEnterprises/

World Bank. 1988. *Education in Sub-Saharan Africa: Policies for Adjustment, Revitalization and Expansion.* Washington, DC.

World Bank. 1994. *Higher Education: The Lessons of Experience.* Washington, DC.

World Bank. 1995. *Priorities and Strategies for Education: A World Bank Review.* Washington, DC.

World Food Program. July 25, 2006. "Food Aid Urged for Thousands Fleeing Havoc and Hardship in East." posted on *allAfrica.com.*

Wrong, Michela. 2001. *In the Footsteps of Mr. Kurtz: Living on the Brink of Disaster in Mobutu's Congo*. New York: HarperCollins/Perennial. A top U.S. government official under the Johnson and Nixon administrations, Roger Morris revealed that Mobutu received close to $150 million from the CIA during the first decade or so of his regime.

Yesufu, Ted. 1973. *Creating the African University*, Ibadan: Oxford University Press.

Young, Crawford. 1965. *Politics in the Congo: Decolonization and Independence*. Princeton, NJ: Princeton University Press. It is interesting to note in this regard that following the Battle of Ambwila in which the Portuguese defeated King Antonio I of Kongo, thus permanently compromising the independence of the Kongo State, the Kingdom was divided from 6 into 22 provinces; the Congo now has 11 provinces, to be increased to 26 (each with locally elected provincial assemblies) according to the new constitutional provisions.

Young, Crawford. October 11, 2006. "Britain Now to Reject Nigerians' Stolen Money." *Nigerian Tribune*.

Young, Crawford. *The Economist*. September 16, 2006.

About the Authors

Abdul Karim Bangura is professor of International Relations and researcher-in-residence at the Center for Global Peace in the School of International Service at American University in Washington, DC. Bangura holds a PhD in Political Science, a PhD in Development Economics, a PhD in Linguistics, and a PhD in Computer Science. He is the author of 53 books and more than 400 scholarly essays. He is the recipient of many teaching and other scholarly and service awards. He also is fluent in about a dozen African and six European languages and now studying intensively to increase his proficiency in Arabic and Hebrew.

Ciyata Dinah Coleman is a former associate professor of Economics in the School of International Affairs and Development at Clark Atlanta University in Atlanta, Georgia and is currently employed by the Federal Government. She holds a PhD in Economics from Southern Illinois University n Carbondale and a MS in Business/Cooperative Economics from the Philipps University in Marburg/Lahn in the Federal Republic of Germany. The content of this paper is not associated with the institution and organization with which the author is associated, but rather reflective of her training and professional experiences as an economist and a social scientist.

Doyin Coker-Kolo received her BA in Educational Administration from the University of Lagos in Nigeria and her MEd and PhD in Educational Administration from the University of South Carolina, Columbia. Kolo's research interests include Integrative Learning, Global and Multicultural Education, and School-Community Collaborations. She serves as a consultant to the Habitat for Humanity African Program, has participated in numerous workshops, seminars and conferences on global developments, and is the author of several articles published in peer-reviewed scholarly journals. Courses that she teaches include The Learner and Learning Process in a Multicultural Context, and Third World Education and Development Studies Seminar. She participated in Fulbright Hays International Scholar Summer Programs in Brazil (2002) and Southeast Asia (2006). Kolo, a member of several professional organizations, serves as Treasurer of the Association of Third World Studies (ATWS). Active in community work, she serves as a mentor in a K-12 school program and as a member of the Board of Directors of New Horizons Habitat for Humanity.

Peter A. Dumbuya is associate professor of history at Fort Valley State University. He received his PhD in History from the University of Akron, and JD from Jones School of Law in Montgomery, Alabama. He is the author of *Tanganyika Under International Mandate, 1919-1945* (1995). His research focuses on colonial and postcolonial state formation in Sierra Leone, international relations in West Africa, international criminal courts, and foreign relations of Africa and the United States.

James T. Gire received a doctorate degree in Experimental Psychology from McMaster University, Hamilton in Ontario, Canada. He is currently a Colonel, Professor and Chair in the Department of Psychology and Philosophy at the Virginia Military Institute. His research interests are in the areas of aging and adult development, cross-cultural social psychology, the psychological study of social issues, substance use and misuse, especially alcohol and tobacco. He has published numerous book chapters and articles in several peer-review journals covering these areas. He also has published a book (Frank Eyetsemitan, co-author) on adult development and aging in the developing world with Greenwood Press.

John Patrick Afam Ifedi is the executive director of the Council on African Word Affairs, a foreign Affairs organization based in Washington, DC, which focuses on educating the public about issues pertaining to the African world, and is also on the managerial staff of the Federal Government's Independent Executive Agency, Court Services Agency for the District of Columbia. He is also a lecturer in Political Science at Howard University, where he has taught a variety of courses in Political Science to include American Presidency and National Government of the United States. His BA is from the State University of Minnesota, Moorhead; his MA is from the University of North Dakota, Grand Forks; and his PhD in Political Science is from Howard University. He recently co-authored a peer-reviewed article, "West African Gas Pipeline Project and Economic Development in the West Africa Region," that appears in the *Journal of Development Alternatives and Area Studies* (June 2005). His areas of specialization are International Relations, International Political Economy, Comparative Politics and Methodology.

George Klay Kieh, Jr. is currently professor of Political Science and African Studies at Grand Valley State University and Senior Research Fellow in the Program in Ethnic and Federal Studies at the University of Ibadan in Nigeria. Previously, he served as Dean of International Affairs at Grand Valley State University and Chair and Professor of Political Science and International Studies at Morehouse College. His research interests are in the areas of conflict and peace studies, security studies, African Politics, American Foreign Policy, political economy and international cooperation. He has published extensively in these areas. His most recent book is an edited volume (with Pita Ogaba Agbese) on Reconstituting the State in Africa, Palgrave-Macmillan, 2007.

Oluseyi Kuforiji has a doctorate degree in Applied Economics from The University of Pittsburgh in Pittsburgh, Pennsylvania. He has outstanding decision science, quantitative and management skills. Currently, he is an Associate Professor at Tuskegee University in Alabama, where he is teaching Managerial Economics (with Six Sigma Managerial Techniques). Kuforiji is a member of many national and international professional associations in his research areas and has presented at many conferences of high academic repute. Additionally, he has authored a number of scholarly articles as well as co-authored a few economic textbooks. Kuforiji is the founding editor of the *Journal of Economics and Business Studies*. He is the 2005-2006 EEOC Labor Economics Fellow and the recipient of the 2002 Georgia University System Chancellor's Russian Faculty Development Fellowship to St. Petersburg State Technical University in Russia. His training, skills and experiences cut across the public, private and academic sectors. In the public sector, he served as Assistant Secretary for General Administration and Financial Matters in Lagos, Nigeria. With regards to the private sector, he worked in the various capacities both as consultant and director of specific national and international projects. In the academics, he is currently a senior faculty member at Tuskegee University.

Guy Martin is professor of Political Science at Winston-Salem State University in North Carolina. Martin holds degree in Political Science (with an African Studies minor) from the University of Grenoble in France (BA), London University's School of Oriental and African Studies (MA), and Indiana University-Bloomington (MA & PhD). He has taught for the past thirty years in Africa (universities of Botswana, Yaoundé, Nairobi and Western Cape) and in the United States (American University, Clark Atlanta University, University of Virginia, New York University and Georgia State University). He is the author of

Africa in World Politics: A Pan-African Perspective (Trenton, NJ: Africa World Press, 2002) and co-editor (with Chris Alden) of *France and South Africa: Towards a New Engagement with Africa* (Pretoria: Protea Book House, 2003). His textbook, *African Political Thought* will be published in 2009 by Palgrave-Macmillan.

Mueni wa Muiu studied at Howard University (MA, African Studies; PhD, Political Science). Muiu's articles have been published by *Journal of African Policy, Journal of Third World Studies,* and *Journal of African and Asian Studies.* Muiu's review articles have been published in *Africa Development* and *African Studies Review.* She teaches Political Science at Winston Salem State University.

Ishmael I. Munene was born and raised in Nairobi, Kenya. Munene received university education in Kenya, Germany, India and the United States where he obtained a PhD in Higher Education Administration and Policy Studies at the State University of New York-Albany. Having taught Educational Foundations at the University of Nairobi, he now teaches Educational Research and Foundations at Northern Arizona University with continuing research interests in African Higher Education. He has published widely in this area, in journals, book chapters and encyclopedia entries.

Godwin Ohiwerei is Chairman of the Department of Sociology and Anthropology at New Jersey City University in Jersey City. He is a Board Member of the Organization for the Protection of Children in Canada. He was a Visiting Scholar at Dartmouth College's Ethical Institute for the Genome Research in 2005. He also is the author of various articles and books.

978-0-595-45197-5
0-595-45197-7

www.ingramcontent.com/pod-product-compliance
Lightning Source LLC
Chambersburg PA
CBHW022243290526
45785CB00015B/149